SECURING CANADA'S FUTURE

Vital Insights from Women Experts

Edited by Aisha Ahmad

After decades of uncontested dominance, the era of American hegemony is ending and a new multipolar world order is emerging in its place. This transformation is also occurring alongside uncontrolled climate change and the development of volatile new technologies. Together, these factors dramatically complicate the global threat landscape.

Securing Canada's Future offers a comprehensive analysis of the most serious challenges that Canada will face in the near future. Written by leading Canadian women scholars and security experts, this collection covers the most critical risks and threats on the horizon, including rising Chinese power, resurgent Russian aggression, escalating competition in the Arctic, the near irreversibility of climate change, disaster management and mitigation, evolving cybersecurity threats, and gendered violence.

Securing Canada's Future explores what this future threat landscape will look like for Canadians and shows how Canada can prepare for and mitigate upcoming risks. This practical, forward-thinking volume maps out the most urgent national and international security issues that Canada is destined to face in the foreseeable future.

AISHA AHMAD is an associate professor in the Department of Political Science at the University of Toronto, a senior fellow at Massey College, and a member of the Royal Society of Canada's College of New Scholars, Artists, and Scientists.

UTP insights

UTP Insights is an innovative collection of brief books offering accessible introductions to the ideas that shape our world. Each volume in the series focuses on a contemporary issue, offering a fresh perspective anchored in scholarship. Spanning a broad range of disciplines in the social sciences and humanities, the books in the UTP Insights series contribute to public discourse and debate and provide a valuable resource for instructors and students.

For a list of the books published in this series, see page 291.

SECURING CANADA'S FUTURE

Vital Insights from Women Experts

Edited by Aisha Ahmad

UNIVERSITY OF TORONTO PRESS
Toronto Buffalo London

© University of Toronto Press 2024
Toronto Buffalo London
utorontopress.com

All rights reserved. No part of this publication may be reproduced, stored in or introduced into a retrieval system, or transmitted in any form or by any means (electronic, mechanical, photocopying, recording, or otherwise) without the prior written permission of both the copyright owner and the above publisher of this book.

ISBN 978-1-4875-4202-3 (cloth)   ISBN 978-1-4875-4205-4 (EPUB)
ISBN 978-1-4875-4203-0 (paper)   ISBN 978-1-4875-4204-7 (PDF)

Library and Archives Canada Cataloguing in Publication

Title: Securing Canada's future : vital insights from women experts / edited by Aisha Ahmad.
Names: Ahmad, Aisha (Aisha S.), editor.
Series: UTP insights.
Description: Series statement: UTP insights | Includes bibliographical references and index.
Identifiers: Canadiana (print) 20240419340 | Canadiana (ebook) 20240419359 | ISBN 9781487542023 (cloth) | ISBN 9781487542030 (paper) | ISBN 9781487542054 (EPUB) | ISBN 9781487542047 (PDF)
Subjects: LCSH: National security—Canada—Forecasting.
Classification: LCC UA600 .S426 2024 | DDC 355/.033071—dc23

Cover design: Gareth Lind
Cover image: muratart/Shutterstock.com

We wish to acknowledge the land on which the University of Toronto Press operates. This land is the traditional territory of the Wendat, the Anishnaabeg, the Haudenosaunee, the Métis, and the Mississaugas of the Credit First Nation.

University of Toronto Press acknowledges the financial support of the Government of Canada, the Canada Council for the Arts, and the Ontario Arts Council, an agency of the Government of Ontario, for its publishing activities.

Canada Council for the Arts   Conseil des Arts du Canada

ONTARIO ARTS COUNCIL
CONSEIL DES ARTS DE L'ONTARIO
an Ontario government agency
un organisme du gouvernement de l'Ontario

Funded by the Government of Canada   Financé par le gouvernement du Canada

Contents

Acknowledgments ix

Introduction

   Canada and the Next World Order   3
   AISHA AHMAD

Part 1: Changing Systems

1 The Enemy Within: Polarization Risks for US Hegemony and the Liberal International Order   31
   CARLA NORRLÖF

2 Canada and NATO   49
   STÉFANIE VON HLATKY AND HANNAH HOLLANDER

3 Balancing Priorities along the Defence, Security, and Safety Continuum in the Canadian Arctic   62
   DANIELLE CHERPAKO AND ANDREA CHARRON

4 Canada-China Trade: Economic Interdependence and Coercion   75
   LYNETTE H. ONG

5 The Middle East and North Africa and the Future of Canadian Security   86
   BESSMA MOMANI

Part 2: Evolving Threats

6 UN Peacekeeping at a Crossroads   99
   KATHARINA COLEMAN AND LOU PINGEOT

7 Cyberspace: A Dangerous Game with Uncertain Rules   111
   LEAH WEST

8 Is the Canadian Emergency Management System Prepared for Evolving Threats?   125
   NIRUPAMA AGRAWAL

9 Climate Change and Canada's Economic Security   138
   KATHRYN HARRISON

10 Knitting a Sweater with a Hammer: Tensions and Opportunities That Emerge from Securitizing Climate Change   148
   SARAH BURCH AND JANETTA MCKENZIE

Part 3: Inclusive Security

11 Leveraging Diversity to Mitigate Groupthink   163
   AISHA AHMAD

12 Gender and Security: Tackling Insecurity Inside the Canadian Military   178
   MEGAN MACKENZIE AND NICOLE WEGNER

13 Indigenous Security   188
   CHELSEA PARKER AND SHERYL LIGHTFOOT

14 Islamophobia in Canada: The Security-Industrial Complex   203
   JASMIN ZINE

15 Refugees and Security in Canada: Invisibility, Crisis, and Discretion   217
   LAMA MOURAD

Conclusion

    Security amid Transition: Canada in the
    Next Decade   237
    AISHA AHMAD

Appendix: Must-Read Books List   263

Contributors   273

Index   285

Acknowledgments

This book was co-created by a team of extraordinary women security scholars across Canada. As editor, I was privileged to work with such remarkable researchers, each of whom enlightened me with their expert contributions to this volume. I am grateful for their intellectual leadership and excellence, as well as their generous mentorship of junior women scholars in the field. To those junior scholars who co-authored chapters in this book, you are our rising stars, and we look forward to reading more of your original work. I also thank the many young women who worked as research assistants on this project behind the scenes, most especially Chantel Cole, Calen Knakowski, Kauthar Mohammad, and Josyl Singh, who stewarded this book from inception to completion. I also thank Mohamed Serageldin for editing and indexing. This book would not have been possible without the generous support of the Social Science and Humanities Research Council of Canada and Women in International Security-Canada. I give special thanks to the wonderful team at University of Toronto Press, especially our editor, Dan Quinlan, for his unbridled enthusiasm for this project. Finally, on a personal note, I am forever grateful for my husband, Simon Wells, who brings so much love and laughter to my life that it counterbalances the weight of our troubled world.

SECURING CANADA'S FUTURE

Vital Insights from Women Experts

Introduction

Canada and the Next World Order

AISHA AHMAD

An Evolving Global Landscape

This book comes at a time of great peril, not only for Canada, but for the world. After decades of unipolar dominance, the era of American hegemony is ending. In its place emerges a multipolar world order in which several powerful countries vie for regional and global dominance. Great power transitions are dangerous times, and shifts in the balance of power are especially volatile when rising powers seek to challenge a waning hegemon. Russia has already lashed out in an effort to remain a superpower contender. China has developed surprisingly advanced new weapons technologies. War has already erupted in Europe, the Middle East, and parts of Africa, and the risk of conflict escalation and contagion is high.

As Canadians look to secure their futures amid this tumultuous period of transition, they must understand and prepare for a very different threat landscape than that which existed from 2002 to 2022. The painful fact is that Canada and its allies spent twenty years embroiled in various counter-insurgency and counterterrorism campaigns that cost a fortune in blood and treasure while largely failing to bring about the desired results. The Middle East remains at high risk of regional war, which could embroil the Americans. Meanwhile, China has thus far managed to avoid many of these costly quagmires and has instead used its resources to develop new capabilities to balance against US power on the world stage.

Although the United States remains the world's most powerful actor in raw military terms, it has suffered a series of international failures and domestic crises that signal its weakening position. It is no secret that Russia has perceived America's defeat in Afghanistan as analogous to its own humiliation in that country, which arguably triggered the collapse of the Soviet Union. Even if this historical analogy is faulty, the mere perception of American hegemonic decline can embolden ambitious competitors. The fact that Russia and China now believe that the era of US hegemony is coming to an end is enough to alter how these states will behave, and what opportunities they may pursue.

Canada must pivot quickly to adapt to this rapidly evolving global landscape. Not only is the balance of power among the most powerful nuclear-armed countries in the world changing, but so, too, are the threats that Canada will face in the years ahead. Enemy states have found ways to penetrate and disrupt democracies using covert cyberwar and disinformation campaigns. Identity-based conflicts and ethnic hatreds now threaten to unravel the fabric of liberal societies. The coronavirus pandemic highlighted critical vulnerabilities in Canada's emergency preparedness. The window to reverse climate change is rapidly closing, with little indication that states will meet their ambitious targets for emissions reduction. Meanwhile, confidence in the institutions that have upheld the international order since 1945 is deteriorating.

This survey of our global landscape looks dire, but it is not without hope. As far back as Vimy Ridge and Dieppe, Canada has known the brutal costs and consequences of great power conflict. Since those dark days, our country has learned how to wield its soft power influence to promote stability and order in global affairs. We have leveraged our status as a mid-sized power to champion international laws and institutions that have upheld international peace and security, even amid intense Cold War hostility. That industrious and creative energy must now be rerouted to address the unprecedented threats and vulnerabilities that lie ahead, including but not limited to the emergence of renewed great power conflict.

At this critical juncture in our history, this edited volume offers a comprehensive survey of the security challenges Canada will face in the near future. The book covers the most pertinent topics in the field, including renewed great power competition, climate change, disaster management, cyber warfare, and human security. Each of the fifteen core chapters highlights a significant security issue that Canada and the wider world will face in the decade ahead, and offers guidance on how Canadians can assess, adapt, and respond to the evolving threat landscape. The authors of these chapters are among the most prestigious and decorated security experts in the country. Their contributions to this volume represent decades of high-level academic research, years of field experience working in complex disaster and war zones, and many hundreds of hours of specialized consultations with governments, militaries, and international institutions around the world.

Given the calibre of the contributors, the book serves as a well-researched resource for experienced scholars, policymakers, and practitioners. However, this practical volume will benefit not only those working in niche areas of security, but also informed non-specialist readers who are interested in how evolving security issues may affect the future of business, politics, or social welfare. Written in an accessible, jargon-free style, the book serves as a general introduction to a range of essential topics within the Canadian security landscape that everyone should know about. Keen learners will also find the appendix, which provides a list of "must-read books," a helpful guide for additional study.

Global Issues, Expert Insights

To provide a comprehensive assessment of these diverse security issues, the book brings together leading scholars from across Canada, each with a unique specialization in a pressing area of international or national security. As the editor of this volume, it was my privilege to recruit such an exceptional team of experts. Although each chapter is headlined by a heavyweight in the field of security, some are also co-authored with graduate students who are rising stars in the field.

Part 1: Changing Systems

The collection is organized into three main sections, which structure the discussions and debates among the chapters. The first section of the volume is called "Changing Systems" and covers a range of traditional security issues, such as great power politics, alliances, and international competition. Opening this first section is Carla Norrlöf, a professor of political Science at the University of Toronto, a senior fellow of Massey College, and a non-resident senior fellow with the Atlantic Council. Dr. Norrlöf is a renowned specialist in great power competition, and most especially in US hegemony in the areas of money, trade, and security. Her research on hegemony has been published in top-tier academic journals in both the international security and international political economy subfields, and her book *America's Global Advantage: US Hegemony and International Cooperation* was field-defining in the study of hegemonic power.[1] She has since published cutting-edge work on how race and inequality can affect great power politics, including a trailblazing piece published in the top journal *International Affairs*.[2] In this volume, she leverages her insights from multiple studies to explain how domestic political problems inside the United States have undermined its otherwise unmatched global power, with serious implications for core US allies such as Canada.

Although its friendship with the United States is of paramount importance to Canada's security, it is also important to understand changes affecting our other key alliances. To provide urgently needed context on the future of NATO, we next hear from Stéfanie von Hlatky, who is the Canada Research Chair on Gender, Security and the Armed Forces, an associate professor of political studies at Queen's University, and the director of the Centre for International and Defence Policy. Among her many top-tier publications, Dr. von Hlatky has three prestigious books on the NATO alliance: *American Allies in Times of War*, *The Future of Extended Deterrence*, and *Deploying Feminism*.[3] She has extensive experience working with NATO and is the honorary colonel at the Princess of Wales' Own Regiment in Kingston, Ontario. In this volume, she co-authors a chapter with Hannah Hollander, an officer in the Canadian Armed Forces with a bachelor's in political science from the Royal Military College of Canada and a master's in political studies from Queen's University. Written at a time when Russian aggression has pushed European security to the edge, von Hlatky and Hollander's chapter directly addresses the big challenges that the NATO alliance will face in the years ahead, and what this will mean for Canadian security.

Canada's security concerns vis-à-vis Russia are especially acute in our contested Arctic region. To explain how Canada must approach both defence threats and human security concerns in the Far North, Danielle Cherpako and Andrea Charron offer an essential chapter on Arctic security. Dr. Charron is a multiple award–winning associate professor in international studies in the Political Studies Department and the director of the Centre for Defence and Security Studies at the University of Manitoba.[4] With a doctorate in war studies from the Royal Military College, Dr. Charron serves as vice chair of the Defence Advisory Board of the Canadian Department of National Defence, providing the government with expertise on the North American Aerospace Defense Command (NORAD), Arctic security, and foreign and defence policy. She wrote this chapter in between expeditions into a deep ice tunnel in Canada's Arctic. Dr. Charron's co-author, Danielle Cherpako, is an associate political affairs officer with the United Nations Department of Peace Operations, specializing in the evaluation of peacekeeping missions. She received the Governor General's Gold Academic Medal for her master's research on sanctions and human rights, and has previously worked with the North American and Arctic Defence Security Network, the Centre for Defence and Security Studies, and the Canadian International Council. Charron and Cherpako's chapter in this book provides a masterful assessment of how Canada must balance its defence concerns over Russia and its safety concerns for remote Indigenous populations living in the Far North.

Of course, Russia is not the only power challenging Western interests; China has also emerged as an economic and military powerhouse that poses a grand challenge to US primacy. To understand how China's rise might affect Canadian security, Lynette Ong provides a brilliant chapter on how Beijing has used economic coercion to advance its political interests, especially when it has an asymmetric power advantage over the other party. Dr. Ong is an associate professor of political science at the University of Toronto, jointly appointed to the Munk School of Global Affairs and Public Policy, and a leading scholar on authoritarianism and contentious politics. She has held multiple fellowships at the Fairbank Center for Chinese Studies and the Weatherhead Center for International Affairs, both at Harvard University. Fluent in Mandarin and other Chinese dialects, Dr. Ong has extensive experience working across China, as well as in the wider Southeast Asia region and India. She is the author of three prestigious academic books, the most recent of which include *Outsourcing Repression: Everyday State Power in Contemporary China* and *The Street and the Ballot Box: Interactions between Social Movements and Electoral Politics in Authoritarian Contexts*.[5] Her publications have also appeared in leading journals, such as *Perspectives on Politics*, *Comparative Politics*, *International Political Science Review*, *Political Studies*, and *Foreign Affairs*.[6] Her chapter in this volume shows how China uses different coercive economic instruments to achieve its goals, and explains how this economic coercion could affect Canadian security.

Finally, given the high level of violent conflict in the Middle East and North Africa (MENA), it is imperative that Canada be prepared to address security in this region as the global balance of power changes. Since the outbreak of war in Israel and Palestine in October 2023, the risk of conflict contagion across the MENA region has dramatically spiked. To help outline the key issues ahead, Bessma Momani's chapter provides an essential guide for those seeking to understand this politically volatile region. Dr. Momani is a professor of political science at the University of Waterloo, a senior fellow at the Centre for International Governance and Innovation, a non-resident fellow at the Arab Gulf States Institute in Washington, DC, and a Fulbright Scholar. She is also a governor on the Board of the International Development Research Centre and an executive member of the board of the Pierre Elliott Trudeau Foundation. She has worked as a consultant for the International Monetary Fund and served as a visiting scholar at Global Affairs Canada in its International Assistance Research and Knowledge Division. An internationally recognized leader in global finance, Canadian foreign policy and defence, and Middle Eastern politics, Dr. Momani is the author and co-editor of ten books and over eighty additional academic publications.[7] Her most recent co-authored and co-edited volume (with Thomas Juneau) is *Middle Power in the Middle East: Canada's Foreign and Defence Policies in a Changing Region*.[8] Building on this exceptional work, Dr. Momani's chapter in this volume explains how Canada has attempted to balance its global economic and strategic interests in the MENA region, but in an increasingly perilous local context. Looking ahead, she advises that Canada must support MENA citizens in their quest for greater freedom in their own countries, even while balancing its other geo-strategic interests and pressures from allies.

Part 2: Evolving Threats

Competition among the great powers shapes every other aspect of global affairs; yet, in addition to these important system-level changes, there are other non-traditional security threats that Canada must consider. The second section of this book, titled "Evolving Threats," covers a range of these security concerns. It begins with Katharina Coleman and Lou Pingeot's co-authored chapter on peacekeeping. Canada has a long history of involvement in peacekeeping, but there are important questions about whether and how much Canada should engage in such missions in the future. Dr. Coleman is an associate professor of political science at the University of British Columbia and specializes in international organizations, peace operations, and sub-Saharan Africa. She is the author of *International Organizations and Peace Enforcement: The Politics of International Legitimacy*,[9] and has published extensively on international peacekeeping missions, especially in Africa.[10] She co-authors this chapter with Dr. Pingeot, a postdoctoral fellow in the School of Public and International Affairs at the University of

Ottawa, where she investigates international policing and peacekeeping missions. Her work has appeared in prestigious journals such as *Small Wars & Insurgencies*, *International Peacekeeping*, *European Journal of International Security*, and *Globalizations*.[11] Coleman and Pingeot's contribution to this volume highlights several key obstacles to peacekeeping, including but not limited to increasing pressures from Russia and China in the UN Security Council, and it offers advice on how Canada can encourage an inclusive new approach to international peacekeeping in the future.

The rest of this section explores new and emerging security threats, which Canada has far less experience tackling. The next chapter, by Leah West, covers cyberspace. Dr. West is an assistant professor of international affairs at the Norman Paterson School of International Affairs at Carleton University, where she teaches public international law, national security law, and counterterrorism. She completed her SJD at the University of Toronto Faculty of Law in 2020, where her research explored the application of criminal, constitutional, and international law to state conduct in cyberspace. She previously served as counsel with the Department of Justice in the National Security Litigation and Advisory Group, where she appeared before the Federal Court in designated proceedings and the Security Intelligence Review Committee. Dr. West was also the inaugural recipient of the Captain Nichola Goddard "Game Changer" Award, which honours a Canadian trailblazer who has made a significant contribution to Canadian security and defence. As a legal scholar and practitioner in national security, she has a research specialization in the laws of cyberspace, has co-authored (with Craig Forcese) the book *National Security Law*, and has published extensively on legal matters pertaining to both terrorism and cybersecurity.[12] Dr. West also served as a captain in the Canadian Armed Forces and has direct combat and military leadership experience. Her chapter in this volume highlights Canada's serious lack of preparedness in dealing with emerging cyber threats and recommends how it can prepare a coherent set of laws and policies aimed at improving cybersecurity at home and cyber foreign policies abroad.

Building on this discussion about unpreparedness, the next chapter turns our attention to the question of Canada's emergency management system and its ability to respond to large-scale and concurrent events. To evaluate Canada's disaster preparedness, Nirupama Agrawal offers an essential chapter on the institutions and frameworks that govern Canada's response to emergencies, and where they must be improved for future success. Dr. Agrawal is a professor in the School of Administrative Studies at York University, and a founding faculty member of its prestigious Disaster and Emergency Management Program. With a PhD in water resources from Kyoto University, Japan, and a master's degree in hydrology from the Indian Institute of Technology Roorkee, Dr. Agrawal brings a much-needed global and interdisciplinary scientific perspective to disaster response policies. Dr. Agrawal's research and teaching focus on understanding nature-triggered extreme events, hazard risk modelling using qualitative and quantitative methods for prevention and mitigation of disaster impacts, climate change, risk perception, disaster resilience and adaptation through engagement, and decision support tools using geographic information systems and remote sensing. She has published scholarly articles and an essential textbook titled *Disasters and Risk Management in Canada*.[13] Agrawal's chapter, written amid the rollout of various national emergency measures to contain the coronavirus pandemic, is an essential primer on how Canada should develop a balanced and whole-of-society approach to managing emergencies, one that emphasizes resilience, adaptation, and risk mitigation.

Most scholars and practitioners are well aware that climate change is projected to increase the frequency and magnitude of natural disasters, which Agrawal's chapter aptly addresses. However, there are other serious security concerns stemming from climate change, and these are outlined in the next two outstanding chapters. The first looks at how climate change presents a real and serious threat to Canada's *economic* security, as global efforts at decarbonization could undercut oil- and gas-producing countries like Canada. This novel chapter is authored by Kathryn Harrison, a multiple award–winning professor of political science at the University of British Columbia who specializes in environmental, climate, and energy policy in Canada. Dr. Harrison has authored and co-authored several books, including (with Lisa McIntosh Sundstrom) *Global Commons, Domestic Decisions: The Comparative Politics of Climate Change*, and has over fifty other academic publications to her name, including in top science journals like *Nature*.[14] Moreover, before she became an award-winning academic, Harrison received master's degrees in chemical engineering and political science from MIT, and then worked as an engineer in Canada's oil industry, beginning in the tar sands in the early 1980s. She has committed the last several decades of her career to undoing the damage done by fossil fuels. Before entering academia, Dr. Harrison also worked as a policy analyst for both Environment Canada and the United States Congress. She therefore brings a unique perspective that connects the science, economics, and politics of the energy industry. Her chapter in this volume provides an exceptional analysis of how the Canadian economy could be threatened by global climate change policies and explicitly outlines what can be done to mitigate potential damage.

Notably, in 2021 the Pentagon announced that it would henceforth prioritize climate change in its risk assessments and would incorporate these considerations into its war gaming and analysis for US national defence. However, in our next chapter on climate change, Sarah Burch and Janetta McKenzie argue that while climate change action is imperative, framing the problem as a security threat as the Pentagon has done may not lead to better results. Dr. Burch is a highly decorated associate professor in the Department of Geography and Environmental Management and the Canada Research Chair in Sustainability Governance and Innovation at the University of Waterloo, as well as a senior fellow at the Centre for International Governance Innovation at the Balsillie School of International Affairs. In addition to her many impactful academic publications, she is the co-author of the essential book *Understanding Climate Change*,[15] as well as a lead author of the *Sixth Assessment Report* of the Intergovernmental Panel on Climate Change (IPCC), which was the winner of the Nobel Peace Prize in 2007. Dr. Burch leads the international partnership-based research project TRANSFORM: Accelerating Sustainability Entrepreneurship Experiments in Local Spaces, and is the director of the Sustainability Policy Research on Urban Transformations Lab. She was inducted into the Royal Society of Canada's College of New Scholars, Artists and Scientists in 2017, was included among Canada's Top 40 Under 40 in 2018, and was named one of Canada's "Clean 50" in 2021. She co-authored her chapter in this volume with Janetta McKenzie, a senior analyst at the Pembina Institute, a clean energy think tank in Canada. Dr. McKenzie received a PhD in geography from the University of Waterloo for research on the efficacy of pipeline regulation in Canada and the United States. She currently works on energy policy development, natural gas certification, and industrial decarbonization in Canada, and has contributed to a variety of research projects on international climate governance. Burch and McKenzie's essential chapter in this volume explains why and how Canada should pursue climate change action through a more nuanced human security lens.

Part 3: Inclusive Security

Building on this discussion of inclusivity, the third group of chapters in the book focuses specifically on how gender, race, and Indigeneity transform how we understand and approach Canadian security. This final section of the book, called "Inclusive Security," clearly explains why defence and security communities urgently need to address these issues. As a concept, inclusive security emerged in response to growing awareness that our security and defence communities have often overlooked perspectives and insights from women, civilians, Indigenous communities, and other minorities. Correcting this bias is not merely an ethical or equity issue; rather, a lack of diversity and diverse perspectives hurts operational effectiveness and can result in serious vulnerabilities and even ghastly errors. Indeed, the fact that there were zero Pashto-speakers working at the US State Department in 2001 unquestionably disadvantaged the American operation in Afghanistan. The miscalculations made at the outset of that deployment resulted in twenty years of frustration in the theatre, and eventual mission failure. This is one of countless examples of how a lack of inclusivity in security and defence communities can result in disastrous outcomes.

The chapters in the "Inclusive Security" section present a range of analyses aimed at remedying these problems. I open this section with a chapter that delves into the Afghanistan example and other similar cases. I am an associate professor of political science at the University of Toronto specializing in international security, and I have advised senior leaders from the Canadian Armed Forces and other allied nations on international interventions and counterinsurgency operations around the world. I am the author of the award-winning book *Jihad & Co.: Black Markets and Islamist Power*, and multiple academic articles on jihadist insurgencies, most of which draw upon direct fieldwork in such countries as Afghanistan, Pakistan, Mali, Kenya, Somalia, Lebanon, and Iraq.[16] My chapter in this volume reveals how a lack of diversity has caused decision makers to fall victim to groupthink and cognitive bias. Learning from past mistakes suggests ways that Canada could fare better if it taps into its diversity as a strategic asset.

Continuing with the theme of how Canada can undermine its own national security, the next chapter in this section looks at the consequences of gendered and racialized violence inside the Canadian Armed Forces (CAF). Co-written by Megan MacKenzie and Nicole Wegner, the chapter illustrates how unchecked internal violence in the CAF turns our military institutions into agents of insecurity for those who serve in them. Dr. MacKenzie is a professor and the Simons Chair in International Law and Human Security at the School for International Studies at Simon Fraser University, and she has over a decade of experience working on military culture and gender, including work on military sexual violence and military suicide. Among her many publications on gender and security, Dr. MacKenzie is the author of *Beyond the Band of Brothers: the US Military and the Myth That Women Can't Fight*.[17] She has also co-edited with Nicole Wegner the volume *Feminist Solutions to Ending War*.[18] Dr. Wegner is a postdoctoral research fellow at the University of Auckland. She has published research on militarized masculinities, feminist pedagogy, affective militarism, and intra-military violence, and was the 2019 recipient of the prestigious Cynthia Enloe Award for her research on the political use of the "helpful hero" image in the CAF. MacKenzie and Wegner's chapter in this book examines how gender and racial bias constitutes an institutional vulnerability within the CAF and has resulted in an increased prevalence of post-traumatic stress disorder, veteran suicide, and military sexual violence.

Building on this discussion of Canada's domestic failures, in the next chapter, Chelsea Parker and Sheryl Lightfoot present a hard-hitting analysis of how Canada's treatment of Indigenous populations creates a number of serious economic and political risks. Dr. Lightfoot is an associate professor of First Nations and Indigenous studies and political science, a former Canada Research Chair in Global Indigenous Rights and Politics, and was previously the senior adviser to the president on Indigenous affairs at the University of British Columbia. She is the author of *Global Indigenous Politics: A Subtle Revolution*, and several other high-impact publications on Indigenous rights.[19] Dr. Lightfoot is Anishinaabe, a citizen of the Lake Superior Band of Ojibwe, enrolled at the Keweenaw Bay Indian Community in Baraga, Michigan, and has fifteen years of experience with a number of Indigenous tribes and community-based organizations in the Minneapolis–St. Paul area, including nine years as chair of the Board of the American Indian Policy Center, a research and advocacy group. Dr. Lightfoot's chapter in this volume is co-authored with Chelsea Parker, a researcher specializing in critical Indigenous studies. Their chapter aptly explains how Canada's abysmal treatment of Indigenous populations not only causes serious international reputational damage, but also negatively affects Canadian economic security, including but not limited to relations with foreign investors. Parker and Lightfoot then provide guidance on how Canada can address this long-standing problem by bringing Canadian laws and policies in line with the UN Declaration on the Rights of Indigenous Peoples.

In addition to its deeply fraught relationship with Indigenous people, Canada also has problematic interactions with other communities. In the next chapter, Jasmin Zine presents a compelling analysis of how Canada has profiled and surveilled Canadian

Muslims for over two decades, resulting in poor domestic and international security outcomes. Dr. Zine is an award-winning professor of sociology at Wilfrid Laurier University and an affiliate faculty member with the Islamophobia Research and Documentation Project at the University of California, Berkeley. She specializes in post-9/11 domestic security policies and their effects on Muslim communities, especially at-risk youth, and has advised multiple international organizations on how to rectify Islamophobia and anti-Muslim racism in their policy making. She has worked as a consultant with the Office for Democratic Institutions and Human Rights at the Organization for Security and Cooperation in Europe, the Council of Europe, and the United Nations Educational, Scientific and Cultural Organization, developing guidelines for educators and policymakers on combating Islamophobia and anti-Muslim racism. She was also the co-chair of the Islamophobia subcommittee of the Ontario Anti-Racism Directorate and testified at the 2017 Canadian Heritage parliamentary sub-committee meetings on Motion 103 addressing Islamophobia, systemic racism, and religious discrimination. Dr. Zine is the author of multiple books and articles, her latest being *Under Siege: Islamophobia and the 9/11 Generation*.[20] This cutting-edge book is based on Dr. Zine's extensive field research with surveilled Muslim youth in Canada and unpacks the consequences of that surveillance on targeted communities and Canadian security. Her chapter in this volume leverages insights from *Under Siege* and speaks directly to how the Canadian security and defence community needs to change course in terms of how it engages with Muslim populations in this country.

The final chapter in the book also addresses the securitization of communities, but this time looking at how Canada approaches refugee claimants. Written by Lama Mourad, this chapter shows that, while Canada enjoys a reputation as a haven for refugees, it has also securitized refugees in ways that prevent asylum-seekers from finding safety in Canada. Dr. Mourad is an assistant professor of political science at the Norman Paterson School of International Affairs at Carleton University, and was formerly a fellow with the Middle East Initiative at the Belfer Center for International Affairs at the Harvard Kennedy School. Her doctoral research, which examined the local politics of refugee governance in Lebanon, was awarded the prestigious American Political Science Association's Migration and Citizenship Best Dissertation Award in 2020. Dr. Mourad specializes in forced migration and Middle Eastern politics, has conducted extensive international field research, is fluent in Arabic and French, and is published in the *European Journal of International Relations*, *Forced Migration Review*, and the *Journal of Refugee Studies*.[21] Her important chapter in this volume explains why Canada is "generous" towards refugees under some conditions but not others, and how Canada could reimagine its approach to asylum-seekers without compromising its security interests.

Taken together, the chapters in this book build an overarching story about the future of Canadian security. Yet, while the keen learner may wish to read this volume cover to cover, the individual chapters also serve as a resource for scholars and practitioners looking for issue-specific analyses of contemporary issues. While each chapter is short and punchy, they all point to the contributors' larger body of published works for follow-up reading. These citations, plus the curated "Must-Read Books List" in the appendix, serve as guides for keen learners who wish to probe deeper into the research on major security issues facing Canada.

All-Women All-Stars

One of the unique features of this book is that it features an all-star roster of women experts, who are not necessarily writing about gender per se, but rather about a wide range of substantive security issues. The expert contributors to this volume have each published top-tier research on contemporary security issues and have advised governments and international organizations on how to resolve them. This volume thus features some of the most-decorated women security scholars in Canada, several of whom have co-authored their chapters with women graduate students who are emerging stars in their fields.

Why does this book showcase an all-women team of security experts? First and foremost, it is because they are the best in the business. But an equally important reason is that the study and practice of security and defence have, historically, excluded women. It was only in 1989 that all military occupations in the Canadian Armed Forces became open to women, and the submarine service only accepted women in 2001.[22] In its entire history, Canada has had only two female defence ministers out of a total of forty-three: former prime minister Rt. Hon. Kim Campbell (in 1993), and Rt. Hon. Anita Anand (in 2021). In academia, both international security and war studies have historically been male-dominated areas of study. Much like the Women in STEM movement, a number of academic and professional organizations have been developed to counteract gender inequities and biases in security studies, including Women in International Security, Women in Defence and Security, and Women Also Know Stuff.

Despite these many laudable efforts to correct gender inequities in security and defence studies, even well-intentioned scholars and practitioners can accidentally replicate these long-standing biases. Too often, organizers of expert panels, advisory committees, and task forces short-list talent from their usual contact lists, only to realize that they have inadvertently created an all-male (and often all-white) team. Research suggests that gender and racial diversity in teams can improve decision making and performance outcomes,[23] whereas more homogenous teams are at risk of cognitive biases and groupthink.[24] Moreover, having an all-male panel – mockingly called a "manel" – can become a source of embarrassment and criticism. Equally so, if a professor has not updated their syllabus in years, they might find themselves assigning an all-male reading list. This, too, can stir up controversy in classrooms, university departments, and beyond.

This book offers a solution. In addition to presenting rigorous research, the chapters are also a handy reference for scholars, practitioners, and decision makers who need quick access to the best security research by women experts across the country. As the former chair of the board of Women in International Security Canada, I am privileged to have helped build a network of women security researchers in Canada, and I am familiar with the scholarship of the top women researchers across the country. I was thus well-positioned to identify academic heavy hitters in the security field and invite them to be contributors to the book.

Of course, this volume is comprehensive, but not exhaustive. In addition to the expert contributors gathered here, there are many other leading women security scholars who ought to be spotlighted. Stephanie Carvin's (Carleton University) excellent book *Stand on Guard* explains how Canada should evaluate national security threats.[25] Diana Fu's (University of Toronto) prize-winning book *Mobilizing Without the Masses* offers readers a rare inside look into politics in China.[26] Juliet Johnson's (McGill University) *Priests of Prosperity* provides important context on how money works in Russia and eastern Europe.[27] On civil wars and genocide, the late great Lee Ann Fujii's (University of Toronto) *Killing Neighbors* should be considered essential reading.[28] Pam Palmater's (Toronto Metropolitan University) *Beyond Blood* is a foundational text on Indigenous politics in Canada.[29] Debra Thompson's (McGill University) multiple award–winning *The Schematic State* is one of the most influential books on race and security in North America.[30] These are but a few of the many senior women scholars in Canada whose research speaks to the important security issues covered in this book. Although I did invite several of these experts to contribute to this volume, some were indisposed during the pandemic; moreover, to include everyone on my long list would have been impossible. Therefore, to ensure that our readers have every opportunity to find and discover more of these important works, the concluding chapter and the "Must-Read Books List" in the appendix offers a guide to finding these and many other essential scholarly resources.

In the decade to come, our world will undergo a number of seismic transformations. The balance among the great powers is shifting, as a resurgent Russia and a rising China compete against a declining American hegemon. Conflict among these three giants – whether through conventional war, cyber warfare, or even nuclear war – will have serious implications for Canada and the wider world. Meanwhile, the international community is desperately trying to coordinate action to mitigate severe climate change crises. Canada must therefore also prepare for a world of fossil fuel divestment, increased forced migration, and heightened risk of natural disasters at home. To meet these challenges successfully, it will need to contend with crucial matters of bias and inequity that have created vulnerabilities in Canadian security.

Fortunately, Canada's diversity is a valuable strategic asset that can be leveraged to meet these challenges. As I explain in detail in chapter 11 of this volume, tapping into this asset allows leaders and decision makers to avoid dangerous cognitive biases and strategic miscalculations. Enhancing diversity and inclusion in the field of security is not about progressive optics. It is about being optimally prepared to face the challenges of a volatile and complex world. Echo chambers are dangerous in any context, but most especially in global security. Given the enormity of the challenges ahead, Canada simply does not have the luxury to replicate woefully outdated gender biases that keep top women experts out of the conversation. With the storms of great power conflict and climate crisis on the horizon, Canada will fare better with the country's best experts at the helm. Now is the time to take full advantage of our strategic assets. The expert contributors to this volume are some of our best.

NOTES

1 Carla Norrlöf, "Dollar Hegemony: A Power Analysis," *Review of International Political Economy* 21, no. 5 (2014): 1042–70, https://doi.org/10.1080/09692290.2014.895773; Carla Norrlöf, "Hegemony, Hierarchy, and Unipolarity: Theoretical and Empirical Foundations of Hegemonic Order Studies," in *Oxford Research Encyclopedia of Politics*, 27 July 2017, https://doi.org/10.1093/acrefore/9780190228637.013.552; Carla Norrlöf and William C. Wohlforth, "Raison de l'Hégémonie (The Hegemon's Interest): Theory of the Costs and Benefits of Hegemony," *Security Studies* 28, no. 3 (2019): 422–50, https://doi.org/10.1080/09636412.2019.160498 2; Carla Norrlöf, "Is COVID-19 the End of US Hegemony? Public Bads, Leadership Failures and Monetary Hegemony," *International Affairs* 96, no. 5 (2020): 1281–1303, https://doi.org/10.1093/ia/iiaa134. See also Carla Norrlöf, *America's Global Advantage: US Hegemony and International Cooperation* (Cambridge: Cambridge University Press, 2010).

2 Carla Norrlöf, "Hegemony and Inequality: Trump and the Liberal Playbook," *International Affairs* 94, no. 1 (2018): 63–88, https://doi.org/10.1093/ia/iix262.
3 Stéfanie von Hlatky, *American Allies in Times of War: The Great Asymmetry* (Oxford: Oxford University Press, 2013); Stéfanie von Hlatky and Andreas Wenger, *The Future of Extended Deterrence: The United States, NATO, and Beyond* (Washington, DC: Georgetown University Press, 2015); Stéfanie von Hlatky, *Deploying Feminism: The Role of Gender in NATO Military Operations* (New York: Oxford University Press, 2022). See also Stéfanie von Hlatky and Justin Massie, "Ideology, Ballots, and Alliances: Canadian Participation in Multinational Military Operations," *Contemporary Security Policy* 40, no. 1 (2019): 101–15, https://doi.org/10.1080/13523260.2018.1508265; Stéfanie von Hlatky and Michel Fortmann, "NATO Enlargement and the Failure of the Cooperative Security Mindset," *International Politics* 57, no. 3 (2020): 554–72, https://doi.org/10.1057/s41311-020-00240-w; Heidi Hardt and Stéfanie von Hlatky, "NATO's About-Face: Adaptation to Gender Mainstreaming in an Alliance Setting," *Journal of Global Security Studies* 5, no. 1 (2020): 136–59, https://doi.org/10.1093/jogss/ogz048.
4 Andrea Charron, "The Northwest Passage: Is Canada's Sovereignty Floating Away?," *International Journal* 60, no. 3 (2005): 831–48, https://doi.org/10.2307/40204066; Andrea Charron, Joël Plouffe, and Stéphane Roussel, "The Russian Arctic Hegemon: Foreign Policy Implications for Canada," *Canadian Foreign Policy Journal* 18, no. 1 (2012): 38–50, https://doi.org/10.1080/11926422.2012.674384; Andrea Charron, "Canada and the Arctic Council," *International Journal* 67, no. 3 (2012): 765–83; Andrea Charron, "Canada, the Arctic, and NORAD: Status Quo or New Ball Game?," *International Journal* 70, no. 2 (2015): 215–31; Andrea Charron and James Fergusson, "Beyond NORAD and Modernization to North American Defence Evolution," *Policy Commons*, 1 May 2017, https://policycommons.net/artifacts/2327166/beyond-norad-and-modernization-to-north-american-defence-evolution/3087796/; Andrea Charron and James Fergusson, "Canada and Defence against Help: The Wrong Theory for the Wrong Country at the Wrong Time," in *Canadian Defence Policy in Theory and Practice*, ed. Thomas Juneau, Philippe Lagassé, and Srdjan Vucetic (Cham, Switzerland: Springer, 2020), 99–115, https://doi.org/10.1007/978-3-030-26403-1_7.

5 Lynette H. Ong, *Outsourcing Repression: Everyday State Power in Contemporary China* (Oxford: Oxford University Press, 2022); Lynette H. Ong, *The Street and the Ballot Box*, new ed. (Cambridge: Cambridge University Press, 2022); Lynette H. Ong, *Prosper or Perish: Credit and Fiscal Systems in Rural China*, ill. ed. (Ithaca, NY: Cornell University Press, 2012).

6 Lynette H. Ong, "Fiscal Federalism and Soft Budget Constraints: The Case of China," *International Political Science Review* 33, no. 4 (2012): 455–74, https://doi.org/10.1177/0192512111414447; Lynette H. Ong, "Between Developmental and Clientelist States: Local State-Business Relationships in China," *Comparative Politics* 44, no. 2 (2012): 191–209, https://doi.org/10.5129/001041512798838030; Lynette H. Ong, "'Thugs-for-Hire': Subcontracting of State Coercion and State Capacity in China," *Perspectives on Politics* 16, no. 3 (2018): 680–95, https://doi.org/10.1017/S1537592718000981; Lynette H. Ong and Donglin Han, "What Drives People to Protest in an Authoritarian Country? Resources and Rewards vs Risks of Protests in Urban and Rural China," *Political Studies* 67, no. 1 (2019): 224–48, https://doi.org/10.1177/0032321718763558; Lynette H. Ong, "Thugs and Outsourcing of State Repression in China," *China Journal* 80 (July 2018): 94–110, https://doi.org/10.1086/696156.

7 For a selection of Dr. Momani's work related to her contribution to this volume, see the following: Bessma Momani, *Arab Dawn: Arab Youth and the Demographic Dividend They Will Bring* (Toronto: University of Toronto Press, 2015); Bessma Momani and Tanzeel Hakak, "Syria," in *The Oxford Handbook of the Responsibility to Protect*, ed. Alex J. Bellamy and Tim Dunne (Oxford: Oxford University Press, 2016), https://doi.org/10.1093/oxfordhb/9780198753841.013.48; Bessma Momani, "Canadian Foreign Policy from the Roaring 1990s," *International Journal* 72, no. 2 (2017): 192–202; Melissa Finn and Bessma Momani, "Building Foundations for the Comparative Study of State and Non-state Terrorism," *Critical Studies on Terrorism* 10, no. 3 (2017): 379–403, https://doi.org/10.1080/17539153.2017.1287753; Bessma Momani, "Economic Development: Bread, Jobs, and Beyond," in *The Societies of the Middle East and North Africa*, 2nd ed., ed. Sean Yom (London: Routledge, 2021); Bessma Momani and Nawroos Shibli, "Canada and the Middle East," in *The Palgrave Handbook of Canada in International Affairs*, ed. Robert W. Murray and Paul Gecelovsky, Canada and International Affairs (Cham, Switzerland: Springer, 2021), 729–47, https://doi.org/10.1007/978-3-030-67770-1_32.

8 Thomas Juneau and Bessma Momani, eds., *Middle Power in the Middle East: Canada's Foreign and Defence Policies in a Changing Region* (Toronto: University of Toronto Press, 2022).
9 Katharina P. Coleman, *International Organisations and Peace Enforcement: The Politics of International Legitimacy*, ill. ed. (Cambridge: Cambridge University Press, 2007).
10 Magnus Lundgren, Kseniya Oksamytna, and Katharina P Coleman, "Only as Fast as Its Troop Contributors: Incentives, Capabilities, and Constraints in the UN's Peacekeeping Response," *Journal of Peace Research* 58, no. 4 (2021): 671–86, https://doi.org/10.1177/0022343320940763; Katharina P. Coleman and Brian L. Job, "How Africa and China May Shape UN Peacekeeping beyond the Liberal International Order," *International Affairs* 97, no. 5 (2021): 1451–68, https://doi.org/10.1093/ia/iiab113; Katharina P. Coleman, "African Peacekeeping," *International Affairs* 98, no. 5 (2022): 1828–29, https://doi.org/10.1093/ia/iiac180; Katharina P. Coleman, "Peacekeeping Financing," in *Handbook on Peacekeeping and International Relations*, ed. Han Dorussen (Cheltenham, UK: Edward Elgar, 2022), 27–45, https://www.elgaronline.com/display/book/9781839109935/book-part-9781839109935-12.xml.
11 Lou Pingeot, "In Whose Interest? The UN's Strategic Rapprochement with Business in the Sustainable Development Agenda," *Globalizations* 13, no. 2 (2016): 188–202, https://doi.org/10.1080/14747731.2015.1085211; Lou Pingeot, "International Peacebuilding as a Case of Structural Injustice," *International Peacekeeping* 27, no. 2 (2020): 263–88, https://doi.org/10.1080/13533312.2019.1673739; Lou Pingeot, "The Multilateral Production of Global Policing: UN Peace Operations as Hubs for Protest Policing," *Small Wars & Insurgencies* 33, nos. 4–5 (2022): 846–67, https://doi.org/10.1080/09592318.2021.1961374; Lou Pingeot and Colleen Bell, "Recentring the Coloniality of Global Policing," *Third World Quarterly* 43, no. 10 (2022): 2488–2508, https://doi.org/10.1080/01436597.2022.2102475.
12 Craig Forcese and Leah West, *National Security Law*, 2nd ed. (Toronto: Irwin Law, 2020). See also Leah West and Craig Forcese, "Judicial Supervision of Anti-terrorism Laws in Comparative Democracies," in *Research Handbook on International Law and Terrorism*, ed. Ben Saul (Cheltenham, UK: Edward Elgar, 2020), 465–78, https://www.elgaronline.com/display/edcoll/9781788972215/9781788972215.00041.xml; Jessica Davis, Leah West, and Amarnath Amarasingam, "Measuring Impact, Uncovering Bias? Citation Analysis of Literature on Women

in Terrorism," *Perspectives on Terrorism* 15, no. 2 (2021): 58–76; Leah West, "The Perilous Prerogative: An Argument for Legislating Defence Intelligence in Canada," *Canadian Public Administration* 65, no. 4 (2022): 585–600, https://doi.org/10.1111/capa.12498.

13 Nirupama Agrawal, *Natural Disasters and Risk Management in Canada: An Introduction* (New York: Springer Nature, 2018). See also Nirupama Agrawal and Robin Cox, "Natural Disasters and 150th Commemoration of Canada as a Country," *Natural Hazards* 98, no. 1 (2019): 3–7, https://doi.org/10.1007/s11069-019-03751-9; Nirupama Agrawal, Mark Elliott, and Slobodan P. Simonovic, "Risk and Resilience: A Case of Perception versus Reality in Flood Management," *Water* 12, no. 5 (2020): 1254, https://doi.org/10.3390/w12051254; Amar Deep Regmi and Nirupama Agrawal, "A Simple Method for Landslide Risk Assessment in the Rivière Aux Vases Basin, Quebec, Canada," *Progress in Disaster Science* 16 (December 2022): 100247, https://doi.org/10.1016/j.pdisas.2022.100247; Peter Tsasis, Nirupama Agrawal, and Natalie Guriel, "An Embedded Systems Perspective in Conceptualizing Canada's Healthcare Sustainability," *Sustainability* 11, no. 2 (2019): 531, https://doi.org/10.3390/su11020531.

14 Kathryn Harrison and Lisa McIntosh Sundstrom, eds., *Global Commons, Domestic Decisions: The Comparative Politics of Climate Change* (Cambridge, MA: MIT Press, 2010). See also Kathryn Harrison, "The Politics of Carbon Pricing," *Nature Climate Change* 8, no. 10 (2018): 852, https://doi.org/10.1038/s41558-018-0289-4; Kathryn Harrison, "Political Institutions and Supply-Side Climate Politics: Lessons from Coal Ports in Canada and the United States," *Global Environmental Politics* 20, no. 4 (2020): 51–72, https://doi.org/10.1162/glep_a_00579; Navroz K. Dubash, Kathryn Harrison, et al., "National Climate Institutions Complement Targets and Policies," *Science* 374, no. 6568 (2021): 690–93, https://doi.org/10.1126/science.abm1157; Kathryn Harrison and Guri Bang, "Supply-Side Climate Policies in Major Oil-Producing Countries: Norway's and Canada's Struggles to Align Climate Leadership with Fossil Fuel Extraction," *Global Environmental Politics* 22, no. 4 (2022): 129–50, https://doi.org/10.1162/glep_a_00682; Matto Mildenberger, Erick Lachapelle, Kathryn Harrison, and Isabelle Stadelmann-Steffen, "Limited Impacts of Carbon Tax Rebate Programmes on Public Support for Carbon Pricing," *Nature Climate Change* 12, no. 2 (2022): 141–7, https://doi.org/10.1038

/s41558-021-01268-3; Parrish Bergquist, Gabriel De Roche, Erick Lachapelle, Matto Mildenberger, and Kathryn Harrison, "The Politics of Intersecting Crises: The Effect of the COVID-19 Pandemic on Climate Policy Preferences," *British Journal of Political Science* 53, no. 2 (2023): 707–16, https://doi.org/10.1017/S0007123422000266.

15 Sarah Burch and Sara Harris, *Understanding Climate Change: Science, Policy, and Practice* (Toronto; Buffalo; London: University of Toronto Press, 2021). See also Daniel Rosenbloom, James Meadowcroft, Stephen Sheppard, Sarah Burch, and Stephen Williams, "Transition Experiments: Opening Up Low-Carbon Transition Pathways for Canada through Innovation and Learning," *Canadian Public Policy* 44, no. 4 (2018): 368–83, https://doi.org/10.3138/cpp.2018-020; Linda Westman, Janetta McKenzie, and Sarah Lynn Burch, "Political Participation of Businesses: A Framework to Understand Contributions of SMEs to Urban Sustainability Politics," *Earth System Governance* 3 (March 2020): 100044, https://doi.org/10.1016/j.esg.2020.100044; Sarah L. Burch and Sara E. Harris, *Understanding Climate Change: Science, Policy, and Practice*, 2nd ed. (Toronto: University of Toronto Press, 2021); Sarah Burch et al., "Building Urban Resilience through Sustainability-Oriented Small- and Medium-Sized Enterprises," *Urban Transformations* 4, no. 1 (2022): 12, https://doi.org/10.1186/s42854-022-00041-9; Jose DiBella, Sarah Burch, et al., "Exploring the Potential of SMEs to Build Individual, Organizational, and Community Resilience through Sustainability-Oriented Business Practices," *Business Strategy and the Environment* 32, no. 1 (2023): 721–35, https://doi.org/10.1002/bse.3171.

16 Aisha Ahmad, *Jihad & Co.: Black Markets and Islamist Power* (Oxford: Oxford University Press, 2017). See also Aisha Ahmad, "The Security Bazaar: Business Interests and Islamist Power in Civil War Somalia," *International Security* 39, no. 3 (2015): 89–117, https://doi.org/10.1162/ISEC_a_00187; Aisha Ahmad, "Going Global: Islamist Competition in Contemporary Civil Wars," *Security Studies* 25, no. 2 (2016): 353–84, https://doi.org/10.1080/09636412.2016.1171971; Aisha Ahmad, "'We Have Captured Your Women': Explaining Jihadist Norm Change," *International Security* 44, no. 1 (2019): 80–116, https://doi.org/10.1162/isec_a_00350; Aisha Ahmad, "The Long Jihad: The Boom-Bust Cycle behind Jihadist Durability," *Journal of Global Security Studies* 6, no. 4 (2021): ogaa048, https://doi.org/10.1093/jogss/ogaa048; Aisha Ahmad,

Tanya Bandula-Irwin, and Mohamed Ibrahim, "Who Governs? State versus Jihadist Political Order in Somalia," *Journal of Eastern African Studies* 16, no. 1 (2022): 68–91, https://doi.org/10.1080/17531055.2022.2075817; Aisha Ahmad and Ousmane Diallo, "A Winning Team of Losers: The Logic of Jihadist Coalitions in Civil Wars," *Journal of Global Security Studies* 8, no. 1 (2023): ogac029, https://doi.org/10.1093/jogss/ogac029.

17 Megan MacKenzie, *Beyond the Band of Brothers: The US Military and the Myth That Women Can't Fight* (Cambridge: Cambridge University Press, 2015). See also Megan MacKenzie, "Securitization and Desecuritization: Female Soldiers and the Reconstruction of Women in Post-conflict Sierra Leone," *Security Studies* 18, no. 2 (2009): 241–61, https://doi.org/10.1080/09636410902900061; Megan MacKenzie, "Empowerment Boom or Bust? Assessing Women's Post-conflict Empowerment Initiatives," *Cambridge Review of International Affairs* 22, no. 2 (2009): 199–215, https://doi.org/10.1080/09557570902877976; Megan Mackenzie, "Securitizing Sex?," *International Feminist Journal of Politics* 12, no. 2 (2010): 202–21, https://doi.org/10.1080/14616741003665250; Megan MacKenzie and Alana Foster, "Masculinity Nostalgia: How War and Occupation Inspire a Yearning for Gender Order," *Security Dialogue* 48, no. 3 (2017): 206–23, https://doi.org/10.1177/0967010617696238; Megan MacKenzie, "Why Do Soldiers Swap Illicit Pictures? How a Visual Discourse Analysis Illuminates Military Band of Brother Culture," *Security Dialogue* 51, no. 4 (2020): 340–57, https://doi.org/10.1177/0967010619898468.

18 Nicole Wegner and Megan MacKenzie, *Feminist Solutions for Ending War* (London: Pluto Press, 2021).

19 Sheryl Lightfoot, *Global Indigenous Politics: A Subtle Revolution* (London: Routledge, 2016). See also Sheryl Lightfoot, "Indigenous Peoples and Canadian Defence," in *Canadian Defence Policy in Theory and Practice*, ed. Thomas Juneau, Philippe Lagassé, and Srdjan Vucetic (Cham, Switzerland: Springer, 2020), 217–31, https://doi.org/10.1007/978-3-030-26403-1_13; Sheryl Lightfoot, "A Leopard Cannot Hide Its Spots: Unmasking Opposition to the UN Declaration on the Rights of Indigenous Peoples Special Issue: British Columbia's Declaration on the Rights of Indigenous Peoples Act," *UBC Law Review* 53, no. 4 (2021): 1147–84; Sheryl R. Lightfoot, "Decolonizing Self-Determination: Haudenosaunee Passports and Negotiated Sovereignty," *European*

Journal of International Relations 27, no. 4 (2021): 971–94, https://doi.org/10.1177/13540661211024713; Sheryl Lightfoot, "Indigenous Disruptions: How Indigenous Self-Determination Practices Can Deepen and Expand International Theory," in *Globalizing International Theory: The Problem with Western IR Theory and How to Overcome It*, ed. A. Layug and John Hobson, (London: Routledge, 2022), 200–18.

20 Jasmin Zine, *Under Siege: Islamophobia and the 9/11 Generation* (Montreal: McGill-Queen's University Press, 2022). See also Jasmin Zine, "Between Orientalism and Fundamentalism: Muslim Women and Feminist Engagement," in *(En)Gendering the War on Terror*, ed. Krista Hunt and Kim Rygiel (London: Routledge, 2008), 27–49; Jasmin Zine, *Islam in the Hinterlands: Muslim Cultural Politics in Canada* (Vancouver: UBC Press, 2012); Jasmin Zine, "The Canadian Islamophobia Industry: Islamophobia's Ecosystem in the Great White North," *Islamophobia Studies Journal* 7, no. 2 (2022): 233–49.

21 Maja Janmyr and Lama Mourad, "Modes of Ordering: Labelling, Classification and Categorization in Lebanon's Refugee Response," *Journal of Refugee Studies* 31, no. 4 (2018): 544–65, https://doi.org/10.1093/jrs/fex042; Maja Janmyr and Lama Mourad, "Categorising Syrians in Lebanon as 'Vulnerable,'" *Forced Migration Review*, no. 57 (February 2018): 19–21; Lama Mourad and Kelsey P. Norman, "Transforming Refugees into Migrants: Institutional Change and the Politics of International Protection," *European Journal of International Relations* 26, no. 3 (2020): 687–713, https://doi.org/10.1177/1354066119883688; Lama Mourad, "Brothers, Workers or Syrians? The Politics of Naming in Lebanese Municipalities," *Journal of Refugee Studies* 34, no. 2 (2021): 1387–99, https://doi.org/10.1093/jrs/feab012.

22 Kevin Cox and Jeff Sallot, "Navy to Let Women Sail on Submarines," *Globe and Mail*, 9 March 2001, https://www.theglobeandmail.com/news/national/navy-to-let-women-sail-on-submarines/article4145469/.

23 Alistair Edgar, Rupinder Mangat, and Bessma Momani, *Strengthening the Canadian Armed Forces through Diversity and Inclusion* (Toronto: University of Toronto Press, 2019). See also L.E. Gomez and Patrick Bernet, "Diversity Improves Performance and Outcomes," *Journal of the National Medical Association* 111, no. 4 (2019): 383–92, https://doi.org/10.1016/j.jnma.2019.01.006; Akshaya Kamalnath, "Gender Diversity as the

Antidote to 'Groupthink' on Corporate Boards," *Deakin Law Review* 22, no. 1 (2018), https://dx.doi.org/10.2139/ssrn.3097396; Nathalie Allen, Leonor Díaz Córdova, and Natalie Hall, "'If Everyone Is Thinking Alike, Then No One Is Thinking': The Importance of Cognitive Diversity in Arbitral Tribunals to Enhance the Quality of Arbitral Decision Making," *Journal of International Arbitration* 38, no. 5 (2021), https://kluwerlawonline.com/api/Product/CitationPDFURL?file=Journals\JOIA\JOIA2021029.pdf; Ayman Issa and Nasrine Bensalem, "Are Gender-Diverse Boards Eco-Innovative? The Mediating Role of Corporate Social Responsibility Strategy," *Corporate Social Responsibility and Environmental Management* 30, no. 2 (2023): 742–54, https://doi.org/10.1002/csr.2385.

24 Irving Lester Janis, *Groupthink: Psychological Studies of Policy Decisions and Fiascoes*, 2nd ed. (Boston: Houghton Mifflin, 1982).

25 Stephanie Carvin, *Stand on Guard: Reassessing Threats to Canada's National Security* (Toronto: University of Toronto Press, 2021).

26 Diana Fu, *Mobilizing without the Masses: Control and Contention in China* (Cambridge: Cambridge University Press, 2017).

27 Juliet Johnson, *Priests of Prosperity: How Central Bankers Transformed the Postcommunist World*, ill. ed. (Ithaca, NY: Cornell University Press, 2016).

28 Lee Ann Fujii, *Killing Neighbors: Webs of Violence in Rwanda*, ill. ed. (Ithaca, NY: Cornell University Press, 2011).

29 Pamela D. Palmater, *Beyond Blood: Rethinking Indigenous Identity* (Saskatoon: Purich Publishing, 2011).

30 Debra Thompson, *The Schematic State: Race, Transnationalism, and the Politics of the Census*, repr. ed. (Cambridge: Cambridge University Press, 2018).

PART 1

Changing Systems

chapter one

The Enemy Within: Polarization Risks for US Hegemony and the Liberal International Order

CARLA NORRLÖF

The widely accepted notion of an imminent power shift risks becoming a self-fulfilling prophecy. China's emergence as an economic powerhouse, coupled with the geopolitical manoeuvres of both China and Russia, reinforces the perception of an irreversible decline in US influence. In the words of the 2017 *National Security Strategy*, "after being dismissed as a phenomenon of an earlier century, great power competition [has] returned."[1] Even Russia's invasion of Ukraine and the epic sanctions imposed by the United States and its allies in response are said to weaken the United States by creating a backlash and strengthening the potential Sino-Russian alliance against US financial dominance.[2] While academics and policymakers have been debating US decline since the 1970s, the Trump administration framed this decline in a way that none of its predecessors had before. It attributed US relative decline to unfair foreign economic competition and inadequate burden sharing within the security sphere. Having diagnosed the problem, the solution was clear: negotiating more favourable terms for US foreign economic engagement and reducing the tolerance for free riding on US offensive capabilities. Foreigners would no longer be allowed to take advantage of the United States. This narrative of free-loading economic partners and security allies was wrapped in belligerent language towards foreigners and hostile imagery about their attitudes and circumstances. Given that Canada is a key ally and trading partner of the United States, these changes in US policy towards allies and the broader changes in the global balance of power have significant implications for the future of Canadian security.

American decline will unquestionably affect Canadian national security, as well as the security of the wider world. Nevertheless, the breakdown of America's social fabric and its neglect of the hard task of restoring the domestic foundations of American power have brought about this reckoning, one that has been a long time coming for the United States and that will have far-reaching reverberations. This chapter explains why the United States is in a period of hegemonic decline and what this decline means for the international order. First, it examines the decline hypothesis and explains that the causes of US decline are more domestic than foreign. It then explains why shoring up the domestic sources of US power and cultivating social cohesion is the key to sustaining US dominance and the liberal international order. As Canadian national security is inextricably tied to the United States, it is imperative that Canada understand and adapt to these changes in the years ahead.

Foreign and Domestic Drivers of US Decline

The United States is widely perceived to be losing its standing as the world's dominant power. Indeed, in certain areas, the United States no longer commands the strong lead it once had, notably in the trade area, where China has emerged as a formidable competitor. Long before China made its mark as a commercial colossus on the world stage, the European Union had started to nudge away at the United States' advantage. For several decades, Chinese growth outpaced that of the United States, and this, too, is taken as a sign of waning US hegemony. Starting from a low level of GDP, Chinese growth has been spectacular. The United States also faces starker competition on the security scene. China and Russia have significantly ramped up their military capabilities over the last decades and have become more forceful, pressing territorial demands in their respective regions. But Russia's Ukraine invasion stunned the world as much for its naked aggression as for the country's substandard great power performance and inability to break Ukrainian resistance.

Despite the rising challenges from China and Russia, these explanations do not adequately explain the relative decline in US hegemonic power. While Chinese growth has been impressive, whether China will outpace US GDP as its economy matures remains to be seen. Moreover, quantifying the loss of US commercial power requires a more elaborate assessment than subtracting merchandise exports from imports. In addition, often absent from the great power scorecard is an evaluation of financial power where China lags behind, particularly with regard to cross-border finance and international currency provision. The United States remains the only country to provide a global currency, offering a range of perks other countries, even great powers, do not possess. The United States still dominates international financial markets, and despite geopolitical challenges, the dollar remains the dominant reserve currency for official actors and the most global currency for private actors.[3] To be sure, China has made some inroads in the currency area; however, its distance from the United States is far too wide to pose any immediate or even medium-term threat. Russia lags even further behind and is reeling after its Ukraine aggression. Russia may continue to pose a security threat, but it is even less of a contender for great power dominance than it has been in the last quarter century. US privileges are not written in stone, and over the very long term, the Chinese currency, or perhaps the euro, could displace the US dollar as the primary global currency, particularly if China expands third-party trade in yuan, becomes more financially sophisticated and open, and leads the way in supplying a central bank digital currency. While great power scholars largely ignore these metrics, they are important measures to consider when weighing up great power competition. When they are factored into the balance, it is evident that we are a long way from a bipolar or multipolar order.

To fully explain US decline, it is therefore necessary to look inward to domestic politics, the rise in populism, and the social divisions on issues ranging from immigration, discrimination, gender, sexuality, abortion, and gun control in the United States. The 2016–20 Trump administration, which promised to "Make America Great Again," embodied the prevailing angst about US slippage. Acting on declinist sentiment, President Trump pushed hard to preserve US primacy abroad and white primacy at home. His administration's discourse about US decline blamed foreign countries for outcompeting the United States and made foreigners the principal cause of flailing US prosperity and standing in the world.

A clear ethnic hierarchy underpinned President Trump's attacks. On the campaign trail, he often said China was engaging in "trade rape" against the United States.[4] In 2015, during his official campaign kick-off event, Trump called Mexicans rapists and thugs as he unveiled his plan to build a wall along the southern border.[5] He also took to Twitter to share inaccurate crime statistics disaggregated by "Black" and "white" Americans and called for a ban on Muslims from entering the United States.[6] Within the very first week of taking office, he made good on this promise, issuing an executive order suspending US entry from seven Muslim-majority countries for ninety days. Most troubling of all, he pushed forward with his promise to construct a wall along the southern border and failed to disassociate himself from white nationalist protestors in Charlottesville, Virginia, while introducing a policy separating Latin American migrant children from their parents before withdrawing it in the face of mass rebuke. When he gained office, Trump continued to insist that America's economic exchange with China amounted to one of the "greatest thefts in the history of the world."[7] Calling the coronavirus the "kung flu" virus, he was slow to accept the gravity of its threat to public safety but was quick to associate China with the tragedy it caused.[8] The most telling difference in his view of categories of foreigners was the contrast he made between immigration from Latin American and African countries, on the one hand, and immigration from Norway, on the other, allegedly calling the former "shithole" countries while welcoming immigration from Scandinavia.[9]

In essence, Trump's xenophobic rhetoric aimed to pit "foreign-looking" Americans against Americans of European descent in an "us" versus "them" bid welcomed by right-wing populists worldwide. When Trump clinched the 2016 election, far-right populists such as Marine Le Pen (France), Viktor Orbán (Hungary), Gábor Vona (Hungary), Nikolaos Michaloliakos (Greece), Frauke Petry (Germany), Heinz-Christian Strache (Austria), Christoph Blocher (Switzerland), and Geert Wilders (Netherlands) rejoiced and pledged a new world order. In common, these far-right populist leaders have anti-immigration platforms characterized by xenophobia and nativism. They anticipated that a Trump presidency would legitimize policies considered unsavoury in the past. And they were right. In Austria, Hungary, Italy, Poland, and the United States, far-right populist parties and candidates have entered government. In France, Germany, Greece, the Netherlands, Sweden, and the United Kingdom, they have won record levels of support and reshaped the political landscape. Canada was not at all immune to this rise in right-wing populism, with some leading Canadian political figures signalling their support for Trump's xenophobic messages. The far-right People's Party of Canada (PPC), formed in 2018, committed to "ending official multiculturalism and preserving Canadian values and culture."[10]

Trump's xenophobia at home also aligned with his confrontational stance on the world stage. Soon after taking office, the administration labelled China a "strategic competitor,"[11] and slapped punitive tariffs on Chinese goods. Stoking a trade war with China proved counterproductive. It not only triggered retaliatory threats and tariffs, but also failed to close the bilateral trade deficit, create a manufacturing boom in the United States, or incentivize China to change its WTO-inconsistent trade policies on subsidies, intellectual property, and forced technology transfers.[12] Moreover, the *National Defense Strategy* accuses China of "using predatory economics to intimidate its neighbors while militarizing features in the South China Sea"[13] (a development addressed by Lynette Ong in this volume). Nevertheless, America's more confrontational approach towards China – economically and militarily – has neither cowed the Chinese leadership nor halted its advances in the South China Sea.[14] The Trump administration did increase its naval dispatch to that area, but failed to mount an international coalition to push back against China's maritime expansion.[15]

Under Trump, US power and influence also declined in Europe, especially as a result of security disengagement. Asking allies to pay their "fair share" of alliance costs while threatening to withdraw US participation took a toll on transatlantic relations. The threat was made explicit in a *New York Times* interview in which Trump chided those allies who failed to make sufficient contributions towards the defence burden: "Congratulations, you will be defending yourself."[16] He doubled down on this promise in his inaugural address, saying that the United States "subsidized the armies of other countries while allowing for the very sad depletion of our military. We've defended other nations' borders while refusing to defend our own."[17] Shortly after, in his February address to Congress, he said, "We expect our partners – whether in NATO, the Middle East, or in the Pacific – to take a direct and meaningful role in both strategic and military operations, and pay their fair share of the cost."[18] These signals were not lost on an increasingly belligerent Putin, who, following years of complaints about NATO expansion, welcomed fissures within the North Atlantic Alliance.[19] While other US presidents had expressed concerns about NATO burden sharing, President Trump made the security bargain a more direct quid pro quo.

After stoking ethnic tensions for four years, Trump's campaign of racial and political division in the United States culminated in the infamous Capitol Hill insurrection and occupation of Congress on 6 January 2021. Although Canada watched in shock at these incidents, it soon thereafter experienced a comparable domestic crisis. In February 2022, Canada experienced a month-long occupation of its capital city of Ottawa. The "Freedom Convoy" protests not only occupied the capital, but also blocked off the Ambassador Bridge, a key trade route connecting Canada and the United States. Although the protestors claimed to be dissenting against vaccine mandates, the ethnically divisive undercurrent was just as inescapable as the xenophobia undergirding the January 2021 attacks on the US capitol. Several organizers are associated with white nationalism.[20] As in the United States, anti-Muslim rhetoric features prominently in their messaging.

According to a 2019 EKOS poll, 40 per cent of Canadians said there are "too many visible minorities coming to Canada."[21] The

UK-based Institute for Strategic Dialogue claims that more than 6,600 right-wing extremist social media pages, channels, and accounts have been linked to Canadians, and that more than 6,300 Canadian users were "closely connected" to extremist Twitter accounts.[22] Most recently, Canada saw a rise in the popularity of the far-right PPC, headed by Maxime Bernier, who is frequently compared to Trump. Importantly, what makes the emergence and victories of these populist leaders so disturbing are the common characteristics that unite far-right populists: the rejection of liberal values and the recourse to discriminatory overtones.

Although economic inequality plays a part in stoking populism, underlying material concerns have been co-opted by right-wing extremists to blame racial minorities for these economic woes. Having opened the floodgates of xenophobic populism and normalized discriminatory discourse and policies, redistributive economic measures are now less likely to be effective than if they had been implemented earlier. Far-right groups, once on the fringes of society, have been galvanized by Trump's presidency and the populist surge around the globe. Social acceptance of discriminatory practices is on the rise, as is a certain fatigue on the part of erstwhile self-ascribed allies. The reignition of racist and xenophobic ideas within society has led to the planning, and sometimes execution, of devastating events.

A white nationalist "threat from within" has emerged in the United States and has spread beyond its border. Hate crimes inflamed by Trump's rhetoric and rallies surged in connection with these campaigns.[23] These have increased in Canada as well, and right-wing extremism has become more organized in the country.[24] Network analysis of these social ties shows how right-wing extremist leaders in Canada actively work to create bonds within their communities after establishing themselves as authoritative voices.[25] In Canada, this "threat from within" resulted in the horrific Quebec City mosque shooting of 29 January 2017, when an individual with white nationalist and anti-Muslim views shot and fatally injured worshippers at a local mosque. In 2021, the Afzaal family was murdered in London, Ontario. (For a comprehensive discussion of Islamophobia, see the chapter by Jasmin Zine in this volume.) Xenophobia is not only a threat to communities and societies, but one that cannot be reconciled with the values at the heart of the liberal international order.

Inequality and the Liberal International Order

A key tenet of the liberal international order is the equal treatment of individuals regardless of race, ethnicity, or religion. With few exceptions, the debate about the future of the liberal international order reduces the liberal component to "democracy." In an early work, Daniel Deudney and G. John Ikenberry listed ethnic tolerance as a requirement for leadership of this liberal order.[26] However, their later scholarship, and the subsequent literature, made little to no room for discussion of discrimination in debates surrounding the future of US hegemony and the liberal international order. Instead, they focused on the strength of US domestic political institutions in other respects, with much of the discussion bracketed under the heading "democracy." Very little thought was given to how the regular human rights infringements posed by discrimination might erode democracy or directly threaten the liberal international order in other ways. As a matter of policy, the United States expended considerable resources and even went to war to promote democracy abroad. Often, it advocated for greater observance of human rights in foreign countries as well. Domestically, however, discrimination-related human rights abuses were allowed to continue, sometimes sanctioned by domestic laws and institutions.

In *An American Dilemma*, Gunnar Myrdal described the contradiction between American liberal ideals and the reality of racial discrimination.[27] Today, the conflict between liberal institutions' mission statements and the reality of discrimination is particularly stark within higher education.[28] Long considered a bastion of liberal values and a site for oppressive "woke" policies, colleges and universities trumpet their support for non-discrimination. Institutional leaders and faculty teach and research colonialism, microaggressions, and institutional racism, create diversity bureaus, and "educate" society about the high standards from which they exempt themselves. Unsurprisingly, a study of Canadian universities shows how faculty and university leadership, advocating inclusiveness and diversity, persistently fail to hire, promote, support, and celebrate racialized faculty.[29]

Research has shown a relationship between the higher rates of punitive actions against Black students (as compared to white students) and the degree of racial bias against them, increasing their likelihood of negative life experiences.[30] Disproportionate punishment tends to lower students' sense of belonging and therefore academic performance, adversely affecting social outcomes, even encouraging criminal involvement.[31] In some high-profile cases, faculty have also been disciplined for raising complaints about discrimination. For example, at Penn State University, a Black associate professor in the Department of Political Science asked the administration to intervene to put a stop to decades of discrimination.[32] A university investigation was conducted and came to the conclusion that his claims were unsubstantiated.[33] Instead, the white female department chair accused the Black male complainant of harassment.[34] Even higher-ranking administrators, including the university president, denied the substance of the charges.[35] The associate vice-president of affirmative action supported the faculty, who had mobilized against the complainant, alleging that his allegations had created a "hostile environment" for them, which then led to the complainant being charged with discrimination and subjected to a series of punitive actions.[36] Whatever the merits of the case, accusing a Black man of discrimination and harassment in response to his complaint of racial discrimination is an absurd outcome.

The killing of George Floyd saw university leadership issuing statements about the legacy of racism and its pernicious effects. In this climate, the president of Penn State, who had denied the complainant's charges of discrimination in the above-mentioned case, issued a statement calling for a campus-wide reckoning with racism.[37] So, despite having disciplined the complainant for drawing attention to racial bias, the president's community address noted that to stop university incidents of hate, "we cannot exact a legal punishment without both violating the law or giving up the rights that protect our democracy."[38] The complainant filed a lawsuit, and the case was mediated and settled.[39] This seems to be representative of broader problems with racism at Penn State.[40] It also reflects the experience of countless Black academics in the United States who choose to resign instead of being slammed by the inevitable conclusion of a university-controlled "investigation" into their institution's failure to guarantee a discrimination- and harassment-free environment.[41] Similar discriminatory practices and incidents of university leadership retaliating against complainants plague Canadian higher education.[42]

Today, Black professors account for only 4 per cent of professors in the United States. Liberal academics continue to attribute this lack of diversity to a pipeline problem, which they claim will self-correct when new students are admitted and mentored.[43] Yet only 8 per cent of assistant professors in the United States are Black, suggesting more profound challenges.[44] In Canada, the situation is far worse. Black professors across all ranks account for only 2 per cent of the whole.[45] Most people associate Canada with multiculturalism and believe the country is more open, immigration-friendly, and tolerant than the United States. However, Black people in both societies report similar rates of racism relative to their populations. In Canada, 41 per cent of Blacks say they have encountered discrimination based on their race or colour.[46] In the United States, 43 per cent say they have experienced racism by individuals and 52 per cent due to racism enshrined in laws.[47]

Black academics have an entirely different view of the underlying problem. They point to the myriad obstacles skewing remuneration, awards, honours, promotions, and job offers.[48] The societal effects are significant, with the lingering racial divide in higher education constituting the primary cause of the imbalance in elite representation within culture, politics, the economy, science, media, and public policy.[49] The problem lies with a status quo in which everyone knows discrimination exists but assumes no one they know could possibly act in a discriminatory way because no one really knows what qualifies as a discriminatory act.

For many people, discrimination involves slurs and/or physical violence. They are unable to see the myriad ways in which more subtle forms of discrimination occur. In academia, gatekeeping networks, flexible criteria, opportunism, exclusion, authority pandering, and confidential procedures provide fertile ground for discriminatory behaviour with plausible deniability.[50] While many scholars say they are concerned about anti-Black racism in the academy, they do little to counter it, and sometimes even exploit marginalization to further their own careers. Instead of any consequential change, the system keeps humming along under a thin veneer of DEI (diversity, equity, and inclusion) campaigns aimed at whitewashing institutions' reputations, infuriating most conservatives (for its political correctness) and Black scholars (for its hypocrisy).[51]

To understand how inequality relates to American hegemonic decline, we can draw on the ideas of the fourteenth-century Arab philosopher and historian Ibn Khaldûn and his concept of *asabiyyah*, which offers valuable insights into our current predicament.[52] *Asabiyyah* refers to a strong "we" feeling, a shared identity, which could refer to group solidarity based on ancestral "blood" ties, or a shared purpose and sense of belonging on a basis broader than identity. Khaldûn uses the concept of *asabiyyah* to illuminate how a socially cohesive group gains power before withering away in the face of decadence and extravagance. By this logic, internal social divisions pose a grave threat to group solidarity and cohesion, rendering them less proactive and effective externally. As a direct parallel, the "threat from within" of right-wing extremism acts as a corrosive force on American power, both at home and abroad. Great power rivals, particularly Russia, recognize this lack of social unity as a weakness.[53] They fan the flames of division using covert information campaigns on social media, particularly during elections, as they did in both 2016 and 2020.[54] (See Leah West's chapter on cybersecurity for further analysis of this dynamic).

This internal corrosion allows tribal logic to inform America's domestic and foreign policies, causing the hegemon to forego mutually beneficial outcomes through cooperation for zero-sum gains, ultimately contributing to its own decline. This self-destruction jeopardizes America's ability to compete with key rivals and carries three additional risks for the United States and the liberal international order. First, "white" identity-based politics fuels resentment of foreigners both abroad and at home, sowing divisions that undermine the domestic foundations of US power. Second, "white" identity-based politics privileges zero-sum policies over mutually beneficial ones, effectively weakening America's ability to come out on top effectively in great power competition. Third, conflict between warring "tribes" at home creates discontinuity and incoherence in the United States' grand strategy for managing external competitors.

An increasingly polarized, unequal, and unpredictable United States reflects a country that has lost sight of its common purpose and vision, and a weakening of *asabiyyah* in the broader sense of the term. After defeating Trump in 2020, Biden attempted to portray himself as "a president for all Americans," and he took actions to diminish the "us and them" social and political climate, such as choosing Kamala Harris as vice-president and advancing racially, ethnically, and religiously diverse cabinet and Supreme Court nominations. However, the real challenge will be to go beyond virtue signalling to address core systemic issues.

Moreover, Biden's unconditional support for Israel's Gaza campaign, following Hamas's brutal attack, has resulted in a widening partisan, ethnic, and generational divide within the United States. With the overwhelming majority of countries (153) supporting the non-binding UN General Assembly resolution calling for an "immediate humanitarian ceasefire" in Gaza, and the United States voting against it, Biden's policy is out of step with global sentiment.[55] This deep rift may play towards a Trump victory in the 2024 presidential race.[56] Given the divisiveness that was unleashed in 2016, we may be in for an alternating cycle of discriminatory and liberal forces for some time to come.

If America fails to reverse course and heal its deepening racial and social divisions, it will continue to experience decline on the world stage. Canada is not only watching this erosion of American power from the sidelines but also experiencing a similar "threat from within." Some populist narratives have been mainstreamed. The Conservative Party of Canada saw Pierre Poilievre elected as leader. Poilievre has adopted some of the same far-right populist themes as the PPC – for example, with his support of the so-called Freedom Convoy.[57] The composition of immigrants has become a partisan issue in Canada, with a supermajority of Conservatives characterizing the portion of visible minorities as too big.[58] Even more than the United States, Canada depends on the maintenance of the liberal international order and its alliances with other democratic countries to uphold its security interests. The corrosive and contagious force of xenophobia threatens not only American hegemony – it also endangers the democratic allies of the United States, including Canada, as they confront similar challenges.

NOTES

1 Donald J. Trump, *The National Security Strategy of the United States of America* (Washington DC: White House, 2017).
2 Carla Norrlöf, "The New Economic Containment: Russian Sanctions Signal Commitment to International Order," *Foreign Affairs*, 18 March 2022.
3 Carla Norrlöf, "Currency, Conflict, and Global Order," *Project Syndicate*, 14 July 2023, https://www.project-syndicate.org/onpoint/will-multi polarity-follow-global-dollar-hegemony-by-carla-norrlof-2023-07; Carla Norrlöf, "The Dollar Still Dominates: American Financial Power in the Age of Great-Power Competition," *Foreign Affairs*, 21 February 2023, https://www.foreignaffairs.com/united-states/dollar-still-dominates.
4 Jeremy Diamond, "Trump: 'We Can't Continue to Allow China to Rape Our Country'," *CNN*, 2 May 2016, https://www.cnn.com/2016/05/01/politics/donald-trump-china-rape/index.html.
5 Michelle Ye Hee, "Donald Trump's False Comments Connecting Mexican Immigrants and Crime," *Washington Post*, 8 July 2015.
6 Carla Norrlöf, "Hegemony and Inequality," *International Affairs* 94, no. 1 (2018): 63–88.
7 Jordan Fabian and Morgan Chalfant, "Trump Expands Anti-China Effort," *The Hill*, 10 September 2018.
8 Li Zhou, "Trump's Racist References to the Coronavirus Are His Latest Effort to Stoke Xenophobia," *Vox*, 23 June 2020, https://www.vox.com/2020/6/23/21300332/trump-coronavirus-racism-asian-americans.

9 Josh Dawsey, "Trump Derides Protections for Immigrants from 'Shithole' Countries," *Washington Post*, 12 January 2018.
10 Moira Warburton, "Canadian Right-Wing Party Calls for End to 'Official Multiculturalism,'" Reuters, 9 August 2019, https://www.reuters.com/article/idUSKCN1UZ1WR/.
11 Jim Mattis, *Summary of the 2018 National Defense Strategy of the United States of America* (Washington DC: Department of Defense, 2018).
12 Philip H. Gordon, "What Should Come after Trump's Failed China Policy?," *War on the Rocks*, 6 July 2020, https://warontherocks.com/2020/07/what-should-come-after-trumpsfailed-china-policy/.
13 Mattis, *Summary of the 2018 National Defense Strategy*, 1.
14 Gordon, "What Should Come after Trump's Failed China Policy?"
15 Michael Schuman, "Why China Wants Trump to Win," *The Atlantic*, 7 July 2020.
16 "Transcript: Donald Trump on Nato, Turkey's Coup Attempt and the World," *New York Times*, 21 July 2016.
17 "Remarks of President Donald J. Trump – as Prepared for Delivery, Inaugural Address Friday, January 20, 2017, Washington, D.C.," White House, accessed 19 March 2024, https://trumpwhitehouse.archives.gov/briefings-statements/the-inaugural-address/.
18 "Remarks by President Trump in Joint Address to Congress, Issued on February 28, 2017," White House, accessed 19 March 2024, https://trumpwhitehouse.archives.gov/briefings-statements/remarks-president-trump-joint-address-congress/.
19 Carla Norrlöf, "A New Iron Curtain Splits Russia from the West," *World Politics Review*, 19 April 2022. For a full discussion of how NATO enlargement impacts Canadian security, see von Hlatky and Hollander's chapter in this volume.
20 Rachel Gilmore, "Some Trucker Convoy Organizers Have History of White Nationalism, Racism," *Global News*, 29 January 2022, https://globalnews.ca/news/8543281/covid-trucker-convoy-organizers-hate/.
21 Ekos Politics, "Increased Polarization on Attitudes to Immigration Reshaping the Political Landscape in Canada," *Ekos Politics*, 15 April 2019, https://www.ekospolitics.com/index.php/2019/04/increased-polarization-on-attitudes-to-immigration-reshaping-the-political-landscape-in-canada/.

22 Jacob Davey, Cécile Guerin, and Mackenize Hart, *An Online Environmental Scan of Right-Wing Extremism in Canada* (London: Institute for Strategic Dialogue, 2019).
23 Ayal Feinberg, Regina Branton, and Valerie Martinez-Ebers, "The Trump Effect: How 2016 Campaign Rallies Explain Spikes in Hate," *PS: Political Science & Politics* 55, no. 2 (2022): 257–65.
24 Davey, Guerin, and Hart, *An Online Environmental Scan of Right-Wing Extremism in Canada.*
25 Bessma Momani and Ryan Deschamps, "Canada's Right-Wing Extremists: Mapping Their Ties, Location, and Ideas," *Journal of Hate Studies* 17, no. 2 (2021): 36–46.
26 Daniel Deudney and G. John Ikenberry, "The Nature and Sources of Liberal International Order," *Review of International Studies* 25, no. 2 (1999): 179–96.
27 Gunnar Myrdal, *An American Dilemma: The Negro Problem and Modern Democracy* (New York: Harper and Row, 1944).
28 Lawrence Goodman, "How Diversity Can Blind Us to Society's Underlying Racism," *BraneirNOW*, 14 December 2020, https://www.brandeis.edu/now/2020/december/diversty-race-mayorga.html; Meredith Kolodner, "Students Sick of 'Lip Service' from Universities over Racism," *Hechinger Report*, 20 June 2020, https://hechingerreport.org/students-sick-of-lip-service-from-universities-over-racism/.
29 Frances Henry, Enakshi Dua, Carl E.James, Audrey Kobayashi, Peter Li, Howard Ramos, and Malinda S. Smith, *The Equity Myth: Racialization and Indigeneity at Canadian Universities* (Vancouver: University of British Columbia Press, 2017).
30 Travis Riddle and Stacey Sinclair, "Racial Disparities in School-Based Disciplinary Actions Are Associated with County-Level Rates of Racial Bias," *Proceedings of the National Academy of Sciences* 116, no. 17 (2019): 8255–60.
31 Ming-Te Wang and Juan Del Toro, "For Black Students, Unfairly Harsh Discipline Can Lead to Lower Grades," American Psychological Association, 7 October 2021, https://www.apa.org/news/press/releases/2021/10/black-students-harsh-discipline.
32 John Beaugue, "Disciplined Penn State Professor Sues, Accuses the University of Discrimination," *PennLive*, 12 May 2021, https://www.pennlive.com/news/2021/05/disciplined-penn-state-professor-sues-accuses-the-university-of-discrimination.html.

33 John Beauge, "Black Professor Given Chance to Amend Federal Civil Rights Suit against Penn State," in *PennLive*, 22 March 2022, https://www.pennlive.com/news/2022/03/black-professor-given-chance-to-amend-federal-civil-rights-suit-against-penn-state.html.
34 Maddie Seelig, "Black Penn State Professor Settles Federal Lawsuit with the University," *Daily Collegian*, 3 February 2023, https://www.psucollegian.com/news/black-penn-state-professor-settles-federal-lawsuit-with-the-university/article_6c726856-a438-11ed-92d0-67e2aae4cb51.html.
35 Seelig, "Black Penn State Professor Settles Federal Lawsuit."
36 Beaugue, "Disciplined Penn State Professor Sues."
37 Eric J. Barron, "A Message from Penn State President Eric J. Barron," (Pennsylvania: Penn State, 10 June 2020, https://www.psu.edu/news/administration/story/message-penn-state-president-eric-j-barron-2/.
38 Barron, "A Message from Penn State President."
39 John Beaugue, "Ex-professor's Suit That Accused Penn State of Racism Is Settled through Mediation," *PennLive*, 30 January 2023, https://www.pennlive.com/news/2023/01/ex-professors-suit-that-accused-penn-state-of-racism-is-settled-through-mediation.html; Seelig, "Black Penn State Professor Settles Federal Lawsuit."
40 Nick Anderson, "Black Professors Push a Major University to Diversify and Confront Racism," *Washington Post*, 16 June 2021.
41 Colleen Flaherty, "Why They Left," *Inside Higher Ed*, 2 May 2021.
42 Sarah Nafisa Shahid, "Black Faculty Exposes Systemic Racism in Canadian Higher Education," *Spring*, 12 April 2021.
43 Tyrell Connor, "Black Faculty and Radical Retention," *Footnotes: A Magazine of the American Sociological Association* 50, no. 2 (2022), https://www.asanet.org/footnotes-article/black-faculty-and-radical-retention/.
44 Connor, "Black Faculty and Radical Retention."
45 Josh Kozelj, "Black People Make Up Just Two Per Cent of University Instructors in Canada. What Needs to Change?," *The Pigeon*, 6 November 2020, https://the-pigeon.ca/2020/11/06/black-professors/.
46 Adam Cotter, "Experiences of Discrimination among the Black and Indigenous Populations in Canada, 2019," Statistics Canada, 16 February 2022, https://www150.statcan.gc.ca/n1/pub/85-002-x/2022001/article/00002-eng.htm.

47 Katherine Schaeffer and Khadijah Edwards, "Black Americans Differ from Other U.S. Adults over Whether Individual or Structural Racism Is a Bigger Problem," Pew Research Center, 15 Novebver 2022, https://www.pewresearch.org/short-reads/2022/11/15/black-americans-differ-from-other-u-s-adults-over-whether-individual-or-structural-racism-is-a-bigger-problem/.
48 Colleen Flaherty, "The Souls of Black Professors," *Inside Higher Ed*, 20 October 2020.
49 Carla Norrlöf, "Educate to Liberate," *Foreign Affairs*, 12 February 2019, https://www.foreignaffairs.com/united-states/educate-liberate.
50 Lee Ann Fuji, "The Real Problem with Diversity in Political Science," *Duck of Minerva*, April 2017, http://duckofminerva.com/2017/04/the-real-problem-with-diversity-in-political-science.html; Carla Norrlöf and Cheng Xu, "The Networks and Hidden Procedures that Keep Discrimination Alive in Academia," *Duck of Minerva*, 12 July 2020, https://www.duckofminerva.com/2020/07/the-networks-and-hidden-procedures-that-keep-discrimination-alive-in-academia.html.
51 Rodney D. Coates, "Diversity and the University: A Call for Transformation and Reformation," *Footnotes: A Magazine of the American Sociological Association* 50, no. 2 (2022), https://www.asanet.org/footnotes-article/diversity-and-university-call-transformation-and-reformation/.
52 Carla Norrlöf, "The Ibn Khaldûn Trap and Great Power Competition with China," *The Washington Quarterly* 44, no. 1 (2021): 7–28.
53 For NATO and Canada's response, see Stéfanie von Hlatky and Hannah Hollander's chapter in this volume.
54 P.R. Lockhart, "How Russia Exploited Racial Tensions in America during the 2016 Elections," *Vox*, 17 December, 2018, https://www.vox.com/identities/2018/12/17/18145075/russia-facebook-twitter-internet-research-agency-race; Julian E. Barnes and Adam Goldman, "Russia Trying to Stoke U.S. Racial Tensions before Election, Officials Say," *New York Times*, 10 March, 2020, https://www.nytimes.com/2020/03/10/us/politics/russian-interference-race.html.
55 "Un General Assembly Votes by Large Majority for Immediate Humanitarian Ceasefire During Emergency Session," *UN News*, 12 December 2023, https://news.un.org/en/story/2023/12/1144717.

56 Eric Levenson, Whitney Wild, and Bill Kirkos, "Landlord Accused of Killing 6-Year-Old Palestinian American Boy Pleads Not Guilty to Murder and Hate Crime Charges," *CNN*, 30 October 2023, https://www.cnn.com/2023/10/30/us/palestinian-american-boy-stabbed/index.html; Andrea Shalal, "Biden's Israel Stance Angers Arab, Muslim Americans; Could Jeopardize 2024 Votes," Reuters, 24 October 2024, https://www.reuters.com/world/bidens-israel-stance-angers-arab-muslim-americans-could-jeopardize-2024-votes-2023-10-24/; "Americans' Views of the Israel-Hamas War," Pew Research Center, 8 December 2023, https://www.pewresearch.org/politics/2023/12/08/americans-views-of-the-israel-hamas-war/.

57 "Canadian Conservatives Elect "Right-Wing Populist" Pierre Poilievre to Lead Fight against Justin Trudeau," *CBS News*, 12 September 2022, https://www.cbsnews.com/news/pierre-poilievre-canada-conservatives-elect-right-wing-populist-vs-justin-trudeau/.

58 Ekos Politics, "Increased Polarization on Attitudes to Immigration Reshaping the Political Landscape in Canada."

chapter two

Canada and NATO

STÉFANIE VON HLATKY AND HANNAH HOLLANDER[1]

The North Atlantic Treaty Organization (NATO) is Canada's only treaty-based multilateral alliance and the cornerstone of its security and defence policy, along with the North American Aerospace Defense Command, which is focused on North American continental defence.[2] Canada's vast territory and limited defence budget, in an era of increasing threats to its security and sovereignty, means that its national and international interests are best pursued through the prism of bilateral and multilateral cooperation.[3] Consequently, Canada's involvement in NATO, and NATO's endurance over time, are central to the pursuit of its foreign and defence policy objectives. As an original member of NATO, created in 1949 at the outset of the Cold War, Canada's participation has ensured that the alliance harnesses both its military *and* political dimensions to promote transatlantic security.

This chapter will look at the importance of NATO membership within Canada's foreign and defence policy, highlight the security challenges that have driven the depth of its involvement through the alliance, and examine how the international security environment might evolve over the next decade. An overarching consideration throughout this discussion is the importance of alliance cohesion, given the tension between NATO's consensus-based decision-making process and the multiplicity of interests landing on its agenda since the Cold War. Russia's 2022 invasion of Ukraine has solidified the alliance's sense of common purpose, but intra-alliance disagreements about contributions remain, and ultimately these are a testament to NATO's institutional resilience. Indeed, NATO's security interests have broadened since the end of the Cold War because threat perceptions have changed and because NATO embarked on a process of enlargement.[4] NATO enlargement has been a particularly sensitive topic both within the alliance and in the context of the NATO-Russia relationship, even in the case the accession of Sweden and Finland, countries that have been close NATO partners for years.[5] Scholars continue to debate the merits of enlargement, as well as the specific terms upon which it was undertaken in the 1990s and 2000s.[6] The intensification of great power competition, with Russia but also China (see the chapter by Lynette Ong in this volume), has renewed the alliance's raison d'être as a defensive organization and more solidly anchored its open-door policy. Yet security challenges are not limited to traditional collective defence considerations; they also include cybersecurity threats, climate change (see chapter by Kathryn Harrison), the enduring effects of the COVID-19 pandemic, and human security, as outlined in the *NATO 2030* document (discussed further below) and other high-level policy documents. Indeed, since the end of the Cold War, NATO and Canada have broadened their focus from strictly defence and deterrence to include human security, pursued primarily through capacity-building operations and partnerships, both within the North Atlantic space and globally, from Colombia to Mongolia. Human security translates into a people-centric, rather than a narrow state-centric, conception of security, consistent with NATO's Policy on Women, Peace, and Security. Security challenges in Kosovo, Afghanistan, Libya, and Iraq, and NATO's subsequent involvement in those countries, has pushed the alliance to broaden its conception of security, drawing from the claim that insecurity in other regions destabilizes transatlantic security (see chapter by Bessma Momani, for example). During the post–Cold War era, this expanding security agenda created intra-alliance disagreement. However, and as previously stated, Russia's war in Ukraine has motivated greater alliance cohesion and a renewed focus on NATO's eastern flank.

Canada and NATO's History

When NATO was created in 1949, there were debates about its identity as a traditional military alliance. For example, Canada's lead diplomat (and future prime minister) Lester B. Pearson pushed for the North Atlantic Treaty to have a political article, committed to promoting peace through political and economic cooperation. This resulted in article 2, which is sometimes referred to as the "Canadian Article."[7] While many other founding members opposed this, article 2 was adopted and eventually proved to be critical to NATO's success and ongoing relevance, especially as the nature of international conflict has evolved over the alliance's seventy plus years of existence.

After the collapse of the Soviet Union in 1991, there was uncertainty about the purpose of the alliance and what its role in international security would be going forward. An alliance in the traditional sense may have dissolved, but NATO embarked on an enlargement process, broadening its membership to fill the political security vacuum in central and eastern Europe.[8] While broadening the alliance to what it is today, an organization of thirty-two member states (and counting), has no doubt contributed to political stability and economic prosperity in many former Soviet republics and Warsaw Pact countries, enlargement has been a major point of contention between Russia and NATO. Russia has even made enlargement one of its main *casus belli* in its war in Ukraine, a formal NATO partner. While much of the present focus is on Russia, NATO has also been called upon to intervene militarily in response to the humanitarian catastrophe that followed the breakup of Yugoslavia, a presence that continues to this day with approximately 3,500 troops in Kosovo.[9] The al-Qaeda terrorist attack of 11 September 2001 signified another shift in NATO's focus with the launch of counterterrorism and counter-insurgency operations in Afghanistan, through the United Nations–sanctioned International Security Assistance Force (ISAF) and, after, the Resolute Support Mission (RSM). Although the Afghan mission ended poorly, with the government's collapse following the hasty American troop drawdown in August 2021, ISAF was the biggest and most visible manifestation of NATO's role in regional and global security, as well as of Canada's involvement within NATO.

NATO Operations – Past to Present

Canada has contributed to all NATO operations since the 1990s and has often been tasked with important command positions. This was the case during ISAF, when in 2003, Brigadier General P.J. Devlin commanded the Kabul Multinational Brigade, the operational headquarters for ISAF, for six months, Major-General A. Leslie was the deputy commander of ISAF for six months, and Lieutenant General R. Hillier was the commander of ISAF for six months in 2004.[10] Lieutenant General C. Bouchard took command of Operation Unified Protector in Libya in March 2011, serving in that position until the end of the operation in October 2011,[11] and Major Generals D. Fortin and J. Carignan each commanded the NATO Mission Iraq for a year, starting in 2018.[12] Canada is also a lead ally, or Framework Nation (in NATO parlance), for Enhanced Forward Presence (EFP) on NATO's northeastern front. Canada has led the battlegroup in Latvia since it was established in 2017, and this multinational NATO presence has been upgraded since 2022.[13] Operation Unified Protector lasted all of eleven months and had a rather narrow mandate focused on the Responsibility to Protect, and NATO wrapped up its military operation in Afghanistan in 2021 after two decades of extensive involvement; however, Canada is still a contributor to the missions in Iraq and Latvia.

NATO's record of military operations is, at best, mixed and certainly uneven. The abrupt end to NATO's training mission in Afghanistan illustrates this. The democratically elected government in Kabul was overthrown by the Taliban much faster than any intelligence analysts, academics, or politicians could have reasonably predicted following the American withdrawal of troops in August 2021. Despite two decades of extensive military operations and high costs both in blood and dollars, the West was unable to secure a stable outcome, in either political or security terms.

Although it was clear in 2020 that the Afghanistan government and Afghan National Army were struggling to maintain control of the country, in February 2020, President Donald Trump signed a peace agreement with the Taliban, stating that the United States would completely withdraw its troops from Afghanistan within fourteen months. Following the 2020 election, which brought Joe Biden to the White House, this withdrawal time frame was extended to 11 September 2021, thereby imposing the United States' deadline on the rest of its NATO allies and partners, who could not run RSM without a substantive American presence. While Canada withdrew its combat troops from Afghanistan in 2011 and wrapped up its training role in 2014, the end of NATO's military presence in the country was a significant milestone for all allies and partners who had committed troops and money to this endeavour over the past two decades.

In Iraq, the United States formally ended its combat mission in December 2021, though it continues to maintain 2,500 troops to serve in advisory, training, and assistance roles. Despite the reduction in American contributions, during the February 2021 NATO defence ministerial, the alliance announced that contributions would be ramped up, indicating that the troop presence could increase from 500 to 4,000.[14] Russia's war in Ukraine has interfered with those plans. While Canada renewed its involvement in Iraq through Operation Impact, Russia's invasion of Ukraine forced a re-evaluation of all of NATO's out-of-area operations.

Beyond these operations, Canada continues to support NATO objectives through contributions to the standing maritime groups and other activities, such as Enhanced Forward Presence and its own training and capacity efforts with NATO partners. Canada has been conducting training and capacity-building efforts in Ukraine since 2014 under the banner of Operation Unifier. The training was briefly paused in February 2022, but the mission then quickly expanded to include the training of Ukrainian troops in Poland and the United Kingdom. In addition to its contributions to NATO operations, Canada participates in NATO exercises throughout the year and across the globe. These exercises are essential to enhance NATO's interoperability so that large and small members alike are prepared to respond to a diverse range of security threats across domains (e.g., land, air, sea, cyber, and space).

Canada and NATO in an Evolving Security Environment

Russia's invasion of Ukraine in February 2022 affirmed many experts' predictions that NATO would face greater instability due to more intense great power competition. This instability took the form of a full-scale conventional war right on NATO's doorstep, along with millions of refugees seeking safety in neighbouring countries. This war, alongside China's increasingly adversarial relationship with NATO allies, has resulted in intensified adversarial tactics directed at the alliance. Individual allies, including Canada, are attacked daily in the cyber and information domains (see chapter by Leah West). Rapid technological advancements have created new hybrid means for adversarial states to attack NATO members, making it more challenging for NATO to respond when the nature and actor behind the attack are unclear. Indeed, NATO adversaries are increasingly willing to exploit this space between peace and war, what is often referred to as the grey zone of conflict.[15] NATO allies have been facing an increase in the number and severity of cyberattacks, both against public and private entities, as well as disinformation campaigns that aim to undermine Western democracies and amplify national divisions, not least through interference attempts during elections.[16] As an alliance, NATO has sought to counter this disinformation and to build greater resilience among its member states by opting for transparent communication and systematically debunking myths and accusations through its public diplomacy efforts.[17] Most of these non-conventional attacks come from Russia, China, Iran, and North Korea, and they can be used in tandem with traditional state-based aggression as a means of hybrid warfare, as Russia has done in Ukraine. Grey zone and hybrid strategies create an opportunity for states in the underdog position to act aggressively towards more powerful states, with a lower risk of repercussions compared to traditional state-based aggression through the use of conventional armed forces. What has been surprising with Russia's 2022 invasion of Ukraine is the extent to which, after successfully exploiting the grey zone for decades, Moscow opted for a full-scale war that exposed it to massive losses and diplomatic and economic isolation on the world stage, through concerted action by NATO, the European Union, and key global partners.

Even if Russia's war in Ukraine has brought a renewed focus on NATO's eastern flank, activities on the southern flank, dubbed Projecting Stability, have continued to monitor and counter threats in the Middle East and North Africa. These activities entail strengthening defence cooperation with partner countries, but NATO continues to update its approach to the southern neighbourhood at each summit and in response to events, such as Israel's war with Hamas. NATO, more than at any other time since the end of the Cold War, is now faced with more acute and diverse threats, whether it looks north, east, or south. Anticipating such changes, NATO laid the groundwork for a concerted strategic response by launching a consultation process with experts during the 2019 London Summit. Then, the NATO secretary general outlined the mandate for NATO going forward, which culminated in the 2020 release of *NATO 2030: United for a New Era*.[18] The document highlights the unpredictability of the current security environment but falls short of articulating specific predictions:

> The world of the next ten years will be very different than the world that the Alliance inhabited either during the Cold War or the decades that immediately followed. It will be a world of competing great powers, in which assertive authoritarian states with revisionist foreign policy agendas seek to expand their power and influence, and in which NATO Allies will once again face a systemic challenge cutting across the domains of security and economics.[19]

The *NATO 2030* document highlights how the broad variety of threats that might impact NATO's activities and its strategic focus can lead to varying threat perceptions within the alliance, and shows that this could be an important political challenge to manage, especially when it comes to managing cohesion among the various member states:

> Against this changing backdrop, NATO has experienced internal strains. Recent years have seen Allies engaged in disputes that partly reflect anxieties about their long-term strategic futures. Some Europeans worry that the United States is turning inward – or that its commitment to their continent will diminish as it increases focus on the Indo-Pacific. Some Americans worry that Europeans will shirk their responsibilities for the common defence – or even pursue a path of autonomy in a way that splinters the Alliance. Inside NATO, societal divisions have arisen and representative democracy is being challenged. In many ways, the Alliance could be said to be formidable in military strength; but it is far from invulnerable to such political turbulence.[20]

While Russia's war with Ukraine has fostered greater unity, this does not solve the underlying tensions and disagreements that have bedevilled the alliance politically. Indeed, if alliance disagreements reach NATO's core values and norms, it will certainly derail political consultation and decision making, which occurs by consensus. Individual allies such as Turkey, Hungary, and Poland, but also the United States under the Trump presidency, have repeatedly challenged NATO cohesion and unity (see chapter by Carla Norrlöf). Indeed, the *NATO 2030* document underscores the growing importance of having robust mechanisms for political consultation to manage this uncertainty, with the ultimate goal of preserving alliance cohesion and ensuring strategic coherence.[21]

Canada, therefore, might find a role for itself when it comes to negotiating the strategic and normative priorities of NATO in the years to come. Canada's feminist foreign policy makes it a leader on human security issues and the Women, Peace and Security agenda. As such, it can make a distinct contribution in a range of areas, from NATO's public diplomacy efforts to its operations.[22] Canada, then, should work with its allies to find the right balance between human security, traditional deterrence, and defence priorities, a balance that remains possible even with the 2022 articulation of the

NATO *Strategic Concept*, a foundational document for the articulation of alliance priorities.

Canada and NATO

While the challenges outlined in the previous section might appear daunting, it is worth pointing out that across the alliance, there is strong domestic public support of NATO. Although there are fears the United States will be a fair-weather ally, so long as Trump remains an influential political figure, his threats to withhold support for NATO members spending less than 2 per cent of their GDP on defence may have influenced Canadian public opinion. A 2024 study found that 53 per cent of Canadians believed Canada needs to increase its defence spending to 2 per cent of the GDP or beyond, with 30 per cent supporting the current spending level (1.38 per cent of GDP). The number of Canadians who believe that military preparedness and presence on the world stage should be Canada's top priority has risen from 12 per cent to 29 per cent over the past decade.[23] Proud to be known internationally as "friendly" and "peaceful," Canada's strategic culture envisions an outward-looking role for the Canadian Armed Forces (CAF). While there have been heated debates about whether that role should support combat or non-combat aspects of alliance or coalition operations, there is usually agreement among the major parties that the CAF should contribute to those multilateral operations and that Canada should have a seat at the table. In short, Canadians seem to prefer that the CAF exhibit a leadership role in multilateral, non-combat operations that focus on reassuring allies, capacity building, or humanitarian assistance for disaster relief. This makes Canada predisposed to taking on roles within NATO or UN peacekeeping, with more prudent assessments when it comes to combat roles or coalition-led operations.

NATO remains central to Canadian foreign and defence policy because of its collective defence value and its shared commitment to support democracy and the international rules-based order. As a middle power, Canada is able to spend less on security and defence and more on domestic issues by pooling its resources with the transatlantic alliance, though cyclically, there are (mostly unheeded) calls to spend more on defence, emanating from domestic and allied pressure. Canada has shared many of the same security threats and concerns as its fellow members, particularly with the past threat of the Soviet Union and the present threat posed by Russia. The Canadian government's 2024 defence policy, *Our North, Strong and Free*, mentions NATO fifty times, and outlines $8.1 billion in investments that aim to bring Canada's defence spending to 1.76 per cent of GDP by 2029–30, with an agreement to continue to work towards the 2 per cent target. While the new defence policy places Arctic security and sovereignty at the forefront of Canada's defence strategy, it does so through the lens of strengthening Canada's role within NATO and being a leader in defending NATO in the North.[24]

Conclusion

Although NATO is facing new security threats, from climate change to cybersecurity, Russia's full-scale war in Ukraine has underscored the alliance's original purpose as a collective defence organization, as stated in the 2022 *Strategic Concept*. NATO continues to adapt, as it has done throughout the Cold War, with the Suez Crisis, then weathering internal division over the wars in Vietnam and Iraq, and, more recently, the democratic backsliding of its member states.[25] NATO has survived these ups and downs, and security community scholars would point out that common values and a sense of shared identity can help in overcoming such disagreements through ongoing consultation and dialogue.[26] The return of great power competition brings the focus back to Russia as a common adversary, and this has fostered greater convergence when it comes to threat perceptions within the alliance compared to the past three decades. An international security environment characterized by great power competition also makes NATO's cohesion critical for balancing and extended deterrence. Every member, including the United States, needs the alliance to deter aggression and possible escalation of conflict with Russia, while considering the longer-term implications of more acute security competition with China. With a globalized and interconnected world, many contemporary security challenges require multilateral and diplomatic cooperation – towards which NATO is well suited to contribute. NATO will remain at the core of Canada's defence priorities because it remains its best option for responding to this wide array of threats, sharing best practices for managing current and emerging security challenges, tempering the influence of the United States, and mitigating disagreements with close allies and partners through its consultation mechanisms.

NOTES

1 The authors are listed alphabetically.
2 For a historical account of NATO, see Timothy Andrews Sayle, *Enduring Alliance: A History of NATO and the Postwar Global Order* (Ithaca, NY: Cornell University Press, 2019). For an overview of Canada's role within NATO, see Joel J. Sokolsky and Joseph T. Jockel, *Canada in NATO, 1949–2019* (Montreal: McGill-Queen's University Press, 2021).
3 Stéfanie von Hlatky, *American Allies in Times of War: The Great Asymmetry* (Oxford: Oxford University Press, 2013).
4 At its creation, NATO had twenty member states. It now has thirty-two member states.
5 Stéfanie von Hlatky and Michel Fortmann, "NATO Enlargement and the Failure of the Cooperative Security Mindset," *International Politics* 57, no. 3 (2020): 554–72.
6 Joshua R. Itzkowitz Shifrinson, "Deal or No Deal: The End of the Cold War and the US Offer to Limit NATO Expansion," *International Security* 40, no. 4 (2016): 7–44. See also articles in James Goldgeier and Joshua R. Shifrinson, eds., "Legacies of NATO Enlargement: International Relations, Domestic Politics, and Alliance Management," special issue, *International Politics* 57, no. 3 (2020).
7 "Canada and NATO," NATO, accessed 12 March 2024, http://www.nato.int/cps/en/natohq/declassified_161511.htm.
8 Michel Fortmann and Stéfanie von Hlatky, "NATO Enlargement 20 Years On: Some Thoughts," Network for Strategic Analysis, 26 April 2021,

https://ras-nsa.ca/publication/nato-enlargement-20-years-on-some-thoughts/.
9 "Operations and Missions: Past and Present," NATO, last modified 10 July 2023, http://www.nato.int/cps/en/natohq/topics_52060.htm.
10 "International Security Assistance Force (ISAF)," Government of Canada, last modified 24 August 2021, https://www.canada.ca/en/department-national-defence/services/military-history/history-heritage/past-operations/asia-pacific/athena.html.
11 "NATO and Libya: Operation Unified Protector," NATO, last modified 27 March 2012, https://www.nato.int/cps/en/natohq/71679.htm.
12 "Canada Transfers Command of NATO Mission Iraq to Denmark," Government of Canada, last modified 24 November 2020, https://www.canada.ca/en/department-national-defence/news/2020/11/canada-transfers-command-of-nato-mission-iraq-to-denmark.html.
13 Stéfanie von Hlatky, "Canada's Pledge to Latvia and the Bigger NATO Bargain," *RUSI Newsbrief* 38, no. 9 (2018), https://rusi.org/explore-our-research/publications/rusi-newsbrief/canadas-pledge-latvia-and-bigger-nato-bargain.
14 "Online Press Conference by NATO Secretary General Jens Stoltenberg Following the Second Day of the Meetings of NATO Defence Ministers," NATO, last updated 19 February 2021, http://www.nato.int/cps/en/natohq/opinions_181561.htm.
15 Marc Ozawa, "Adapting NATO to Grey Zone Challenges from Russia," in *NATO 2030: New Technologies, New Conflicts, New Partnerships*, ed. Thierry Tardy (Rome: NATO Defense College, 2021), 19–32.
16 John Raine, "Time for NATO to Find a Way Out of the Escalation Trap in Ukraine," International Institute for Strategic Studies, 11 March 2022, https://www.iiss.org/blogs/analysis/2022/03/time-for-nato-to-find-a-way-out-of-the-escalation-trap-in-ukraine.
17 *The Secretary General's Annual Report: 2021* (Brussels: NATO, 2021), 52, https://www.nato.int/nato_static_fl2014/assets/pdf/2022/3/pdf/sgar21-en.pdf.
18 NATO, *NATO 2030: United for a New Era* (Brussels: NATO, 2020), https://www.nato.int/nato_static_fl2014/assets/pdf/2020/12/pdf/201201-Reflection-Group-Final-Report-Uni.pdf.
19 NATO, 5.
20 NATO, 5.

21 NATO, 5.
22 Stéfanie von Hlatky, *Deploying Feminism: The Role of Gender in NATO's Military Operations* (New York: Oxford University Press, 2022).
23 "Canadians Prioritise Importance of Military Readiness," Angus Reid Institute, 5 March 2024, https://www.angusreid.com/intelligence/canadians-prioritise-importance-of-military-readiness/#:~:text=New%20data%20from%20the%20non,cent%20in%20the%20past%20decade.
24 Department of National Defence, *Our North, Strong and Free: A Renewed Vision for Canada's Defence* (Ottawa: Department of National Defence, 2024), https://www.canada.ca/en/department-national-defence/news/2024/04/our-north-strong-and-free-a-renewed-vision-for-canadas-defence.html.
25 NATO, *NATO 2030*, 5.
26 Emmanuel Adler, "The Spread of Security Communities: Communities of Practice, Self-Restraint, and NATO's Post–Cold War Transformation," *European Journal of International Relations* 14, no. 2 (2008): 195–230; Alexandra I. Gheciu, *NATO in the "New Europe": The Politics of International Socialization after the Cold War* (Stanford, CA: Stanford University Press, 2005).

chapter three

Balancing Priorities along the Defence, Security, and Safety Continuum in the Canadian Arctic

DANIELLE CHERPAKO AND ANDREA CHARRON

Introduction

At a time when one of the eight Arctic states,[1] Russia, is seen as a global security threat, it may seem wise to view Canada's Arctic security exclusively through the lens of hard power and military threats. Even before Russia's attack on Ukraine, rhetoric surrounding the North American Arctic security environment had become increasingly alarmist in nature. The war in Ukraine has further adjusted the framing from conceptualizing the Arctic as an exceptional region of cooperation with *some* competition to one facing imminent threats from competitors such as Russia and China. Given that defence-related issues in the Arctic have historically been prioritized by the Government of Canada at the expense of human security threats, such as climate change and food insecurity, this shift in rhetoric risks once again overshadowing these other more immidiate concerns. We argue that while protecting Canada and North America against potential military aggression remains vital, this should not come at the expense of addressing persistent safety and human security challenges facing Canada's Arctic communities. There are many reasons to invest in and expand community preparedness initiatives and infrastructure that would help to address threats along the defence, security, and safety (DSS) continuum.

While the term "defence" typically refers to *hard* security threats that can be addressed by military agencies (e.g., missile defence), the terms "security" and "safety" can be more broadly interpreted. Security can include cyber, environmental, and human security, among other forms. Security typically involves the enforcement of Canadian laws, while safety involves the protection of lives and the environment.

Security and safety issues are the domain of a wide array of Canadian civilian agencies, such as Transport Canada, Parks Canada, the Canadian Ice Service, the Royal Canadian Mounted Police (RCMP), and the Canadian Coast Guard (CCG), as well as Arctic residents and their communities, territorial governments, industry, and non-governmental agencies such as the Civilian Air Search and Rescue Association (CASARA). The Canadian Armed Forces (CAF) and the Canadian Rangers, who form a part of the Canadian Army Reserve, also play an essential supporting role in various security and safety scenarios.

This chapter explains the roles and importance of these different actors operating along the DSS continuum and counsels that the protection of Canadians and Canada requires balancing priorities along this continuum with a whole-of-government approach.

Defence Context

During the Cold War, Canada focused more on traditional defence threats, especially air-breathing ones,[2] including Soviet Bear bombers and cruise missiles. Today, there is a greater awareness of security and safety interests. Nevertheless, given the increased geopolitical competition, and especially due to Russia's aggression against Ukraine, Canada is poised to renew its focus on the defence of the Arctic.

This focus on defence is encouraged by Canada's southern neighbour and closest defence ally, the United States, which is particularly focused on its deterrence credibility and the vulnerability of North America; after all, the Arctic is the fastest avenue of approach to hit North American targets. In 2019, General O'Shaughnessy, then commander of North American Aerospace Defence Command (NORAD)[3] and United States Northern Command, pronounced that "the threats facing our nations are real and significant. The Arctic is no longer a fortress wall, and our oceans are no longer protective moats; they are now avenues of approach for advanced conventional weapons and the platforms that carry them."[4] He also noted that "the strategic threat to the homeland has entered a new era. Key adversaries Russia and China have deployed and continue to advance a range of capabilities to hold the homeland at risk."[5] Statements like these have gained traction in the media and put the spotlight on Canada to contribute resources to bolster North American deterrence.[6] Russia's aggression against Ukraine and the Chinese spy balloon flying across North America in February 2023 have made continental defence impossible to ignore.[7]

Besides renewing the aged North Warning System (a necessary but costly proposition), the United States aims to achieve all-domain awareness by connecting sensors from all US military agencies and allies to share data to achieve "information dominance." This also requires closer coordination between NORAD and NATO (see Stéfanie von Hlatky and Hannah Hollander's chapter in this volume for more on NATO). These and other initiatives, such as extending runways and improving communications in the Arctic, are part of wider initiatives to "modernize" NORAD and to evolve continental defence in a total reimagining of how to deter and defeat threats facing North America. Presidents Trump and then Biden and Prime Minister Trudeau confirmed modernization as a priority, and Biden's address to the Canadian Parliament on 24 March 2023 accelerated Canadian timelines.[8] The extent of resources promised is hopeful; however, the challenges involved in spending the money are many.

Russia has been considered a proximate and persistent threat to North America since the illegal annexation of Crimea in 2014. Russia has invested in Arctic-specific technology and dual-use equipment, such as icebreakers. While often justified as necessary to protect Russian assets in the region and to bolster homeland defence (since Russia has the largest Arctic territory and population living in the region of all of the Arctic states), these investments can also be interpreted as signalling Russia's desire to be seen as an Arctic leader.[9] Some of Russia's recent actions in the Arctic have also revolved around projecting power, such as the testing of hypersonic weapons, performing high-altitude Arctic jumps, increasing flight patrols near NATO airspace, and engaging in the use of "grey zone" tactics such as GPS and radio jamming during NATO exercises.[10] These actions have caused some to sound alarm bells about the possibility of an Arctic conflict between Russia and NATO, even before Russia's recent invasion of Ukraine. While it is still considered unlikely that an armed conflict will originate in or because of the Arctic, there is always the possibility that Russia, should it feel cornered in eastern Europe, will lash out and threaten critical targets in the Arctic to force a de-escalation from NATO.

Canada insists it does not envision peer-to-peer kinetic competition occurring in the North American Arctic with Russia.[11] Rather, Canada seeks deterrence by denial by improving surveillance and domain awareness, thus contributing to the United States' Combined Joint All Domain Command and Control, the Department of Defense's concept to connect sensors from all of the military services – the US Air Force, Army, Marine Corps, Navy, and Space Force – into a single network. Canada was also committed to cooperating with Russia and other Arctic partners on scientific research and search and rescue (SAR) efforts through various Arctic agreements facilitated via the Arctic Council. The war in Ukraine, however, has made cooperation with Russia difficult.[12] Concerns have also been raised about China's pacing role geopolitically in the coming decades (see Lynette Ong's chapter in particular). Despite China's distance from the Arctic, its interest in conducting scientific research, its investment in infrastructure, its expansion of shipping through the Arctic via its "Polar Silk Road" initiative,[13] and its reliance on Russia for oil and gas has positioned it as another competitor.[14] While potential threats from Russia and China will remain important to Canada, most of Canada's security concerns *in* the Arctic are of a safety and constabulary nature, especially those associated with climate change and a lack of health and education services and basic infrastructure. When considering the prioritization of threats, Canada must not only consider those that are most *dangerous* but also those that are most *likely*. Threats along the security–safety continuum represent the latter and are already affecting Canada's Arctic.

Human Security and Safety

Canada's Arctic constitutes 40 per cent of the country's total landmass,[15] and while it is currently sparsely populated, with fewer than 150,000 residents, the population is primarily young and is growing rapidly. Within the four Inuit homelands in Canada's Arctic, Inuit make up 90 per cent of the population in Nunavik, 89 per cent in Nunatsiavut, 84 per cent in Nunavut, and 55 per cent in Inuvialuit.[16] Communities across these regions require better housing, basic and improved infrastructure, food security, and equal access to services, as discussed by Chelsea Parker and Sheryl Lightfoot in this volume. Threats from Russia and China are not the priorities of these communities. Climate change (see Kathryn Harrison's chapter) poses an existential threat to Inuit ways of life in particular, and its rate and scope of effects means that any existing and future infrastructure is in danger of being rendered unusable quickly. These security threats can also lead to safety issues. As animals' migration patterns have changed due to climate change and resource extraction projects, hunters and fishers have had to travel farther out on the land and ice to find them. This means more time spent on the land and sea and greater vulnerability to unpredictable weather and sea ice.[17] At the same time, tourism in the Canadian Arctic is expected to increase in the coming years, and southerners may not be prepared to travel in the Arctic environment safely. These factors mean that demand for SAR missions in the North will likely increase in the next five to ten years.

Communities have also raised concerns about the environmental impacts of mining and other extractive activities. For example, in early February 2021, a public hearing was launched as Inuit hunters protested the expansion of Baffinland's Mary River iron ore mine in Nunavut, citing concerns for local wildlife amid noise pollution, possible oil spills, and railway construction.[18] As extraction, shipping, and tourism are expected to increase in and around the Arctic in coming years, it is vital that Canada's civilian agencies are prepared to assist communities in responding to probable and unforeseen accidents. Such assistance must also be set within the context of reconciliation in Canada and the recognized rights codified in the UN Declaration on the Rights of Indigenous Peoples. The Government of Canada has historically harmed and underserved these communities, and they continue to lack access to basic services and adequate infrastructure.[19]

Moving forward, there are numerous opportunities for Canadian agencies to work with Inuit and other Indigenous peoples, facilitate intergenerational knowledge transfers, and provide supports to communities. In the words of Kaviq Kaluraq, chair of the Nunavut Impact Review Board, "we need to be able to have adequate resources in our community ... not just us being protected, but us having the ability to protect ourselves."[20] While defence-related threats may be top of mind for Canadians in the South, now is also a critical time to imagine how federal agencies might play a supporting role in community-led security and safety initiatives.

Solution? Finding Balance

To achieve its defence, security, and safety goals, Canada needs balance. It has many civilian agencies operating and cooperating with one another in its Arctic. The Canadian Coast Guard and its volunteer auxiliaries play particularly important roles in responding to an ever-increasing number of SAR calls in the Arctic. In 2020, the CCG volunteer auxiliaries responded to thirty-two incidents, the Inshore Rescue Boat station in Rankin Inlet (which trains Indigenous post-secondary students) responded to six SAR cases, and the CCG icebreakers responded to twelve. Known for its safety-supporting role, the CCG also provides marine communications and navigational aids, manages marine traffic, and supports government departments and scientific researchers with equipment for travel. It is relied upon for icebreaking for commercial shipping, maritime SAR missions, and providing supplies to northern communities and Environment Canada and National Defence sites during the summer months. The CCG vessels are also used to support RCMP and customs and immigration officers during surveillance and interdiction missions.[21]

In the event of a marine oil spill, the CCG and Transport Canada are also tasked with leading the response. Yet the CCG might be spread too thinly, preventing an efficient response. The CCG is working with communities to improve local preparedness in the event of oil spills and SAR missions. The CCG Auxiliary program is one example of using community volunteers to great effect. Another example is the Inuit Marine Monitoring Program, an initiative designed by Nunavut Tunngavik Incorporated (NTI) in partnership with Oceans North.[22] Through this program, community members, particularly those who are experienced hunters and fishers, collect data on vessels and their activities (whether suspicious or not), concerns identified by communities (e.g., pollution, oil spills), and behaviour patterns of wildlife.[23] Some of this is achieved by installing real-time vessel tracking technology infrastructure with a community's permission. Participants hope to expand the program by hiring new marine monitors and creating an open-source website to allow community members and government agencies to see data in real time.[24]

Another vital community resource is the Canadian Rangers program, a reserve force of the Canadian Army in operation since 1947. The Rangers' mandate is to "provide lightly-equipped, self-sufficient mobile forces to support CAF, national security and public safety operations within Canada."[25] Some of their work includes patrolling, surveilling, collecting data for the CAF, assisting in SAR missions, and responding to natural disasters. The Rangers not only support the work of the CAF in remote locations but also act as liaisons between communities and the government. As Peter Kikkert and Whitney Lackenbauer write, "Their familiarity with local cultures, fluency in Indigenous languages, and vested interest in the welfare of their fellow community members make them valuable, trusted assets."[26]

Magali Vullierme also finds that the Rangers program and the Junior Canadian Ranger patrols help to strengthen the human security of Inuit communities and facilitate intergenerational transfers of knowledge as youth learn how to navigate and protect the land.[27]

The Canadian Rangers and the CCG Auxiliary are dependent on volunteers and their own equipment. The same volunteers, however, often assume multiple roles, such as volunteer firefighters, and may even be spotters for CASARA.[28] The lament across the CCG Auxiliary and CASARA is that the administrative burden to fill out complicated federal forms for compensation when personal equipment is used or damaged is a major impediment to recruiting new volunteers.

One core difference between the CAF and other agencies is that CAF members have "unlimited liability," meaning that they can, if necessary, be "lawfully ordered into harm's way under conditions that could lead to the loss of their lives."[29] For this reason, the CAF may be more appropriately positioned than the CCG and volunteer agencies to respond directly to the most dangerous SAR missions, such as those in unpredictable ice and weather conditions and in line with their aeronautical SAR mandate. The challenge is that the CAF is unable to respond as quickly as community-based reserves. Moreover, the majority of CAF members and their equipment, indeed the bulk of the resources of all federal agencies, are based in the South. However, if community members in the Arctic can be the "eyes and ears" on the ground and begin immediate triage, detect suspicious activities, warn of impending disasters, and alert the CAF and other agencies, this can save time and lives.

On the defence end of the spectrum, infrastructure is needed in the Arctic, including improved radar coverage (especially in Arctic and polar over-the-horizon radar systems), longer runways, modernized forward-operating locations, and better communication infrastructure. Investing in multi-use equipment and multi-purpose capabilities is the best way to prepare for threats *along* the DSS continuum in an economical way. For example, there is now focused attention on the issue of "agile basing"[30] in the Arctic, as runways are prone to buckling and ice roads are not guaranteed to be safe and usable. These and other infrastructure projects, such as the establishment of ports and refuelling stations, are vital for the communities, needed for federal agencies, and are also important for military use. But there is a limit to what defence funding can provide. Clean drinking water, access to health services, and funding for education in the North all rest with the federal and territorial governments in consultation with rights holders. These are not within the purview of the Department of National Defence.

The interconnectedness of civilian and military agencies in the Canadian Arctic is clear and will only increase in the next few years. There are many reasons outlined here to invest in and expand community preparedness initiatives and infrastructure that relate to defence, security, *and* safety concerns. The need for increased attention to the CAF's ability to contribute to the defence of Canada and North America is not questioned. The concern is that it will come at the expense of tackling the persistent and increasing security and safety concerns that require a whole-of-government and whole-of-society effort.

NOTES

1 The eight state members of the Arctic Council are Canada, Denmark, Finland, Iceland, Norway, Sweden, the Russian Federation, and the United States.
2 Air-breathing threats are those that have an engine requiring the intake of air for combustion of its fuel.
3 NORAD has three missions: aerospace warning, control, and maritime warning. It is North America's first line of defence since the binational agreement was signed on 12 May 1958.
4 "Statement of General Terrence J. O'shaughnessy, United States Air Force Commander, United States Northern Command and North American Aerospace Defense," Senate Armed Services Committee, 13 February 2020, p. 2, https://www.armed-services.senate.gov/imo/media/doc/OShaughnessy_02-13-20.pdf
5 "Statement of General Terrence J. O'shaughnessy," 3.
6 Jim Bell and Krestia DeGeorge, "Defense Expert Slams Ottawa for Ignoring North Warning System Upgrade," *Arctic Business Journal*, 21 January 2020, https://www.arctictoday.com

/defense-expert-slams-ottawa-for-ignoring-north-warning-system-upgrade/; Andrea Charron, "Beyond the North Warning System," *War on the Rocks*, 7 September 2020, https://warontherocks.com/2020/09/beyond-the-north-warning-system/. For more on continental defence and NORAD, see Andrea Charron and Jim Fergusson, "North America's Imperative: How to Strengthen Deterrence by Denial," *Strategic Studies Quarterly* 15, no. 4 (2021): 8–24, https://www.airuniversity.af.edu/Portals/10/SSQ/documents/Volume-15_Issue-4/D-Charron.pdf; Andrea Charron, "Beyond the North Warning System," in *On Thin Ice: Perspectives on Arctic Security*, ed. Duncan Depledge and Whitney Lackenbauer (Peterborough, ON: North American and Arctic Defence and Security Network, 2021), 64–70, https://www.naadsn.ca/wp-content/uploads/2021/04/Depledge-Lackenbauer-On-Thin-Ice-final-upload.pdf; and Andrea Charron, "Arctic Security: NATO and the Future of Transatlantic Relations," in *Turning the Tide; How to Rescue Transatlantic Relations*, ed. Simona Soare (Paris: EU Institute of Security Studies, 2020), 137–53, https://www.iss.europa.eu/content/turning-tide-how-rescue-transatlantic-relations.

7 Mark Gollom, "Why Do Unidentified Objects Seem to Be Popping Up Above North America All of a Sudden?," *CBC News*, 14 February 2023, https://www.cbc.ca/news/world/unidentified-objects-norad-balloon-1.6746860.

8 See "Minister Anand Announces Continental Defence Modernization to Protect Canadians," Government of Canada, 20 June 2022, https://www.canada.ca/en/department-national-defence/news/2022/06/minister-anand-announces-continental-defence-modernization-to-protect-canadians.html, and "NORAD Modernization Timelines," Government of Canada, last modified 24 March 2023, https://www.canada.ca/en/department-national-defence/services/operations/allies-partners/norad/norad-modernization-project-timelines.html.

9 Heather A. Conley, Matthew Melino, and Jon B. Alterman, "The Ice Curtain: Russia's Arctic Military Presence," Center for Strategic and International Studies, 26 March 2020, https://www.csis.org/analysis/ice-curtain-russias-arctic-military-presence.

10 Conley, Melino, and Alterman, "The Ice Curtain."

11 As per the remarks delivered by Chief of the Defence Staff General Eyre on 10 March 2022 at Canada's largest defence gathering, the Ottawa

Conference on Security and Defence. See "Public Record: Chief of the Defence Staff at Ottawa Conference on Security and Defence," CPAC, accessed 19 March 2024, https://www.cpac.ca/public-record/episode/chief-of-the-defence-staff-at-ottawa-conference-on-security-and-defence?id=767c567f-51fb-4e2c-874d-a38e98491316.

12 "Joint Statement on Arctic Council Cooperation Following Russia's Invasion of Ukraine," Government of Canada, 3 March 2022, https://www.canada.ca/en/global-affairs/news/2022/03/joint-statement-on-arctic-council-cooperation-following-russias-invasion-of-ukraine.html.

13 Kong Soon Lim, "China's Arctic Policy & the Polar Silk Road Vision," *Arctic Yearbook 2018*, accessed 2 March 2021, https://arcticyearbook.com/arctic-yearbook/2018/2018-scholarly-papers/290-china-s-arctic-policy-the-polar-silk-road-vision; Sergey Pogodin, "Geopolitical and Geo-Economic Interest of China in the Arctic Region" (paper presented at the 4th International Multidisciplinary Scientific Conference on Social Sciences and Arts SGEM2017, Sofia, Bulgaria, 28–31 March 2017), https://sgemsocial.org/index.php/elibrary-research-areas?view=publication&task=show&id=4711.

14 Department of National Defence, *Strong, Secure, Engaged: Canada's Defence Policy* (Ottawa: Department of National Defence, 2017), 50, http://dgpaapp.forces.gc.ca/en/canada-defence-policy/docs/canada-defence-policy-report.pdf.

15 Canada's definition of the Arctic is all land north of 60°N to include the four Inuit homelands in the three territories, northern Quebec, and Labrador. The other Arctic states use land north of the Arctic Circle (approximately 66°N) as the demarcation line. Inuit, Dene, Cree, Métis, and other Indigenous groups live in Canada's Arctic, but it is defined by the location of the four Inuit homelands.

16 "Aboriginal Peoples in Canada: Key Results from the 2016 Census," Statistics Canada, 25 October 2017, https://www150.statcan.gc.ca/n1/daily-quotidien/171025/dq171025a-eng.htm?indid=14430-4&indgeo=0.

17 Anna Bunce, James Ford, Sherilee Harper, Victoria Edge, and IHACC Research Team, "Vulnerability and Adaptive Capacity of Inuit Women to Climate Change: A Case Study from Iqaluit, Nunavut," *Natural Hazards*, 1 June 2016, https://doi.org/10.1007/s11069-016-2398-6; "What Are Elders Reporting?," Nunavut Climate Change Centre, accessed 13 March 2024, https://www.climatechangenunavut.ca/en/content/what-are-elders-reporting; Gita J. Laidler et al., "Travelling and Hunting in a Changing

Arctic: Assessing Inuit Vulnerability to Sea Ice Change in Igloolik, Nunavut," *Climatic Change* 94, nos. 3–4 (2008): 363–97, https://doi.org/10.1007/s10584-008-9512-z.

18 Sara Frizzell, "Nunavut Mine Blockade to Continue Until Concerns Are Addressed, Say Inuit Hunters," *CBC News*, 5 February 2021, https://www.cbc.ca/news/canada/north/baffinland-blockade-hunters-group-1.5902516.

19 For a good primer on Nunavut's historical relationship with the federal government, see "Key Findings," Qikiqtani Truth Commission, accessed 13 March 2024, https://www.qtcommission.ca/en/key-findings.

20 Kaviq Kaluraq in *Voices from the Arctic: Diverse Views on Canadian Arctic Security*, ed. Dalee Sambo Dorough, Bridget Larocque, Kaviq Kaluraq, and Daniel Taukie (Peterborough, ON: North American and Arctic Defense and Security Network, 2021), 21, https://www.naadsn.ca/wp-content/uploads/2021/01/20-nov-ArcticVoicesProceedings-upload.pdf.

21 Stefan Konrad, "The Canadian Coast Guard and Future Arctic Challenges," NATO Association of Canada, 11 August 2014, https://natoassociation.ca/the-canadian-coast-guard-and-future-arctic-challenges/.

22 NTI is the body created by the Nunavut Land Claims Agreement to ensure that all levels of government adhere to the principles of the agreement and live up to its promises. NTI and Oceans North are NGOs. Oceans North is a charitable organization that supports marine conservation in partnership with Indigenous and coastal communities in Canada and East Greenland. See "Our Story," Oceans North, accessed 13 March 2024, https://www.oceansnorth.org/en/about/our-story/.

23 Erin Abou-Abssi, "A New Way to Track Arctic Vessels," Oceans North, 11 January 2018, https://oceansnorth.org/en/blog/2018/01/nti-monitoring-program/.

24 Daniel Taukie in Dorough et al., *Voices from the Arctic*, 26.

25 "About the Canadian Rangers," Government of Canada, last modified 14 June 2023, https://www.canada.ca/en/ombudsman-national-defence-forces/education-information/caf-members/career/canadian-rangers.html.

26 Peter Kikkert and Whitney Lackenbauer, "Strengthening Search and Rescue in Nunavut: Approaches and Options" (Policy Primer, North American and Arctic Defense Security Network, 27 January 2021), https://www.naadsn.ca/wp-content/uploads/2021/01/21-jan-Policy-Primer-PK-PWL-Search-and-Rescue-in-Nunavut.pdf.

27 Magali Vullierme, "Towards Human Security in the Arctic: Lessons Learned from Canadian Rangers and Junior Canadian Rangers," *Arctic Yearbook 2019*, accessed 2 March 2021, https://arcticyearbook.com/arctic-yearbook/2019/2019-scholarly-papers/309-towards-human-security-in-the-arctic-lessons-learned-from-canadian-rangers-and-junior-canadian-rangers.
28 Kikkert and Lackenbauer, "Strengthening Search and Rescue in Nunavut."
29 "Accepting Unlimited Liability," Government of Canada, last updated 7 October 2019, https://www.canada.ca/en/department-national-defence/corporate/reports-publications/duty-with-honour-2009/chapter-2-statement-of-canadian-military-ethos/section-2-fundamental-beliefs-and-expectations.html.
30 Danielle Cherpako, Nicholas Glesby, and Andrea Charron, "Joint Agile Basing Airpower Seminar (JABAS)" (Virtual JABAS – Joint Agile Basing Airpower Seminar, 22 September 2020), https://umanitoba.ca/centres/media/JABAS_22-September-2020_Key-Takeaways__Final.pdf.

chapter four

Canada-China Trade: Economic Interdependence and Coercion

LYNETTE H. ONG[1]

Canada's trade with China entails benefits as well as risks for Canadian exporters. Canada must be aware of how increased interdependence with Beijing can lead to vulnerabilities. Evidence shows that China uses economic coercion in response to political or security disputes and will retaliate against countries with which it has disagreements. This suggests that Canada must evaluate which of its industries have an asymmetric dependence on China, in order to protect against potential future economic coercion by Beijing. Focusing on the growing security threats stemming from Canada's engagement with China, this chapter makes clear that trade is among the areas of concern.

In a broader context, policy communities in the West have been debating economic decoupling or de-risking vis-à-vis China, not only to reduce economic dependence on the country but also to cut off supplies of critical input materials, such as semiconductors, that could limit the growth of China's technological prowess. The 2023 "spy balloon" incidents underscore the lack of trust and high tension between the United States and China, which led some to speculate on the rising likelihood of an "accidental war" between the two superpowers. This will no doubt have ramifications for Canada.[2]

Trade is believed to improve economic efficiency and promote growth, and trade openness is also commonly believed to have a positive effect on democratization.[3] However, the rise of China as a major trading nation has challenged this conventional wisdom and the rules of global trade governance.[4] When China was admitted to the World Trade Organization in 2001, the West held out hope that greater economic openness would result in the country's political liberalization.[5] Twenty years on, not only has rapid economic expansion not brought about liberalizing political reforms, but the ascendency of President Xi Jinping has introduced an unequivocal trend towards political centralization.

Relatedly, would economic interdependence give rise to power asymmetry between trading countries? When a small or medium-sized country trades with an economic juggernaut like China, does it expose itself to vulnerabilities despite the promise of an enormous consumer market? In this chapter, I tackle the important question of whether economic interdependence subjects smaller nations to the risk of economic coercion, and if so, how and through what mechanisms.

Deepening trade ties with China have brought many benefits to various countries, including access to a large export market; however, political disputes with Beijing can produce negative spillover effects on bilateral economic relations. Beijing's punitive trade measures have escalated since 2013. They include sanctions against Mongolia for hosting a visit by the Dalai Lama,[6] against South Korea for installing a US missile defence system,[7] against Australia for banning Huawei and calling for an independent inquiry into the origins of COVID-19,[8] as well as against Canada for the detention of Huawei's CFO, Meng Wanzhou.[9] Notably, most of these sanctions are "informal" in nature, delivered – in the case of Canada – in response to Canadian imports' "failure to meet" Chinese health and safety protocols. Beijing has denied an explicit link between bilateral political disagreement and economic sanctions in each of these incidents. But the informal nature of these measures has provided Beijing with a degree of plausible deniability while punishing its trading partners for political disagreement. As I have argued in my book *Outsourcing Repression: Everyday State Power in Contemporary China*, outsourced repression carried out by non-state actors provides a veil of deniability for the authorities.[10] These punitive measures amply demonstrate the vulnerability and passivity of the countries that have been victimized by Beijing's retaliation.

Thus, understanding the logic of Beijing's economic coercion will be critical for Canadian security moving forward. This chapter evaluates the nature of the economic interdependence that exposes trading nations like Canada to trade coercion from a larger trading partner like China. It starts by explaining how China uses economic coercion in response to political disputes, using the Terminal High Altitude Area Defense (THAAD) dispute with South Korea as an example. It then examines how these dynamics have played out in China's relations with Canada. It also analyses how Beijing chooses its targets of coercion, and the mechanisms through which it imposes its coercive strategies.

South Korea–China Relations and the THAAD Dispute

This section examines how the Terminal High Altitude Area Defense dispute froze bilateral relations between South Korea and China and led to Beijing's imposition of economic coercion to extract concessions from Seoul.[11] The dispute began in 2016, when South Korea and the United States agreed to deploy the THAAD missile as a deterrent against North Korea's nuclear threat, which led to Chinese fears about the missile defence system's powerful radar potentially being used to spy on mainland China. Beijing responded with informal sanctions on South Korea that ultimately won it three key concessions: South Korea would no longer pursue the installation of THAAD launchers, interceptors, radar, or fire-control units; it would refuse to enter into a potential US regional missile defence system; and it would back out of a proposed trilateral alliance with the United States and Japan.

In response to this military dispute, China employed an economic coercion strategy against two main targets: the South Korean Lotte Group and the country's tourism industry. After the Lotte Group signed a land deal to house THAAD missile batteries, many Lotte Mart stores in China were forcibly closed over alleged fire safety violations, which caused the company to lose US$1.7 billion in revenue. The tourism industry in South Korea – which relies heavily on Chinese tourists, who account for nearly half of all tourist arrivals in the country – also suffered tremendous losses. Evidence suggests that Beijing threatened Chinese travel agencies with fines and licence suspensions if they continued to sell travel packages to South Korea, costing an estimated US$15.6 billion and 402,000 job losses in the retail and hospitality industries. While Chinese tourists could easily substitute South Korea with alternative destinations, South Korea could not easily replace 4.5 million Chinese holidaymakers in the short term. The prospect of costs of this magnitude persisting into the future forced Seoul to make concessions in exchange for a policy reversal.

The evident success of China's strategy in extracting concessions from South Korea illuminates the logic of its economic coercion. At the core of the Chinese strategy is asymmetric interdependence that allows for its weaponization of trading relations – that is, the use of trade or economic leverage to put pressure on other countries that cannot easily pivot away from a reliance on Chinese sources.[12] The enormous control the Chinese party-state wields over its domestic media and business enterprises provides it with a unique leverage compared to other governments.[13]

An Overview of Canada-China Trade Relations

Due to its increased trade relations with China, Canada has also become the target of retaliatory economic coercion by Beijing in response to bilateral political disputes. Prior to being elected prime minister, Justin Trudeau touted the Chinese market as a valuable "third option" to diversify Canada's dependence on the United States. This trade-diversification strategy matches China's desire to erode US hegemony by having greater influence over the United States' neighbour and long-time ally.[14] After overtaking the United Kingdom, Mexico, Japan, and Germany, China is now Canada's second-largest trading partner (the first being the United States). Canada's exports to China have been growing steadily, though at a much slower pace than its imports, which contributed to an annual trade deficit of over C$52 billion in 2020. This could be due to the different structures of the two economies and their distinct comparative advantages, as well as the relatively more open nature of the Canadian economy, reflected in its lower tariffs.

In what is widely believed to be retaliation for the arrest in Vancouver of Meng Wanzhou, Huawei's chief financial officer, on allegations of fraud and violating US sanctions against Iran, Beijing imposed import bans on Canadian pork and canola oil in 2018.[15] Beijing denies this allegation, however, citing health and safety concerns over Canadian imports, notably the residue from restricted feed additives in Canadian pork and pest concerns. This led to the suspension of import licences for Richardson and Viterra, the two major Canadian canola producers.[16] The magnitude of the ban is evident in Figure 4.1, which shows a 17 per cent decrease in the total value of Canadian merchandise exports to China in 2019 compared to a year earlier. This represents a reversal of steady growth in Canada's merchandise trade, with China registered over the preceding years.

The canola ban dealt a significant blow to farmers in the provinces of Alberta, Saskatchewan, and Manitoba, as China once purchased over 42 per cent of Canada's total canola exports. The ban led to a loss of C$2.2 billion in trade, or 20 per cent of the total canola export market, and resulted in falling prices due to the sudden collapse in demand.[17] However, these numbers do not account for market complexities, such as a change in price that boosted demand from other nations. One detailed study estimates that the net loss in total canola exports from 6 March 2019 to 31 July 2020 is between C$859 million and C$1.1 billion when accounting for positive secondary market effects.[18]

The export ban has heightened awareness among Canadian exporters of trade imbalances between the two countries, particularly Canada's reliance on China as a key export market. Three of the top five Canadian exports to China in 2018 (i.e., iron ores and concentrates, chemical wood pulp, pork, canola seeds, and canola oil) were targeted in retaliation. In addition, China accounted for substantial shares of pork (34 per cent), canola seeds (23 per cent),

Figure 4.1. Canada's total merchandise trade with China (C$ billion)

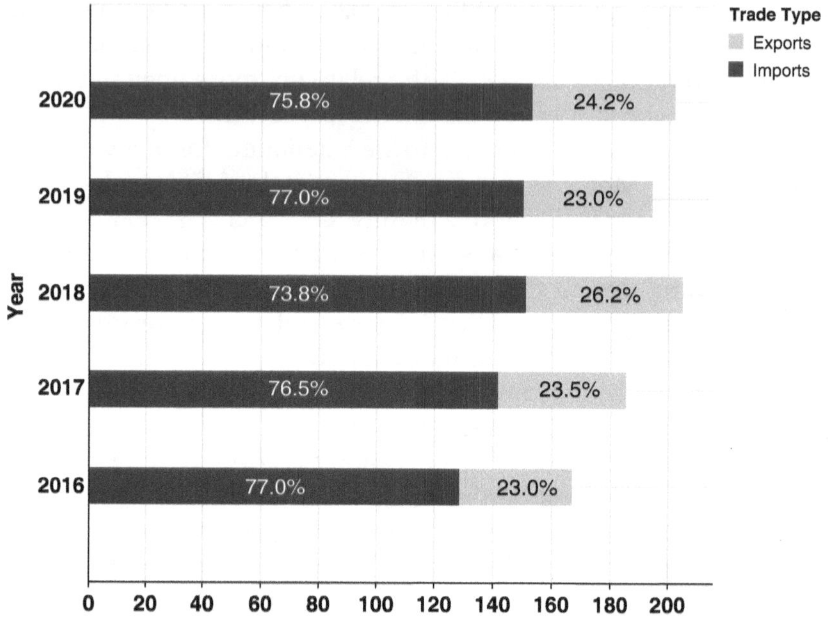

Year	Imports	Exports
2020	75.8%	24.2%
2019	77.0%	23.0%
2018	73.8%	26.2%
2017	76.5%	23.5%
2016	77.0%	23.0%

Source: Statistics Canada

and canola oil (29 per cent), which gave Beijing significant leverage over Canadian exporters as it could substitute these imports from elsewhere. Notably, iron ores and wood pulp, which contributed more dollars to Canadian exports than canola and pork, were not targeted.[19] This is presumably because wood and iron are critical resource inputs in the Chinese industrial economy, as opposed to easily substituted agricultural products.

Asymmetry Interrupted: The Fortunate Case of Canadian Pork and Canola

Even though the export bans on canola and pork share a similar logic to the boycott on the Lotte Group and the South Korean tourism industry, Beijing has been unsuccessful so far in extracting any

Figure 4.2. Canada's pork and canola exports (C$ billion)

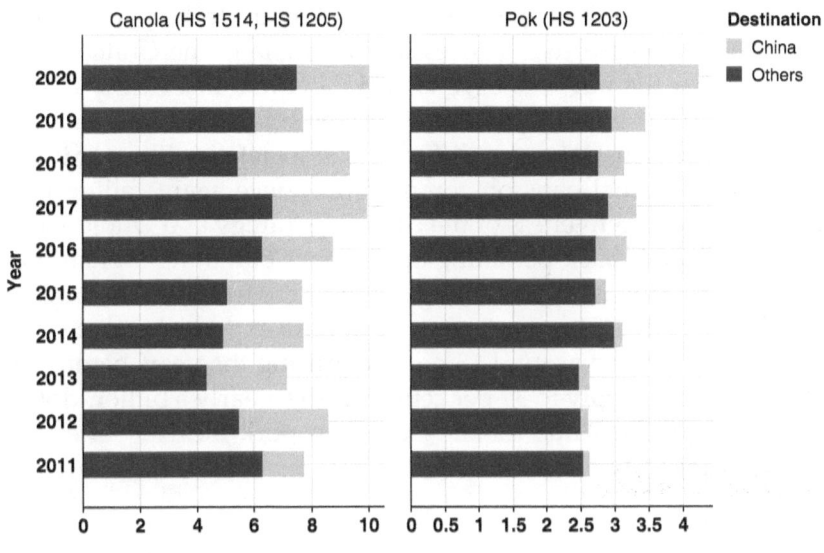

Source: Statistics Canada

concession from Ottawa. This could be partly credited to changes in the external environment that have begun to turn relevant market factors in Canada's favour, such as new European Union biofuel mandates, which have shifted imports of palm to sustainable sources like canola amid some of Europe's worst domestic canola harvests in over a decade.[20] More importantly, Beijing was compelled to quickly reverse the pork ban in late 2019 after an African swine fever outbreak devastated domestic suppliers.[21] As Figure 4.2. indicates, canola exports in 2020 nearly exceeded the historical peak, while pork exports broke records, following the ban's reversal in the fourth quarter of 2019.

Yet, it should be underlined that the negative impact on Canadian exports could have become truly dire had the external environment not disrupted asymmetric interdependence that was not in Canada's favour. From 2018 to 2020, imports from other major canola producers, such as Russia, Australia, Ukraine, and France, quickly substituted for China's imports. That said, the effectiveness of China's import ban is questionable, underscoring its lack of efficacy as a punitive measure. After the trade ban, Canadian exporters increased their processing of canola in the United Arab Emirates for the purpose of re-export,[22] evident in a nearly C$300 million spike in exports to China from the small Gulf state in 2020. This also demonstrates the difficulties associated with coordinating these informal bans on commodities, once again calling into question the effectiveness of the coercive strategy as a whole. Conversely, China's back-pedalling on the pork ban in light of supply constraints demonstrates Beijing's lack of control over the import ban as a punitive measure. The share of pork exports accounted for by China averaged around 13 per cent during the years before the ban and rose sharply to 34 per cent in 2020 – nearly a billion-dollar increase in trade value for the Canadian pork industry after the ban was abruptly lifted.

Conclusion

Drawing on bilateral trade data, this chapter has argued that China's economic coercion is clearly connected to its political or security disagreements with other countries. Looking at the evidence from Canada, it appears that Beijing is strategically targeting sectors that account for a substantial proportion of Canadian exports, and whose products can be easily substituted by switching to imports from other countries. This is consistent with *Canada's Indo-Pacific Strategy*, a document released in November 2022, in which the government has described China as an "increasingly disruptive global power." Given the perceived decline in the US superpower status,[23] as well as the inherent challenge of balancing business interests with concerns about politics in host countries,[24] the issue of economic coercion looms ever larger in the minds of Canadian exporters dealing with China.

Western nations have been urged to shift trade to friendly partners and with like-minded countries in what Chrystia Freeland terms "friend-shoring."[25] However, the lesson to take from Beijing's weaponization of trade is not necessarily that global interdependence is by its very nature a security risk. Trade allows countries to specialize in the creation of goods whose cost of production is low relative to others, resulting in cheaper and more efficient global production. However, how do we maintain global interdependence alongside adversaries that may seek to exploit it? Trade diversification is, of course, the key to reducing the risk of asymmetric dependence. By pre-emptively diversifying exports of easily substitutable products that are vulnerable to asymmetrical transactions, we could reduce the leverage that adversaries might otherwise seek to exploit. This often requires long-term planning by agricultural producers, made possible by guidance from the government and industry associations that can provide macro and strategic perspectives on the global environment. Canada's recent efforts in fostering closer ties with the Association of Southeast Asian Nations, which led to the elevation of its status to that of a "strategic partner," has opened inroads to the region's markets for our agricultural products.[26] This testifies to the importance of trade diversification for our national interests. In contrast to other countries that have similarly been at the receiving end of China's economic coercion, Canada's relatively positive experience suggests that the effect of an import ban is unpredictable because of multiple factors that are not within Beijing's control, and which could in turn offset the intended impact. This calls into question the effectiveness of import bans as a weapon of trade, particularly on a bilateral basis.

NOTES

1 The author would like to thank Brodie Hemphill for providing excellent research assistance, and Darren Touch, Kristen Hopewell, Jiang Wenran, and the other panelists and participants at the 2021 Canadian Political Science Conference panel on Canada-China relations for their helpful comments. Any remaining errors are those of the author.
2 Stephen Roach, *Accidental Conflict: America, China and the Clash of False Narratives* (New Haven, CT: Yale University Press, 2022).
3 Seymour Martin Lipset, "Some Social Requisites of Democracy: Economic Development and Political Legitimacy," *American Political Science Review* 53, no. 1 (1959): 69–105.

4 Kristen Hopewell, *Clash of Powers: US-China Rivalry in Global Trade Governance* (New York: Cambridge University Press, 2020).
5 Yeling Tan, "How the WTO Changed China: The Mixed Legacy of Economic Engagement," *Foreign Affairs*, 16 February 2021, https://www.foreignaffairs.com/articles/china/2021-02-16/how-wto-changed-china.
6 "China Says Hopes Mongolia Learned Lesson after Dalai Lama Visit," Reuters, 24 January 2017, https://www.reuters.com/article/us-china-mongolia-dalailama-idUSKBN158197.
7 Christine Kim and Ben Blanchard, "China, South Korea Agree to Mend Ties after THAAD Standoff," Reuters, 30 October 2017, https://www.reuters.com/article/us-northkorea-missiles-idUSKBN1D003G.
8 Bonnie S. Glaser, "Time for Collective Pushback against China's Economic Coercion," Center for Strategic and International Studies, 13 January 2021, https://www.csis.org/analysis/time-collective-pushback-against-chinas-economic-coercion.
9 "China Suspends Canadian Beef, Pork Imports as Tensions Rise," *BBC News*, 27 June 2019, https://www.bbc.com/news/business-48767399.
10 Lynette H. Ong, *Outsourcing Repression: Everyday State Power in Contemporary China* (New York: Oxford University Press, 2022).
11 This section draws heavily on Darren J. Lim, Victor A. Ferguson, and Rosa Bishop, "Chinese Outbound Tourism as an Instrument of Economic Statecraft," *Journal of Contemporary China* 29, no. 126 (2020): 916–33; Darren J. Lim and Victor Ferguson, "Chinese Economic Coercion during the THAAD Dispute," *Asan Forum*, 28 December 2019, https://theasanforum.org/chinese-economic-coercion-during-the-thaad-dispute/.
12 Henry Farrell and Abraham L. Newman, "Weaponized Interdependence: How Global Economic Networks Shape State Coercion," *International Security* 44, no. 1 (2019): 42–79.
13 Farrell and Newman, "Weaponized Interdependence."
14 Stephen Noakes and Charles Burton, "Economic Statecraft and the Making of Bilateral Relationships: Canada-China and New Zealand–China Interactions Compared," *Journal of Chinese Political Science* 24, no. 2 (2019): 411–31.
15 Tom Alton, "Canada-China Trade: 2019 Year in Review," China Institute, University of Alberta, 13 February 2020, https://www.ualberta.ca/china-institute/media-library/media-gallery/research/analysis-briefs/canada-china-trade-2019-year-in-review.pdf.

16 Andy Blatchford and Stephanie Levitz, "China Lifts Ban on Canadian Pork, Beef Products," *Toronto Star*, 5 November 2019, https://www.thestar.com/news/canada/2019/11/05/china-lifts-ban-on-canadian-pork-beef-products.html; Alton, "Canada-China Trade."

17 David Common and Melissa Mancini, "Canola Growers Caught in Middle as Canada-China Relations Sour," *CBC News*, 15 May 2019, https://www.cbc.ca/news/business/national-canola-canada-china-trade-1.5135241.

18 LeftField Commodity Research, *Case Study – Impacts of the Chinese Trade Restrictions on the Canadian Canola Industry* (Winnipeg: LeftField Commodity Research, February 2021), https://www.canolacouncil.org/wp-content/uploads/2021/03/CCC-Market-Access-Impact-Report-China-Final.pdf.

19 China accounted for high shares of 37 and 42 per cent of Canada's exports of iron ores and wood pulp, respectively, in 2020.

20 "EU to Phase Out Palm Oil from Transport Fuel by 2030," Reuters, 14 June 2018, https://www.reuters.com/article/us-eu-climatechange-palmoil-idUSKBN1JA21F; Rob Nickel and Gus Trompiz, "Shut Out in China, Canada Finds Canola Buyers in Drought-Damaged Europe," Reuters, 22 August 2019, https://www.reuters.com/article/us-canada-canola-europe-idUSKCN1VC1WW.

21 Jason Kirby, "China Lifts Ban on Canadian Pork and Beef Exports," *Financial Times*, 5 November 2019, https://www.ft.com/content/be42bd22-0010-11ea-b7bc-f3fa4e77dd47.

22 Ashley Robinson, "China Goes through UAE 'backdoor' to Buy Canadian Canola Oil," *BNN Bloomberg*, 28 October 2019, https://www.bnnbloomberg.ca/china-goes-through-uae-backdoor-to-buy-canadian-canola-oil-1.1338813.

23 See the chapter by Carla Norrlöf in this volume.

24 Balancing between these concerns features prominently in Canada's foreign policy with the Middle East and North Africa. See the chapter by Bessma Momani in this volume.

25 Steven Chase, "Western Countries Already Embracing 'Friend-Shoring' to Reduce Trade with Authoritarian Regimes, Freeland Says," *Globe and Mail*, 17 October 2022.

26 Lu Xu, "Trudeau's China Talk in Asia," *Middle Powers*, 10 September 2023, https://middlepowers.substack.com/p/trudeaus-china-talk-in-asia.

chapter five

The Middle East and North Africa and the Future of Canadian Security

BESSMA MOMANI

Introduction

The outbreak of war in Palestine and Israel in October 2023 starkly revealed how serious the risk of conflict contagion is across the Middle East and North Africa (MENA) region. Alongside this serious international security concern, the Gaza crisis also further revealed a growing gap between the demands of citizens and the responses of their respective governments across almost every country in the MENA. This ever-worsening rift between citizen and state will affect not only the wider region but will also have significant security implications for Canada and its allies in the foreseeable future.

There is no way that NATO members can overlook the security implications of what is unfolding in the MENA region. Indeed, in 2021 the United States and other NATO allies tried to draw back from the MENA and pivot focus to eastern Europe and the Asia-Pacific, a move that allowed other powers like China and Saudi Arabia to temporarily fill the leadership vacuum (as noted in Carla Norrlöf's and Lynette Ong's chapters in this volume). Yet, after Hamas's attack on Israel on 7 October 2023, the United States has once again been pulled back to the Middle East. This eruption of violence made clear that the region remains relevant to the security of the United States, Canada, and the wider international community. For the foreseeable future, the MENA will be a serious source of conflict, instability, and mass migration – factors that are, in fact, aggravated by the growing gap between MENA citizens and their governments.

More than a decade after the Arab Spring, a series of popular uprisings that swept through the region, domino-like, between 2010 and 2013, MENA citizens are losing trust in their governments, which are becoming increasingly authoritarian and repressive. The ongoing crisis in Gaza not only puts other neighbouring countries at risk of conflict spillover, but also worsens MENA citizens' already serious loss of trust in their governments. Despite this, MENA citizens, particularly the youth, demand, in greater numbers every year, inclusive economic policies that lead to productive employment and political liberalization that leads to good governance. Throughout this time, Canada has attempted to balance its geopolitical and geo-economic interests of seeking continued business ties with these autocratic regimes, claiming its support for a two-state solution in the Palestine-Israel conflict, while also upholding rhetorical support for inclusive growth and democracy in the MENA. Canada's balancing of these interests meant that it appeared publicly at odds with itself in 2017 when it championed its Feminist International Assistance Policy (FIAP). As a feminist agenda with a mandate to support equity, empowerment, and inclusivity for women, the FIAP saw the Canadian government officially oppose many illiberal policy decisions on gender put forward in the MENA region while simultaneously maintaining close ties with the same regimes in other policy areas. This was apparent, for instance, in 2018 when Canada accosted Saudi Arabia for its human rights record while continuing to sell it a significant number of armaments.

This chapter seeks to explain how Canada tries to balance its core interest in preserving its alliances, providing rhetorical support for a two-state solution, and doing business with MENA countries while claiming to support the region's public desire for greater political liberalization. Canada's balancing approach will continue to be tested in the decade ahead, which will no doubt bring further turbulence and instability. As Canada navigates its role in the world, its continued cooperation and investments with MENA governments will put it in the uncomfortable diplomatic situation of having to side with these autocratic regimes at the expense of their citizens, particularly when these agreements and collaborations are in opposition to its FIAP priorities and stated intentions.

Context: A Canadian Balancing Act in the MENA

Living in the shadow of the United States and as an active member of NATO (which, as noted in Stéfanie von Hlatky and Hannah Hollander's chapter, is the cornerstone of Canadian security and defence policy), Canada has often reluctantly participated in the security architecture of the Middle East. Trying to be an active member of the Western alliance and defender of the rules-based international order, Canada has often followed rather than led in the MENA. Hence, to understand Canadian security interests in the region, one must consider the context of the changing liberal international order, Canada's role in security and defence alliances, and our relationship with the United States.

Importantly, Canada has not faced direct threats to its security from the MENA region; thus, its decision to participate in international or US-led coalitions is often shaped more by choice than necessity.[1] Consequently, Canada prioritizes upholding its international alliance responsibilities in its approach to the MENA region, rather than addressing other MENA regional challenges, such as diaspora politics or partisan considerations.[2] Accordingly, in support of these alliance commitments, after the events of 9/11, Canada assumed a more active foreign policy posture in the MENA, moving away from its defensive position and towards a more active combat role.[3] Successive governments valorized the Canadian Armed Forces (CAF) and its combat role abroad, and decreased Canada's traditional emphasis on peacekeeping (see Katharina Coleman and Lou Pingeot's chapter on UN peacekeeping in this volume), a notable shift that started under the 2006 Harper government.⁴ This change in policy is most clearly evidenced by Canadian support for NATO forces seeking out al-Qaeda operatives in Afghanistan, under then prime minister Jean Chrétien, and by the subsequent allocation of increased defence spending to the region under Prime Ministers Paul Martin, Stephen Harper, and Justin Trudeau. Despite its prioritization of alliance commitments, Canada has not always yielded to American pressure, as evidenced in Chrétien's decision not to participate in the United States' 2003 invasion of Saddam Hussein's Iraq, despite significant international pressure. Nevertheless, in other cases, Canada often "went along to get along."

The broader security context in the MENA region shifted again in 2010 with the start of the Arab Spring protests. This bottom-up push for democratic change put Ottawa in the uncomfortable position of debating whether to continue strengthening bilateral economic trade relations with regional governments, or to put strategic policy focus on the people's demand for political liberalization. As I have written elsewhere, these competing interests were most evident in the case of the 2011 conflict in Libya, when Libyan dictator Muammar Ghaddafi vowed to use violence to crush the revolutionaries, throwing Canada and its NATO allies off guard.⁵ The Canadian government agreed to participate in the subsequent NATO mission, and took leadership roles in NATO command to prevent Ghaddafi's annihilation of Benghazi and to prevent his forces from regaining control of Libya. Business contracts between several Canadian firms and the Ghaddafi regime were also brought to light, and Canada was in the awkward position of sidelining important corporate interests to continue its military role in the NATO mission.⁶ Eventually, the Ghaddafi regime was overthrown, and Ghaddafi himself was killed by rebels; the country has since descended into a civil war between competing power centres, each claiming to represent the Libyan people. Broad Canadian public support for military intervention in Libya would steadily decline as time passed, and the war settled into a long stalemate.

More broadly, the Arab Spring created a domino effect across the MENA, as several regimes came under intense public pressure, especially those in Egypt, Tunisia, Yemen, and Syria. Canada rhetorically supported these protest movements; however, after the Libyan experience, the Canadian public was overwhelmingly opposed to any further militarily intervention in the region. Notably, the authoritarian regimes in these countries resisted and fought back against Arab Spring movements, and many looked like they could defeat them with coercive and repressive tactics. The case of Egypt was instructive.[7] The country's long-time ruler, Hosni Mubarak, was overthrown; a democratic government was ushered in only to be overthrown itself by the military.[8] Recognizing that Egypt's military general turned president Abdel Fatah Sisi had consolidated power and control, it became difficult for Canada and its Western allies to continue to fully ostracize and denounce him. They tried to sideline President Sisi for overthrowing a democratically elected government, but as time wore on, they returned to doing business with his regime.

The brutal war in Syria was among the most gruesome examples of the failure of many Arab Spring protests to bring about fundamental change. Nevertheless, because of the disappointing experience in Libya, the Canadian government and public were hesitant about military intervention in Syria. Moreover, because Russia and China vetoed the proposed United Nations Security Council resolutions on intervention, NATO allies failed to win support for an international intervention against Assad and had to content themselves with strong negative rhetoric against his regime. In 2014, however, the rise of the so-called Islamic State in Iraq and Syria (ISIS) changed the allies' calculus of the international threat, particularly after ISIS started targeting Western soft targets, and after citizens of Western countries began travelling to the region to join the group.[9] In response to this new threat, Canada sent 850 CAF troops and, for a limited time, some air power to Iraq and Syria to fight ISIS. As ISIS continued to lose territory and revert from a proto-state to a classic terrorist organization, Canada faced criticism of its continued presence in the region. Nevertheless, the Canadian mission, Operation Impact, has maintained a modest contingency of CAF personnel. Canada has tried to balance domestic scepticism of interventions in the MENA, its commitments to alliances to support international security efforts, the growing demands of MENA citizens for support for their revolutions, and pressure from Canadian business interests to continue working with repressive MENA governments.

Change: A Future of MENA Instability

In the coming decade, Canada will have to contend with an unstable MENA, the resurgence of the Palestinian-Israeli issue on the geopolitical agenda, climate change in the region, and another possible refugee exodus from the region that will put global pressure on Canada to continue to admit more migrants. The war in Gaza, the further entrenchment of autocratic regimes in the MENA, and the rise of populist nationalism in the West have made it more difficult for Canada to push for adherence to the liberal international order. This has been further complicated, of course, by the relative decline of the United States (as noted in Carla Norrlöf's chapter in this volume), which is seen, rightly or wrongly, as the leading proponent of the liberal international order, despite having lost all credibility by supporting Israel's disproportionate use of force in its war in Gaza.

The burgeoning demographic of MENA youth and the inability of regional governments to meet their economic needs and political preferences will continue to test the West's relationship with the region.[10] Without policies and reforms that deliver economic security, MENA governments will face a more demanding and youthful population hungry for change and inclusion. While MENA youth are increasingly educated, the rate of unemployment in the region in most non-oil-exporting states is as high as 50 per cent – an unacceptably high figure that is among the worst in the world. The persistence of such under/unemployment will no doubt negatively affect the region's political stability.[11]

The COVID-19 pandemic has brought further economic hardship for MENA citizens, particularly youth. In 2020, unemployment rose rapidly, household incomes dropped drastically, and livelihoods deteriorated. Prior to the pandemic, trends in extreme poverty were down in all parts of the globe, except the MENA;

current conditions will likely be aggravated by the economic hardships of the pandemic. Due to the global prospects of a slow economic recovery and rising public debt, MENA governments' social protections and spending will be limited, thus foreshadowing rising poverty, food insecurity, and rising unemployment. This will result in further mass frustrations for which MENA governments do not have answers, leading many youth who have unfortunately been met with increased repression and violence in the past to seek out opportunities for migration.

Youth unemployment, deteriorating socio-economic conditions, and decreased hope for the future were all key factors that precipitated the Arab Spring. Similarly, prior to the pandemic, trends in MENA life satisfaction over the post–Arab Spring decade were decreasing while the global average increased. As many young people have lost trust and confidence in their governments, the prospects of political instability in the MENA are high. Notably, a majority of MENA academic experts (76 per cent of a sample of 1,293) believe the region is either still in a state of protest or will experience another wave of mass mobilization in less than ten years.[12]

The Arab Spring was a rude awakening for MENA government leaders who thought the maintenance of the status quo was enough to ensure complacency across their societies. Despite some promises of democratic change, transformational civic debates, and increased activism throughout the MENA, there is far too much regression on almost all indicators of political freedoms across the region, and not just in war-torn countries like Syria, Yemen, and Libya.[13] These conditions will only worsen during the post-pandemic recovery period and as Israel's war against Gaza continues into 2024. The latter has also renewed MENA citizens' desire to see the realization of a Palestinian state.

MENA governments will remain vulnerable to further protests and demonstrations in the decades to come. Protests in Iran against the mandatory hijab and government repression are emblematic of the continued desire among the youth for social and political change. MENA youth will continue to be the driving force for economic, political, and social transformation in their societies. As these youth become more vocal, increasingly due to social media connectivity, the diplomatic relationship between the West and the MENA governments will also need to change. For far too long, Western governments and MENA autocrats have maintained a marriage of convenience, either for oil or for valuable geostrategic reasons, much to the dismay of many MENA citizens.

Canada Should Support MENA Citizens

In the MENA today, people's dissatisfaction with their governments is very high; the vast majority report having very low faith in their governments, and these perceptions are far worse among MENA youth. In Lebanon, only 4 per cent of the surveyed public has faith in their government – a sentiment shared by 15 per cent of Tunisians and 22 per cent of Iraqis.[14] These numbers continue to decline as perceptions of government corruption increase. Disaffected youth in the MENA region is a powder keg that demands serious global attention to mitigate another political implosion and stem irregular migrant flows from the region. While Canada has opted for balance in its broader international security commitments by presenting itself as a "principled power," it will face the predicament of needing to choose between siding with authoritarian MENA governments or with the people. This will be a tough balancing act. The Canadian government and Canadian businesses should not forget that citizens across the MENA are watching their own governments, and, if successful in future democratic transitions, will admonish companies and foreign governments that dealt with the corrupt and autocratic regimes they suffered under. Moreover, as the Israeli-Palestinian issue has reinvigorated global attention to Western policy towards the region after 7 October 2023, Canadian rhetoric will be scrutinized and assessed through the prism of a potential two-state solution. Canada may find it more difficult to be ambivalent about in foreign policy towards this issue when there is global demand for concrete action.

The good news is that Canada can increase investment in the MENA region, but it must do so by meeting the needs of the people. With the right investments, there is immense opportunity for economic prosperity and growth, given the educated and eager workforce found throughout the region. The challenge will be to ensure that Western firms do not appear to be complicit in the political trappings and inefficiencies of MENA bureaucracies, curry favour with the crony capitalists of the region, or support the Israeli occupation of Palestinians. Here, Western businesses must operate in an open investment environment and duly report their dealings with MENA governments. Above all, Canada must do business in a transparent, accountable, and responsible manner. This approach will bring positive returns – financial, political, and diplomatic – to the MENA region.

Conclusion

Since 2011, the events in Tunisia, Libya, Egypt, Yemen, and Syria have revealed a growing gap between the demands of MENA citizens and the narrow self-interests of autocratic elites. As domestic pressure for inclusive economies and political systems grows across the MENA, Canada's seemingly contradictory foreign policy towards the region will be tested. The Arab Spring can be understood as the result not only of domestic causes and conditions within the MENA, but also of the clumsy and inconsistent responses of foreign countries and alliances. The region is far more nationalistic today than before the Arab Spring, and it is led by brazen governments willing to go their own way and defy US hegemonic preferences. This in part explains Saudi Arabia's willingness to have China broker an important act of détente between it and Iran in 2023.

Without simply romanticizing Canadian foreign policy through the prism of idealism, it is fair to say that Canada has faced normative pressure to consider the MENA in its foreign policy decisions, despite lacking a strong national interest in this part of the globe. However, this normative pressure forces Canada to walk a tightrope so as to balance three competing and often contradictory forces: (1) the demands of Canadian voters, especially those who have diaspora ties to the MENA region; (2) the pressure to maintain a consistent foreign policy with other allies, especially the United States; and (3) the need to uphold international laws and norms on the world stage. In practice, this tightrope has meant that Canada has voted inconsistently at the UN General Assembly, in ways that have arguably alienated both domestic voters and key allies, as well as the majority of other member states at the UN. Whether or not Canada is able to show any leadership in the MENA will depend on whether it can more effectively balance these three competing pressures.

Looking ahead, the demands of young people for change in the MENA are guaranteed to intensify in the years ahead, including among the expected new wave of Palestinian refugees. Indeed, the risk and reality of war in the region means that mass migration will remain at the forefront of Canada's security and foreign policy agenda. By bringing more diverse voices to the field of security, we can better appreciate the consequences of Canadian policies beyond the standard geopolitical and geo-economic ones that have governed decisions in the past. Only then can we better assess the long-term implications of sidelining the people of the MENA region, and its consequences for global security.[15]

NOTES

1 Thomas Juneau and Bessma Momani, *Middle Power in the Middle East: Canada's Foreign and Defence Policies in a Changing Region* (Toronto: University of Toronto Press, 2022).
2 Juneau and Momani, *Middle Power in the Middle East*.
3 Prosper Bernard Jr., "Canada and Human Security: From the Axworthy Doctrine to Middle Power Internationalism," *American Review of Canadian Studies* 36, no. 2 (2006): 233–61.
4 Patrick Travers and Taylor Owen, "Between Metaphor and Strategy: Canada's Integrated Approach to Peacebuilding in Afghanistan," *International Journal* 63, no. 3 (2008): 685–702.
5 Bessma Momani, *Arab Dawn: Arab Youth and the Demographic Dividend They Will Bring* (Toronto: University of Toronto Press, 2015).
6 Andrew F. Cooper and Bessma Momani, "The Harper Government's Messaging in the Build-up to the Libyan Intervention: Was Canada

Different than Its NATO Allies?," *Canadian Foreign Policy Journal* 20, no. 2 (2014): 176–88.
7 Bessma Momani and Eid Mohamed, eds., *Egypt beyond Tahrir Square* (Bloomington: Indiana University Press, 2016).
8 Eid Mohamed and Bessma Momani, "The Muslim Brotherhood: Between Democracy, Ideology and Distrust," *Sociology of Islam* 2, nos. 3–4 (2014): 196–212.
9 Melissa Finn and Bessma Momani, "Building Foundations for the Comparative Study of State and Non-state Terrorism," *Critical Studies on Terrorism* 10, no. 3 (2017): 379–403.
10 Momani, *Arab Dawn*.
11 Bessma Momani, "Economic Development: Bread, Jobs, and Beyond," in *The Societies of the Middle East and North Africa*, ed. Sean Yom (London: Routledge, 2021), 139–70.
12 Marc Lynch and Shibley Telhami, "Biden Says He Will Listen to Experts. Here Is What Scholars of the Middle East think," Brookings Institution, 19 February 2021, https://www.brookings.edu/articles/biden-says-he-will-listen-to-experts-here-is-what-scholars-of-the-middle-east-think/.
13 Bessma Momani and Melissa Finn, "Arab Youth Nonmovements," in *The Myth of Middle East Exceptionalism: Unfinished Social Movements*, ed. Mojtaba Mahdavi (Syracuse, NY: Syracuse University Press, 2023), 145–60.
14 "Arab Barometer VI, July 2020–April 2021," Arab Barometer, accessed 14 March 2024, https://www.arabbarometer.org/surveys/covid-19-survey/.
15 Alistair Edgar, Rupinder Mangat, and Bessma Momani, eds., *Strengthening the Canadian Armed Forces through Diversity and Inclusion* (Toronto: University of Toronto Press, 2019).

PART 2

Evolving Threats

chapter six

UN Peacekeeping at a Crossroads

KATHARINA COLEMAN AND LOU PINGEOT[1]

Introduction

Almost seventy years after Canada helped establish the first United Nations peacekeeping force in Egypt, peacekeeping remains a flagship UN activity. In 2022, the UN deployed over 74,000 uniformed peacekeepers and some 10,000 civilians in twelve operations, at an annual cost of US$6.3 billion. Peacekeeping missions can reduce civilian and military deaths during wars, facilitate peace agreements, and prevent conflict recurrence.[2] However, they can also ignore key conflict dynamics, fail to achieve mandated goals, and even have adverse effects.[3] Appropriately, there is ongoing debate about improving UN peacekeeping, including our own work on force generation, financing, use of force, and feedback effects on troop-contributing countries.[4]

Currently, UN peacekeeping also faces two more fundamental challenges. First, its evolution towards stabilization missions has raised foundational questions about the nature and limits of UN peacekeeping. Second, the political environment for UN peacekeeping has deteriorated drastically since the mid-2010s. Longer-term trends of tenuous Western support, frustration over the apparent inability of several large missions to bring lasting peace, and growing contestation of the Western-led international order have been exacerbated by the global COVID-19 pandemic and deep tensions following Russia's invasion of Ukraine, which has also led Canada and other allied states to prioritize NATO engagement. UN peacekeeping, which has contracted sharply since 2015, presently faces deep uncertainty.

UN peace operations are likely to persist, but their nature may shift significantly.[5] Canada has a stake in helping to rebuild a new working consensus around UN peacekeeping that preserves key commitments to promoting human rights and democratic governance while enhancing missions' responsiveness to local conflict management and peacebuilding processes.

Context

Although the UN continues to assert the Cold War peacekeeping principles of consent, impartiality, and minimum use of force, this apparent continuity coexists with profound changes in peacekeeping practice. Starting in the 1990s, UN peacekeeping increasingly focused on helping to implement peace agreements rather than simply patrolling ceasefires. Peacekeeping became multidimensional, with more police and civilian personnel deployed, and it started to champion liberal goals of democratization and human rights promotion. Yet UN peacekeeping also experienced crisis and contraction, as operations in Angola, Somalia, and the former Yugoslavia all failed to halt escalating violence, reaching a nadir with UN inaction during the Rwandan genocide.

As UN peacekeeping resurged in the early 2000s, more missions were deployed to places recognized as having "no peace to keep." Increasingly, UN operations were mandated to use force to protect civilians ("robust peacekeeping"), responding to local demands for protection as well as international expectations. In Haiti (2004–17), the Democratic Republic of the Congo (2010–), Mali (2013–23), and the Central African Republic (2014–), missions were also mandated to use force to support host states against non-state armed groups ("stabilization").[6] Expanding numbers of increasingly demanding operations pushed UN peacekeeping personnel and financial requirements to record highs; by 2015, the UN deployed almost 124,000 peacekeepers in sixteen operations costing US$8.5 billion annually.[7] Stabilization operations also raised profound concerns about the UN's capacity to undertake intensive military operations,[8] the additional risks incurred by peacekeepers,[9] and the inherent tensions with the principles of consent, impartiality, and minimum use of force.[10]

Moreover, as UN peacekeeping expanded, tensions around leadership and burden sharing increased. Western democracies, including permanent Security Council members the United States, France, and the United Kingdom (the P3), dominated peacekeeping mandating and financing decisions. However, they did not re-engage as major UN troop contributors, preferring to address crises in which they perceived significant national interests through non-UN operations. By contrast, the African and Asian states that emerged as the UN's major troop contributors (including Bangladesh, Ethiopia, India, Pakistan, and Rwanda) wielded limited mandating and financing power.[11] This produced recurring contestation as Western states passed ambitious mandates but sought to rein in rising costs, while major troop contributors raised concerns about increased risks to their personnel, sought greater inclusion in mandating decisions, and resented Western states' reluctance to fund peace operations more generously. China, meanwhile, emerged as a major financial and personnel contributor, presenting a stark contrast to Western democracies. In the Security Council, both China and Russia increasingly challenged P3 dominance on peacekeeping decisions.

Since 2015, UN peacekeeping has contracted due to the closure of several long-standing missions, increased Security Council tensions that have prevented the creation of any major new mission since 2014, and continuing demands for peacekeeping cost reductions, notably from the United States. From 2015 to 2022, despite historically high numbers of conflicts worldwide (see below), deployed UN peacekeeping personnel diminished by 30 per cent and UN peacekeeping financing by 26 per cent. At UN Headquarters, Russia and China responded to the contraction by advocating for a reduction in human rights–related peacekeeping activities,[12] highlighting a rift with the P3 over the purposes of peacekeeping as well as its leadership. That rift deepened into a chasm with Russia's 2022 invasion of Ukraine; China's muted reaction; and

Western states' condemnation of the invasion, economic sanctions against Russia, and military aid to Ukraine.

Within operations, meanwhile, repeated cost-cutting and downsizing exercises have frustrated and demoralized peacekeepers.[13] The COVID-19 pandemic exacerbated the difficulties faced by peacekeepers and may have longer-term effects both on the availability of peacekeeping financing and on conflict patterns in affected countries. A divided Security Council and the concentration of global attention and resources on Ukraine – and since October 2023, Israel and Gaza – portend continued austerity for UN peacekeeping.

Medium-Term Challenges

Even before the eruption of war in Ukraine and Gaza, the number of armed conflicts globally was at a "historic high," with fifty-four state-based and seventy-six non-state conflicts in 2021.[14] UN peace operations are not the only – or always the best – means of addressing conflicts. However, they are and will likely remain an important part of the international conflict-management toolkit. Policymakers and academics will thus continue to debate ways to enhance peacekeeping effectiveness. In addition, however, UN peacekeeping faces two major medium-term challenges.

First, while a "robust" use of force may be necessary to protect civilians in ongoing conflicts, the UN's shift towards stabilization operations risks undermining inclusive and negotiated political solutions. It may also produce illiberal effects both in the host states where peace operations deploy and in troop-contributing countries, potentially sowing the seeds of future crises.

In host states, stabilization mandates typically entail UN support for the existing government and the extension of state authority, regardless of these institutions' local legitimacy. The immediate focus on building state strength and stability risks sidelining more ambitious aims of promoting democratic governance, human rights, and locally led, inclusive peace and reconciliation processes. Missions may unintentionally enable unrepresentative and/or abusive regimes by providing resources to incumbent governments and tacitly tolerating authoritarian behaviour.[15] They may also undertake joint operations with state armed forces that have dubious human rights records.[16] Moreover, when missions use force against specific armed actors, their ability to engage these actors politically or act as impartial mediators in peace negotiations decreases.[17] A focus on military operations can also divert attention and resources from efforts to promote political solutions to conflicts.[18] Stabilization operations also escalate the risks to peacekeepers, leading to a focus on force protection at the expense of engagement with local communities. Thus, any short-term successes stabilization may bring must be balanced against the potential long-term effects of abetting authoritarianism and distracting from the search for more sustainable political solutions to conflict.

The impact of stabilization on troop-contributing countries also raises concerns. Scholars and practitioners have long hoped that UN peace operations would socialize participating states to embrace democratic values, especially civilian control over the military. Yet in some troop-contributing countries, including Bangladesh, Brazil, Fiji, and Nepal, UN deployments have unintentionally empowered military actors at home, eroding civilian control.[19] Stabilization missions in particular have, perversely, socialized some troop-contributing countries into illiberal uses of force, while giving their militaries combat experience that can be used for repression or counter-insurgency at home.[20] For example, the Brazilian military's leading role in the stabilization mission in Haiti led to calls for greater military involvement in law enforcement within Brazil and for a loosening of rules of engagement for "pacification" in favelas.[21]

The second major challenge is the fractured political environment surrounding UN peacekeeping. As noted, the P3 and other Western states have lost some leadership status in UN peacekeeping discussions given their reluctance to provide troops and their insistence on cost reductions. Following the Trump administration's scepticism of multilateralism, the Biden administration committed to rebuilding US leadership within the UN, especially against "Member States ... that sought to advance a more authoritarian vision of international order."²² Yet a reassertion of Western states' leadership is challenged both by competing demands on these states' attention and resources – notably COVID-19, fractious domestic politics, the war in Ukraine and consequent renewed emphasis on NATO (see von Hlatky and Hollander's chapter in this volume), and the war in Gaza – and by multiple demands for a fundamental power shift within the UN.

With relations between Russia and Western states at a nadir, Russian critiques of Western dominance of peacekeeping decisions are likely to intensify. China – whose growing economic weight and global influence have increasingly concerned Western states (see Ong's chapter) – has long advanced similar critiques, adding its political weight as a major financial and (unlike the P3) troop contributor. The fault line between Western states on the one hand and Russia and China on the other hand was reinforced by China's abstentions or no votes in six major General Assembly resolutions passed between February 2022 and April 2023 criticizing Russia's actions in Ukraine. The United States, Russia, and China have also been at loggerheads regarding responses to the war in Gaza, opposing and vetoing each other's amendments and resolutions in the Security Council.

Troop-contributing countries, meanwhile, have frequently demanded greater influence on Security Council peacekeeping mandating decisions and are frustrated by the incremental concessions they have received to date. Downsizing trends, late reimbursements, and increased risks to troops have exacerbated these frustrations. African states, often acting through the African Union, have advanced an additional demand to be consulted by the Security Council. Half of the UN's current peace operations are deployed in Africa, and African states and regional organizations have become indispensable strategic partners to UN peacekeeping on the continent. While formally committed to consultation with both (overlapping) sets of actors, permanent Security Council members have historically been reluctant to significantly curtail their own freedom of action. However, individual council members (including France and China) have long sought to bolster their international positions by deepening political alliances with states in the Global South, notably in Africa. China emerged as a major presence in Africa and a rival to Western influence on the continent in the 2000s, while Russia has gained more prominence recently, including through Wagner Group deployments in Mali and the Central African Republic. The invasion of Ukraine has highlighted the extent of Russian and Chinese influence in Africa, with many African states abstaining or voting against General Assembly resolutions critiquing Russia's actions. A flurry of US diplomatic visits to Africa (including by Vice-President Kamala Harris in early 2023) indicates that the Biden administration is seeking to regain influence.[23] The extent to which competition over support from African states will translate into greater African influence over UN peacekeeping remains uncertain, though African states have additional leverage, as regionally led deployments are increasingly favoured for enforcement and counterterrorism operations, including by the UN secretary general.[24]

Until these political power struggles reach a new equilibrium, efforts to re-forge consensus around a set of peacekeeping principles – such as the UN secretary general's 2018 Action for Peacekeeping (A4P) initiative, which became A4P+ in 2021 – will likely have limited impact. Deepening Security Council divisions and shrinking UN peacekeeping commitments risk leaving an increasing number of conflicts unaddressed or resurgent after peacekeeping withdrawals. Where missions are deployed, UN peacekeepers may be increasingly demoralized by the difficulty of implementing ambitious mandates with shrinking resources, the frustrating repercussions of political divisions at UN Headquarters on mission mandates, and, for civilian peacekeepers, job insecurity after successive waves of downsizing.

Canadian Interests and Opportunities

While the Russian invasion of Ukraine has led to a renewed emphasis on NATO, UN peace operations remain an important instrument for addressing a broad range of conflicts, including where NATO intervention is not feasible or desirable. As the UN

Secretariat works to complete the promised "New Agenda for Peace" – with significant bureaucratic disagreements and amid considerable uncertainty about what the document might say about peacekeeping – Canada has an opportunity to shape the further evolution of UN peacekeeping.

Canada has an interest in international peace and security because of its integration in globalized economic, political, and social networks. Canada has also long asserted its commitment to liberal democratic values and claimed status within the UN as a significant multilateral actor with foundational contributions to UN peacekeeping. Canada therefore has a substantial stake in addressing the double challenge to the liberal aspirations of post–Cold War UN peacekeeping created by the turn to stabilization and the fracturing political environment. This means rebuilding a broad coalition around a principled vision of peace operations that defends basic liberal democratic values, which will require a more inclusive peacekeeping governance structure.

Canada has the opportunity to position itself as a principled advocate for a recalibrated version of UN peacekeeping that adequately responds to immediate conflict and civilian-protection concerns while also centring political engagement to secure lasting peace, asserting human rights objectives, and avoiding sowing the seeds to future conflicts in troop-contributing states. For UN stabilization missions deployed to address conflicts in which armed actors systematically attack civilian populations, robust rules of engagement are necessary. However, stabilization should be a last resort in the intervention toolkit and must be accompanied by mitigating measures to ensure that it does not detract from the pursuit of political solutions, enable authoritarianism in host states, or worsen civil-military relations in troop-contributing countries.

Centring political solutions to conflicts aligns with the secretary general's A4P initiative, which Canada should support. In the face of growing challenges to the liberal foundations of UN peacekeeping, Canada should specifically advocate political solutions that support inclusive democracy, human rights, and locally led peace initiatives while also helping to develop strategies to counter possible illiberal consequences of stabilization.

Canada also has an interest in participating in a broader international negotiation about the governance of UN peacekeeping. Unless the demands for more inclusive decision making coming from troop contributors, host states, regional actors, and local populations are more fully addressed, debates on peacekeeping principles are unlikely to produce the necessary rejuvenation of UN peace operations. Revisiting governance structures is necessary both to advance the above vision of peace operations and to lay stronger foundations for a continued central Canadian role in UN (peacekeeping) debates. Despite its historical impact and current status as a major financial contributor, Canada's influence on UN peacekeeping has waned, both because of low Canadian troop contributions – totalling just fifty-two in late 2023 – and because of the broader challenges to historic Western dominance of UN peacekeeping policy discussed above. There is a risk that Russia's invasion of Ukraine will further distract Western states from UN peacekeeping, thus weakening their capacity to lead and making alternative visions proposed by Russia and China more attractive. Canada can counter this risk not only by advocating for continued – or renewed – UN engagement by Western states, but also by fostering an inclusive dialogue between Western and non-Western states on the principles and the governance of peacekeeping. To stay relevant, Western states have to offer their own path to a less Western-dominated UN. Relaxing pressures for financial austerity and allowing non-Western troop contributors and regional states expanded input in UN peacekeeping decision making may be necessary for rebuilding support for a version of UN peacekeeping that is compatible with Canadian interests and values. Seeking to facilitate such a compromise could bolster Canada's own status as a credible participant in UN policy debates, an international bridge-builder, and an effective advocate for liberal internationalism.

NOTES

1 Dr. Coleman's recent research on peace operations has been supported by Canada's Social Sciences and Humanities Research Council and

Sweden's Folke Bernadotte Academy. No funding was sought specifically for this chapter.
2   Barbara F. Walter, Lise Morje Howard, and V. Page Fortna, "The Extraordinary Relationship between Peacekeeping and Peace," *British Journal of Political Science* 51, no. 4 (2021): 1705–22.
3   Séverine Autesserre, *The Trouble with the Congo: Local Violence and the Failure of International Peacebuilding* (Cambridge: Cambridge University Press, 2010); Sarah von Billerbeck. *Whose Peace? Local Ownership and United Nations Peacekeeping* (Oxford: Oxford University Press, 2016).
4   Katharina P. Coleman and Xiaojun Li, *Token Forces: How Tiny Troop Contributions Became Ubiquitous in UN Peacekeeping* (Cambridge: Cambridge University Press, 2023); Katharina P. Coleman, Magnus Lundgren, and Kseniya Oksamytna, "Slow Progress on UN Rapid Deployment: The Pitfalls of Policy Paradigms in International Organizations," *International Studies Review* 23, no. 3 (2021): 455–83; Katharina P. Coleman, "The Political Economy of UN Peacekeeping: Incentivizing Effective Participation," *Providing for Peacekeeping No. 7*, International Peace Institute, May 2014, https://www.ipinst.org/wp-content/uploads/publications/ipi_political_economy.pdf; Lou Pingeot, "United Nations Peace Operations as International Practices: Revisiting the UN Mission's Armed Raids against Gangs in Haiti," *European Journal of International Security* 3, no. 3 (2018): 364–81; Lou Pingeot, "The Multilateral Production of Global Policing: UN Peace Operations as Hubs for Protest Policing," *Small Wars & Insurgencies* 33, nos. 4–5 (2022): 846–67.
5   Katharina P. Coleman and Paul D. Williams, "Peace Operations Are What States Make of Them: Why Future Evolution Is More Likely than Extinction," *Contemporary Security Policy* 42, no. 2 (2021): 241–55; Katharina P. Coleman and Brian L. Job, "How Africa and China May Shape UN Peacekeeping beyond the Liberal International Order," *International Affairs* 97, no. 5 (2021): 1451–68.
6   John Karlsrud, *The UN at War: Peace Operations in a New Era* (New York: Springer, 2017).
7   UN, *Fact Sheet: United Nations Peacekeeping Operations* (June 2015; on file with the authors).
8   Lise Morjé Howard, *Power in Peacekeeping* (Cambridge: Cambridge University Press, 2019).

9 Haidi Willmot, Scott Sheeran, and Lisa Sharland, *Safety and Security Challenges in UN Peace Operations* (New York: International Peace Institute, 2015).
10 Emily Paddon Rhoads, *Taking Sides in Peacekeeping: Impartiality and the Future of the United Nations* (Oxford: Oxford University Press, 2016).
11 Katharina P. Coleman, "United Nations Peacekeeping Decisions: Three Hierarchies, Upward Mobility and Institutionalised Inequality among Member States," *Global Society* 34, no. 3 (2020): 318–34.
12 Colum Lynch, "Russia and China See in Trump Era a Chance to Roll Back Human Rights Promotion at U.N.," *Foreign Policy*, 26 June 2018, https://foreignpolicy.com/2018/06/26/russia-and-china-see-in-trump-era-a-chance-to-roll-back-human-rights-promotion-at-u-n; "Action for Peacekeeping Initiative Making Tangible Progress in Bolstering Peace Operations, Under-Secretary-General Tells Security Council," UN Security Council, Press Release SC/14300 (14 September 2020), https://press.un.org/en/2020/sc14300.doc.htm.
13 Katharina P. Coleman, "Downsizing in UN Peacekeeping: The Impact on Civilian Peacekeepers and the Missions Employing Them," *International Peacekeeping* 27, no. 5 (2020): 703–31.
14 Julia Palik, Anna Marie Obermeier, and Siri Aas Rustad, "Conflict Trends: A Global Overview, 1946–2021," *PRIO Paper* (2022): 9, https://www.prio.org/publications/13178.
15 Sarah Von Billerbeck and Oisín Tansey, "Enabling Autocracy? Peacebuilding and Post-conflict Authoritarianism in the Democratic Republic of Congo," *European Journal of International Relations* 25, no. 3 (2019): 698–722.
16 E.g. Paddon Rhoads, *Taking Sides*.
17 Ralph Mamiya, *Engaging with Non-state Armed Groups to Protect Civilians: A Pragmatic Approach for UN Peace Operations* (New York: International Peace Institute, 2018).
18 Ralph Mamiya, *Protection of Civilians and Political Strategies* (New York: International Peace Institute, 2018).
19 Kai Michael Kenkel, "Stability Abroad, Instability at Home? Changing UN Peace Operations and Civil–Military Relations in Global South Troop Contributing Countries," *Contemporary Security Policy* 42, no. 2 (2021): 225–40.

20 Philip Cunliffe, "From Peacekeepers to Praetorians: How Participating in Peacekeeping Operations May Subvert Democracy," *International Relations* 32, no. 2 (2018): 218–39.
21 Christoph Harig. "Re-importing the 'Robust Turn' in UN Peacekeeping: Internal Public Security Missions of Brazil's Military," *International Peacekeeping* 26, no. 2 (2019): 137–64.
22 "Fact Sheet: Restoring America's Leadership at the United Nations in President Biden's First Year," United States Mission to the United Nations, Office of Press and Public Diplomacy, 20 January 2022, https://usun.usmission.gov/fact-sheet-restoring-americas-leadership-at-the-united-nations-in-president-bidens-first-year/.
23 On the challenges the United States and other Western states face in exercising leadership in the Global South, see Carla Norrlöf's chapter in this volume.
24 "Joint Press Conference by United Nations Secretary-General António Guterres, African Union Commission Chairperson Moussa Faki Mahamat," United Nations, Press Conference SG/SM/22054 (28 November 2023), https://press.un.org/en/2023/sgsm22054.doc.htm.

chapter seven

Cyberspace: A Dangerous Game with Uncertain Rules

LEAH WEST[1]

Introduction

The nature of security and conflict has and will continue to evolve in the twenty-first century thanks to society's intensifying interconnectedness, the exponential growth of social media, the proliferation of Internet-enabled devices, and the widespread deployment of artificial intelligence. In the past several years, security officials have increasingly warned Canadians of the perils of cyber warfare, the use of the Internet by terrorist organizations to recruit and spread their propaganda, and the detrimental impact of cyber espionage on our economic prosperity.[2] However, in recent years, one of the fastest-growing threats to democratic states has not been catastrophic cyberattacks but the rise in online foreign influence activity and the spread of disinformation designed to erode trust in state institutions and enable mass or targeted manipulation. Cyber operations that advance these objectives are unlike traditional espionage; the intent is not to learn something about an adversary or steal intellectual property. Nor are they comparable to a kinetic strike or covert action meant to kill an enemy, destroy a physical target, or render a rival capability inoperable. Instead, cyber operations designed to misinform or misdirect may achieve this objective by merely altering or deleting data. These operations are not the high-drama scenarios that make for blockbuster films, but they are far more likely to arise and have the potential to seriously undermine the population's confidence in their governance, security, financial, economic, and democratic institutions.

In addition to these threats, the international community is, at the time of writing, witnessing the employment of offensive cyber operations connected to the international armed conflict between Russia and Ukraine. Bearing in mind that attribution in cyberspace remains a challenge, Ukraine has been the victim of an onslaught of malicious cyber activity, much of which has been connected directly or indirectly to Russia; but Russia has also suffered attacks, including attacks from non-governmental hacktivists who support Ukraine.[3] The conflict may prove to be a case study for renewed discussions on the application of international law to conflicts fought in part in the cyber domain.

In response to this array of threats, Canada and several other states have expanded their cyber capabilities to defend their national interests and cyber infrastructure, and also actively engage in offensive cyber operations abroad.[4] Unfortunately, the government has not matched this increasingly complex threat environment and Canada's growing willingness and capacity to engage both offensively and defensively with any form of national cyber foreign policy, nor is there any public discussion of a coherent cyberspace strategy. It took until April 2022 before Canada finally articulated its understanding of how international law governs state conduct in cyberspace, but its position is at odds with some of its closest allies, including NATO ally France.

In short, Canada is playing a dangerous game without a full understanding of the rules. This short chapter briefly describes the current cyber threat environment, the recent changes in Canada's cyber operations posture and what they mean for the future, and why Canada needs to set out a clear cyber foreign policy. It concludes with a warning and an optimistic look at Canada's potential in the cyber arena.

Context: The Current Threat Environment

Hostile states, terrorist organizations, and criminal enterprises are increasingly leveraging cyberspace to advance their interests. In a speech to the Economic Club of Canada in December 2018, the Canadian Security Intelligence Service (CSIS) director David Vigneault explained that the threat of terrorism and violent extremism is growing and exacerbated by the "use [of] social media, chatrooms, and file sharing sites to disseminate extremist content for recruitment, training, and fundraising."[5] Vigneault also cautioned that states regularly leverage the Internet to conduct cyber espionage and foreign influence activities. He noted that "the scales, speed, range, and impact of foreign interference has grown as a result of the internet, social media platforms, and the availability of cheaper and more accessible cyber tools."[6] The former minister of public safety, Ralph Goodale, echoed Vigneault's warnings during remarks made in January 2019: "millions of times every day, hackers at home and around the world are trying to break in. The culprits may be foreign states, militaries or spy agencies, or terror groups, or organized crime, or petty thieves, or people with corporate or personal grudges, or sometimes it's the computer wonk next door, just trying to see how far he can get."[7]

The threat of online foreign influence on Canadian democratic institutions, especially the 2019 federal election, was of such concern that the government launched the Security and Intelligence Threats to Elections Task Force in February of that year.[8] In a speech announcing the task force, Minister Goodale explained the need for vigilance because of the recent attacks on Canada's allies. He remarked that "one fifth of all Tweets posted during the final month of the 2016 US campaign were generated by bots. This was not citizens intensely engaged in the democratic process. It was contrived and electronically generated meddling intended to pervert the conversation."[9] In her chapter in this volume, Norrlöf identifies that social cleavages across the United States have intensified since the 2016 election, making Americans even more susceptible to this kind of online manipulation. But this activity is not limited to meddling in the US elections; similar Russian activity was identified in France, Germany, and the Netherlands. And, as von Hlatky and Hollander note in their chapter, NATO allies are increasingly facing cyberattacks aimed at undermining their democratic institutions and amplifying national divisions.

The *CSIS Public Report 2020* (published in April 2021) reiterated that "Cyber-espionage, cyber-sabotage, cyber-foreign influence and cyber-terrorism pose significant threats to Canada's national security, its interests and its economic stability."[10] The report also noted that the rise in working from home that accompanied the COVID-19 pandemic increased the risk of exposure to "malicious cyber activity."[11] In the wake of the pandemic, all manner of hostile actors ranging from low-level criminals to foreign intelligence agencies have sought to leverage the crisis for financial gain, to spread disinformation, and to steal medical research and intellectual property. A June 2020 report from the Canadian Centre for Cyber Security assessed that "national and international public health organizations will almost certainly continue to be targeted by cyber threat activity such as ransomware, information and credential theft, and distributed denial of service (DDoS) attacks."[12] A report published by Canada's Communications Security Establishment (CSE) in conjunction with the United Kingdom's National Cyber Security Centre in July 2020 went so far as to attribute efforts to steal information related to COVID-19 vaccine research and development to APT 29, a cyber espionage unit with established ties to Russia.[13]

In the midst of all this, the end of 2020 revealed the most significant and widespread hack of American government and private institutions in history.[14] The infiltration of the SolarWinds Orion software used by hundreds of US companies and US government departments went undetected for a staggering nine months. There was little debate that Russia was behind the massive infiltration; indeed, the United States and the United Kingdom attributed the attack to Russia's Foreign Intelligence Service in April 2021. What was in doubt, and indeed still remains in question, is whether the hack itself and any subsequent actions taken by Russia inside American networks violate international law.[15]

Cyber operations, like the SolarWinds hack, fall in a legal grey zone, somewhere below the threshold of a use of force or armed attack that is conventionally accepted as unlawful under international law. Grey zone attacks are not designed simply to steal information, destroy infrastructure, or take systems offline, but rather to confuse, misinform, misdirect, or promulgate false information. These types of operations can have massive security implications and jeopardize trust in the systems we rely on to keep us safe.

The RAND Corporation's Project Air Force, for example, was tasked by the US Air Force with looking into the challenge of logistics data corruption. Recognizing that the United States' air superiority is difficult to attack directly, the project outlined how the US Air Force might be vulnerable to attacks targeting its logistics systems, which rely heavily on data in hundreds of information technology systems.[16] These attacks may take the form of cyber operations that destroy or corrupt data, deny access to data, or manipulate computer processes.[17] RAND noted that data corruption has the potential to be far more damaging than other forms of attack because it may allow an adversary to "maintain a longer foothold in the systems" or "mask attribution."[18] Examples of data corruption designed to impact aviation operations could include creating an "erroneous shipping destination for critical spares, incorrect technical data for procedures for aircraft repair, a false diagnosis from automated test equipment, [and] a spurious redistribution order for spare parts."[19]

The possibilities for cyber disruptions of this nature are seemingly endless and extend well beyond military targets, although the international armed conflict between Russia and Ukraine demonstrates how cyber operations will play an increasing role in modern warfare. Imagine for a moment the consequences of simply altering or deleting medical records, voter registration records, securities identification numbers, launch codes for strategic weapons, or the code names and passwords associated with clandestine operations or criminal investigations. The impact these operations could have on our confidence in the systems Canadians rely on every day could be even more damaging to national security and public trust in our institutions than a kinetic attack on the state.[20]

In April 2022, Global Affairs Canada (GAC) issued its legal position on this type of cyber activity, noting that any assessment of legality must occur on a case-by-case basis. According to GAC, this is because several factors determine whether a cyber operation gives rise to a violation of state sovereignty. Specifically, "the scope, scale, impact or severity of disruption caused, including the disruption of economic and societal activities, essential services, inherently governmental functions, public order or public safety must be assessed to determine whether a violation of the territorial sovereignty of the affected State has taken place."[21] Moreover, "cyber activities that have significant harmful effects on the exercise of inherently governmental function" would also violate state sovereignty. For Canada, this means that none of the above examples, without more, would likely constitute an internationally wrongful act.

Change: Canada's New Cyber Capabilities

To respond to the modern threat environment, Canada recently expanded the mandate of Canada's signals intelligence agency, the Communications Security Establishment (CSE), to include the power to engage in defensive and active cyber operations.[22]

Under the Communications Security Establishment Act, passed in 2019, CSE may conduct activities on or through the "global information infrastructure" to help protect the electronic information and information infrastructures of federal institutions and those designated as being of importance to the Government of Canada. CSE's active cyber operations mandate is far more aggressive. Under the act, CSE may "carry out activities on or through the global information infrastructure to degrade, disrupt, influence, respond to or interfere with the capabilities, intentions or activities of a foreign individual, state, organization or terrorist group as they relate to international affairs, defence or security."[23]

Together, the scope of these powers is remarkable. The definition of active cyber operations alone encompasses acts as benign as changing the content of a terrorist supporter's tweet to taking down the entire electrical grid of an enemy state capital. The only prohibited activities are those that "cause, intentionally or by criminal negligence, death or bodily harm to an individual; or willfully attempt in any manner to obstruct, pervert or defeat the course of justice or democracy."[24] Notably, the 2022 federal budget included $263.9 million over five years and another $96.5 million annually to enhance CSE's ability to launch cyber operations.[25]

CSE is not the only Canadian agency that operates in the online environment. Canada's latest defence policy, *Strong, Secure and Engaged*, called on the Canadian Armed Forces (CAF) to adopt a more assertive cyber posture, and stipulates that Canada shall conduct "active cyber operations against potential adversaries in the context of government-authorized military missions."[26]

GAC is also the host and principal coordinating agency for the G7's Rapid Response Mechanism (RRM), established in 2019 following the G7 summit in Charlevoix, Québec. The RRM seeks to detect and identify foreign interference and state-sponsored disinformation efforts that threaten the G7 democracies. Canada also has a national RRM, which is the only known body within the Government of Canada that conducts open-source analysis of social media "to monitor and better understand disinformation as a tool of foreign interference."[27]

Under its mandate, the RRM must focus "on foreign threats, noting tactics and trends; use openly available information; take care to avoid focusing on individuals (except in the case of public figures); and avoid the use of personal information ... for any purpose unless it meets a national security threshold."[28]

Additionally, since 2015, CSIS has had a mandate to directly intervene and act to reduce threats to the security of Canada. Where it has reasonable grounds to believe a particular activity constitutes a threat to the security of Canada, CSIS may take measures, within or outside the country, to reduce that threat.[29] "Threats to the security of Canada" is a defined term under the CSIS Act and includes espionage or sabotage, foreign influence, terrorism, and subversion.

Regardless of the severity of the threat, it is at all times prohibited for CSIS to deploy a threat reduction measure (TRM) that could lead intentionally or by criminal negligence to death or bodily harm; violate an individual's sexual integrity; subject anyone to torture or cruel, inhumane, or degrading treatment or punishment; detain someone; or cause property damage if so doing would endanger the safety of an individual.[30] CSIS is also prohibited from using a TRM to willfully attempt in any manner to obstruct, pervert, or defeat the course of justice. A TRM may, however, violate Canadian law or the Charter if CSIS obtains prior authorization from the Federal Court, including TRMs that would violate Canada's international legal obligations.[31] Moreover, CSIS can leverage its threat disruption powers inside or outside Canada, and the CSIS Act does not specify, limit, or prevent CSIS from carrying out threat disruption measures on or through the "global information infrastructure," the phrase used in Canadian statutes to delineate online conduct from actions carried out in the physical world.

Unlike CSIS, both CSE and CAF are bound by international law when carrying out their operations online and extraterritorially.[32] As such, clearly identifying the international legal boundaries on grey zone operations is crucial for Canadian state actors who operate in cyberspace.

Why? On a macro level, international law is a foundational pillar of the modern international order and is crucial for maintaining international peace and security. Uncertainty regarding the law's application creates opportunities for states to justify destabilizing conduct and leaves affected states without a formal means of seeking recourse, making them more likely to respond to perceived wrongs outside the established legal order.[33] Uncertainty also calls into question the validity of the established legal order. Moreover, at the operational level, without a clear understanding of what actions Canada can legally engage in via cyberspace and under what circumstances, there is a risk that its security agencies will unintentionally commit an internationally wrongful act, opening Canada up to countermeasures from other states. Alternatively, uncertainty of the rules may create a state of paralysis within security agencies, leading them to avoid taking measures in the interest of Canadian security out of fear of violating international law and, consequently, Canadian law.

Canada: Capability without Strategy

What, then, are the rules in cyberspace? The primary sources of international law are treaties between states and customary international law derived from the practice of states. Currently, the only international treaty aimed directly at regulating online activity is the Convention on Cybercrime, which calls on states to implement domestic criminal offences and enhance investigative tools for local law enforcement. No treaties exist specifically governing state conduct in cyberspace, and it is widely believed that states are unlikely to reach the consensus necessary to meaningfully advance existing laws.

There are, however, existing treaties (most significantly the UN Charter and the Geneva Conventions) and customary international law that are widely accepted as generally applicable to online state conduct. In the past decade, there have been major efforts by both the academic and international communities to identify how these existing rules and principles apply in the cyber domain.[34] While these efforts significantly advanced our understanding of international law's application in cyberspace, several important questions about how these instruments apply to state conduct remain unsettled and highly contentious. As noted above, there is no agreement regarding whether a foreign cyber operation that results in neither physical damage nor some loss of functionality in another state amounts to a violation of the target state's sovereignty.[35] Thus, whether international law permits cyber operations that delete or alter data to promulgate false information or drive down confidence in state institutions remains unsettled.

For this reason, since 2018, dozens of states and most of the world's democratic cyber powers have issued statements or policy documents enunciating their governments' interpretations of how customary law and existing treaties govern their actions in cyberspace. States are not in agreement on this question. However, this practice is critical so that their state agencies understand the legal parameters of their mandates. It is also essential for the development of customary international law and norms for online state conduct across the international community.

Canada is one of the world's cyber powers, and Parliament mandates its security agencies to take active and defensive measures in cyberspace against other states.[36] Nevertheless, the Government of Canada delayed the release of its statement on how international law applies in cyberspace until 29 April 2022.[37] The statement, while comprehensive, was released online on a Friday afternoon without fanfare or any opportunity for questions or engagement. This approach is unfortunate as the statement advances some legal positions, especially regarding rules related to the concept of state sovereignty, that are not widely shared by the international community, including some of Canada's Five Eyes and NATO allies. Moreover, the government has yet to establish a public policy on if and when Canadian agencies may take actions that would violate international law to defend Canadian interests.[38] It is not enough to make statements. Canada must demonstrate how its understanding of international law (*opinio juris*) affects and shapes state practice if the government truly wants to shape international cyber law. Absent a clear policy, Canada risks ceding the development of customary law to other international players and paralysing its own agencies in the face of ever-growing online threats.

That said, the release of Canada's international legal position was an important first step. I am optimistic that it will lead to the development of a cyber foreign policy and a cohesive international strategy setting out the government's interests and values in cyberspace.[39] While Canada did update its *National Cyber Security Strategy* in 2018 and released a *National Cyber Security Action Plan* in 2019, these documents are vague and fail to define in detail how Canada intends to advance its interests internationally in a digitalized world.[40] GAC has engaged in international cybersecurity processes within the UN and funded projects in foreign states. However, as Gold, Parsons, and Poetranto make clear, these "ad hoc efforts remain incomplete elements of a larger unarticulated whole."[41] In other words, Canada has the capabilities to defend or advance its interests in cyberspace but has not clearly articulated what those interests are or ought to be.

Conclusion

If international state conduct via cyberspace were hockey, Canada's team would have no general manager but three head coaches: the director of CSIS, the chief of CSE, and the CAF's chief of the Defence Staff. Each coach has their own strategy that they keep to themselves, and a number of highly skilled players, none of whom understand the rules of the game or how to win it. This setup is no way to win a hockey game, and it is certainly no way to advance and defend Canada's national interests.

Canada has long relied on its three oceans and its superpower neighbour to keep it safe from serious national security threats. These barriers will not keep Canada safe from current and future online threats, and our adversaries, particularly Russia and China, will continue to use grey zone operations to undermine democratic values and trust in our institutions. Without an understanding of the law, a coherent national strategy, and cyber foreign policy, Canada is unprepared to respond coherently and consistently in the rapidly evolving cyber threat environment. The future of states' successes and failures is tied to their cyber prowess. Canada has the talent; the focus for the future must be the development of a winning strategy.

At the same time, Canada is failing to take a serious leadership role within the international community to ensure the advancement of democratic norms and values and the rule of law in cyberspace. The good news is that it still has the opportunity to take a leading role. Canada can become a significant player in the development of international law and norms in this arena, making not only Canada's future but also the world's more predictable and secure.

NOTES

1 Sincere thanks go to my amazing research assistant, Gabriella Colavecchio, for all of her work and support. I have no doubt that Gabriella and the other outstanding women in her JD/MA class will be writing a future edition of this book.
2 CSIS, "Remarks by Director David Vigneault at the Economic Club of Canada," Government of Canada, last modified 11 December 2018, https://www.canada.ca/en/security-intelligence-service/news/2018/12/remarks-by-director-david-vigneault-at-the-economic-club-of-canada.html; Canada, Canadian Centre for Cyber Security, *National Cyber Threat Assessment 2020* (Ottawa: CSE, 2020), https://www

.cyber.gc.ca/en/guidance/national-cyber-threat-assessment-2020; Canadian Centre for Cyber Security, *National Cyber Threat Assessment 2018* (Ottawa: CSE, 2018), https://www.cyber.gc.ca/en/guidance/national-cyber-threat-assessment-2018.

3 Rafael Satter, Christopher Bing, James Pearson, "Microsoft Discloses Onslaught of Russian Cyberattacks on Ukraine," Reuters, 27 April 2022, https://www.reuters.com/technology/microsoft-discloses-onslaught-russian-cyberattacks-ukraine-2022-04-27/; Frank Bajak, "Russia Continues Cyberwarfare with Ukraine through Data Collection," *Globe and Mail*, 28 April 2022, https://www.theglobeandmail.com/world/article-russia-continues-cyberwarfare-with-ukraine-through-data-collection/; Joseph Marks with research by Aaron Schaffer, "In Cyber Conflict, Ukraine Has an Underdog Advantage over Russia," *Washington Post*, 2 May 2022, https://www.washingtonpost.com/politics/2022/05/02/cyber-conflict-ukraine-has-an-underdog-advantage-over-russia/.

4 Leah West, "Cyber Force: The International Legal Implications of the Communication Security Establishment's Expanded Mandate under Bill C-59," *Canadian Journal of Law and Technology* 16, no. 2 (2018): 381–415.

5 CSIS, "Remarks by Director David Vigneault."

6 CSIS.

7 Democratic Institutions, "Speech: The Government of Canada's Plan to Safeguard Canada's 2019 Election," Government of Canada, 30 January 2019, https://www.canada.ca/en/democratic-institutions/news/2019/03/speech-thegovernment-of-canadas-plan-to-safeguard-canadas-2019-election.html.

8 Democratic Institutions, "Speech."

9 Democratic Institutions.

10 CSIS, *CSIS Public Report 2020* (Ottawa: Public Works and Government Services Canada, 2021), 24.

11 CSIS, 24.

12 Canadian Centre for Cyber Security, "Cyber Threat Bulletin: Impact of COVID-19 on Cyber Threats to the Health Sector," Government of Canada, last modified 25 June 2020, https://cyber.gc.ca/en/guidance/cyber-threat-bulletin-impact-covid-19-cyber-threats-health-sector.

13 "Advisory: APT29 Targets COVID-19 Vaccine Development," UK National Cyber Security Centre, 16 July 2020, https://www.ncsc.gov.uk/news/advisory-apt29-targets-covid-19-vaccine-development.

14 Herb Lin, "Reflections on the SolarWinds Breach," *Lawfare*, 22 December 2020, www.lawfareblog.com/reflections-solarwinds-breach.
15 Michael N. Schmitt, "Top Expert Backgrounder: Russia's SolarWinds Operation and International Law," *Just Security*, 21 December 2020, https://www.justsecurity.org/73946/russias-solarwinds-operation-and-international-law/.
16 Don Snyder, Elizabeth Bodine-Baron, Mahyar A. Amouzegar, Kristin F. Lynch, Mary Lee, and John G. Drew, *Robust and Resilient Logistics Operations in a Degraded Information Environment* (Santa Monica, CA: RAND Corporation, 2017), 1–2, https://www.rand.org/pubs/research_reports/RR2015.html.
17 Snyder et al., *Robust and Resilient Logistics*, 1.
18 Snyder et al., 2.
19 Synder et al., 2–3.
20 Herb Lin, "Reflections on the SolarWinds Breach."
21 GAC, "International Law Applicable in Cyberspace," Government of Canada, last modified 22 April 2022, https://www.international.gc.ca/world-monde/issues_development-enjeux_developpement/peace_security-paix_securite/cyberspace_law-cyberespace_droit.aspx?lang=eng#a3.
22 *Communications Security Establishment Act*, SC 2019, c 13, s. 15(2).
23 *Communications Security Establishment Act*, s. 19.
24 *Communications Security Establishment Act*, s. 32.
25 Department of Finance, *Budget 2022*, Government of Canada, last modified 7 April 2022, https://www.budget.canada.ca/2022/report-rapport/toc-tdm-en.html.
26 National Defence, *Strong, Secure and Engaged: Canada's Defence Policy* (Ottawa: Department of National Defence, 2017), 15.
27 "TPs for USS- Meeting at CSE," obtained via ATI request no. A-2019–01541.
28 "RRM Canada Protocol for Monitoring and Analyzing Foreign Interference (FI) Activities against October 2019 Election," obtained via ATI request to no. A-2019–01541.
29 *Canadian Security Intelligence Service Act*, RSC 1985, c C-23, s. 12.1.
30 *Canadian Security Intelligence Service Act*, s. 12.2.
31 Craig Forcese, "One Warrant to Rule Them All: Re-conceiving the Judicialization of Extraterritorial Intelligence Collection" (Working Paper No 2015–41, University of Ottawa Faculty of Law, 2015), 49.

32 West, "Cyber Force."
33 Jutta Brunnee and Stephen J. Toope, "A Hesitant Embrace: The Application of International Law by Canadian Courts," *Canadian Yearbook of International Law* 40 (2003): 3–60.
34 Michael N. Schmitt, ed., *Tallinn Manual on the International Law Applicable to Cyber Warfare* (New York: Cambridge University Press, 2013); Michael N. Schmitt, ed., *Tallinn Manual 2.0 on the International Law Applicable to Cyber Operations*, 2nd ed. (Cambridge: Cambridge University Press, 2017); *Report of the Group of Governmental Experts on Developments in the Field of Information and Telecommunications in the Context of International Security*, UNGAOR, 65th Sess, UN Doc A/65/201 (2010); *Report of the Group of Governmental Experts on Developments in the Field of Information and Telecommunications in the Context of International Security*, UNGAOR, 68th Sess, UN Doc A/68/98 (2013); *Report of the Group of Governmental Experts on Developments in the Field of Information and Telecommunications in the Context of International Security*, UNGAOR, 70th Sess, UN Doc A/70/174 (2015).
35 Michael N. Schmitt, "Grey Zones in the International Law of Cyberspace," *Yale Journal of International Law Online* 42, no. 2 (2017): 1–21, https://www.yjil.yale.edu/files/2017/08/Schmitt_Grey-Areas-in-the-International-Law-of-Cyberspace-1cab8kj.pdf; Schmitt, "Top Expert Backgrounder: Russia's SolarWinds Operation and International Law."
36 Julia Voo, Irfan Hemani, Simon Jones, Winnona DeSombre, Dan Cassidy, and Anina Schwarzenbach, *National Cyber Power Index 2020* (Cambridge, MA: Belfer Centre for Science and International Affairs, Harvard Kennedy School, 2020), https://www.belfercenter.org/publication/national-cyber-power-index-2020.
37 GAC, "International Law Applicable in Cyberspace."
38 Beyond simply asserting that international law applies in submissions to the United Nations Group of Governmental Experts and Open-Ended Working Group.
39 Josh Gold, Christopher Parsons, and Irene Poetrano, "Canada's Scattered and Uncoordinated Cyber Foreign Policy: A Call for Clarity," *Just Security*, 4 August 2020, https://www.justsecurity.org/71817/canadas-scattered-and-uncoordinated-cyber-foreign-policy-a-call-for-clarity/.
40 Gold, Parsons, and Poetrano, "Canada's Scattered and Uncoordinated Cyber Foreign Policy."
41 Gold, Parsons, and Poetrano.

chapter eight

Is the Canadian Emergency Management System Prepared for Evolving Threats?

NIRUPAMA AGRAWAL[1]

Introduction

In 2020, General Wayne Eyre, now chief of the Defence Staff, declared that disasters and emergencies jeopardize the ability of the Canadian Armed Forces (CAF) to safeguard Canada from domestic and foreign security threats.[2] Eyre's outlook speaks to an alarming twenty-first-century trend that is reshaping and redefining the future of Canadian security and emergency management systems. As natural, technological, and intentional disasters increase in frequency, intensity, scope, and severity, Canada's dependence on military-led emergency management will fast outpace the CAF's defence capabilities. In fact, over the past decade, the CAF has experienced a 40 per cent increase in weather-related missions, including fires, such as the historic Northwest Territories wildfires of 2023; floods; hurricanes; snowstorms; ice storms; and biological hazards like the COVID-19 pandemic, which has entered an endemic phase.[3]

Welcome to the new abnormal, an emergent reality in which disasters and emergencies represent the most rapidly evolving threats to national and international state and human security. Up until the Russian invasion of Ukraine on 24 February 2022, it was assumed that traditional hard security threats such as war and terrorism had been supplanted by non-traditional soft security threats such as natural hazards and disasters (also discussed by Harrison in chapter 9 and Burch and McKenzie in chapter 10), humanitarian emergencies (analysed with the utmost sensitivity by Mourad in chapter 15), biosecurity threats, and cyber incidents, including cyberattacks on critical infrastructures such as the May 2021 Colonial Pipeline cyberattack that shut down 45 per cent of the United States East Coast fuel supply, to cite one example (cyberattacks are addressed in more detail by West in chapter 7).[4] The human suffering in Ukrainian cities and the 2023 Hamas attack on Israel have laid bare the complex nature of threats while serving as a reminder that hard and soft security threats are not mutually exclusive but rather mutually inclusive, with acts of terrorism and war indivisible from humanitarian emergencies that result in gender-based violence and that displace populations.

More insidious than traditional security threats, disasters are a chimera of systemic risks — changing climate, rapid and haphazard urbanization, accelerating socio-economic inequity, etc. — capable of transcending threat patterns, geographic borders, and securitization strategies and inflicting enduring and multiplicative consequences on civil society and public and private infrastructure (as discussed by Burch and McKenzie in chapter 10 and West in chapter 7). Consider the state of emergency management amid COVID-19 (caused by coronavirus SARS-CoV-2 as described by the World Health Organization[5]), which brought life and the global economy to a standstill and propagated overlapping impacts on regions experiencing additional catastrophes – hurricanes such as Henri, Ida, and Larry; wildfires across the West Coast of the United States and Canada; floods in the Fraser Valley, British Columbia, as well as in Germany, Mexico, and New York; earthquakes in Haiti, Australia, and Japan; volcanic eruptions in La Palma; building collapse in Florida; and cyberattacks on hospitals in Ireland, New Zealand, and San Diego.

While Asia-Pacific governments have long recognized that disasters pose the "greatest threats to our national security and public well-being," Canada has yet to acknowledge or adapt to this new world disorder.[6] Even in the midst of global crises, including the pandemic that saw intermittent blockades of Ottawa and the Ambassador Bridge by disruptive anti-vaccine protests in February 2022, Canadian security agencies such as the Canadian Security Intelligence Service, Public Safety Canada, and the National Security and Intelligence Committee of Parliamentarians remain fixated on legacy threats such as terrorism and espionage, and are failing to develop mandates for disaster security challenges such as pandemic security and threats to Canada's electricity sector.[7]

Further, the world's reliance on the Internet and artificial intelligence has made governments and militaries, health-care and education systems, energy and utility providers, financial and corporate entities, etc., highly vulnerable to cyberattacks. In recent years, Ireland's health-care system was immobilized for a week, delaying COVID-19 testing and forcing cancellations of medical appointments and surgeries. In 2020, there were cyberattacks on the United States Department of the Treasury and the United States Department of Commerce.[8] Similarly, Canada has faced cyberattacks targeting public-sector entities – the CAF, House of Commons, and Elections Canada at the federal level; hospitals, courts, and post-secondary institutions at the provincial level; and libraries, school boards, towns, and cities at the municipal level. In other words, Canada cannot afford a pattern of chronic oversight that amplifies its vulnerability, exposure, and susceptibility to risks (which I discuss in my book on Canadian natural disasters and risk management[9]). Looking forward, these post-pandemic challenges include inflation, sharply rising interest rates, and shortages of skilled workers in critical services and essential goods, weakening the system's capacity and readiness to respond to extreme disasters.

All of this raises a series of crucial questions: How can Canada protect its state and society against the urgent threat of disaster? How can Canada manage a shifting threat that has been systematically diminished, dismissed, and disregarded? How can Canada avoid being caught off guard by the occupation of the doorsteps of the Canadian Parliament by transport trucks for several weeks? How can Canada best support its non-NATO sovereign allies when they are unlawfully invaded? More importantly, can Canada's existing national security and emergency management institutions and frameworks adapt before the country is "unable to support a coordinated response to large-scale and concurrent events affecting the national interest?"[10]

Context

Emergency management, public safety, and national security have in common an overarching objective of protecting people and physical and digital infrastructure from potential threats, as highlighted in my study of spatial disaster risk in urban environments.[11] A variety of triggers can initiate, advance, and compound a threat, including naturally occurring phenomena (meteorological, climatological, geophysical, biological); technological incidents (industrial accidents, oil spills, explosions); hostile acts (terrorism, cyberattacks); and politically induced civil conflicts (as demonstrated by the Canadian anti-vaccine protests).

Since 1900, the International Disaster Database has recorded over 90 Canadian emergencies involving intentional acts, technological failures leading to toxic spills and explosions, and human-error-induced events, and documented over 150 Canadian disasters triggered by natural phenomena, with over 1,000 deaths, 453,831 affected persons, and $28.6 million in economic losses since 2000.[12] These numbers are much higher in the Canadian Disaster Database, where over 1,000 natural hazards and 384 human-induced events have been reported since 2000.[13] The current rare persistence of La Niña conditions for three years in a row was last seen in the 1970s, way past recent memory. It is imperative, therefore, to take stock of the nature and severity of the challenges facing the Canadian emergency management system, which involves all levels of government and consists of partnerships between non-profit humanitarian aid agencies and community-based organizations.

In Canada, 90 per cent of emergencies are addressed at the local or municipal level; however, municipalities can seek assistance from provincial and/or territorial governments should local capacities prove insufficient. Additionally, the federal government, at a province's request, has the power to deploy the CAF to aid in emergency response. This occurred in June 2020 when Ontario and the Northwest Territories were tackling COVID-19 outbreaks in long-term care facilities,[14] and again in October 2021 when intensive care units in Alberta were dealing with the fourth wave of the pandemic. As of March 2022, more than eight out of every ten dollars spent to fight the pandemic have been provided by the Canadian federal government.[15] However, all provinces and territories have dedicated emergency management programs to monitor and prioritize risks and develop mitigation strategies for their jurisdictions.

Canada and the United States have similar emergency management systems in place. The United States Federal Emergency Management Authority (FEMA) is known for both its pioneering inception in 1979 and its ambitious mission to help people before, during, and after disasters. FEMA has evolved over time with every major disaster, financial downturn, and political shift. Similarly, in Canada, the Emergencies Act of 1988,[16] which replaced the War Measures Act, empowers the federal government to provide security and welfare to Canadians during domestic or international crises – whether a natural disaster, state of emergency, or war. February 2022 offered a test case when shortcomings in the emergency management system were exposed during the trucker convoy and blockade of the Ambassador Bridge, a critical transportation corridor along the Canada–United States border. The Ambassador Bridge blockade prompted the use of the Emergencies Act for the first time in Canadian history, sparking a charged political debate and the announcement of the Public Order Emergency Commission to investigate Prime Minister Justin Trudeau's invocation of the act.

In 1999, the Senate of Canada Subcommittee on Canada's Emergency and Disasters Preparedness proposed the Emergency Preparedness Act in consultations with the Canadian Red Cross Society and the Insurance Bureau of Canada.[17] The act allows the federal government to distribute financial aid to provinces and territories affected by a natural disaster through the Disaster Financial Assistance Arrangements. In 2015, the National Disaster Mitigation Program was established to lessen the impacts of natural disasters on communities across Canada by investing in the reduction of recurring flood risks and facilitating private residential insurance coverage for overland flooding.[18] The minister of public safety and emergency preparedness, within the realm of Public Safety Canada (formerly the Office of Critical Infrastructure Protection and Emergency Preparedness), oversees Canada's domestic security department. In addition, the Canadian Standards Association, a non-profit organization, offers over fifteen guidelines and best practices regarding public safety, many of which are referenced in legislation. Standards include psychological health and safety in the paramedic service; protection of first responders from chemical, biological, radiological, and nuclear events; transportation of dangerous goods; and, most importantly, emergency and business continuity management to ensure continuous internal and external operations during emergencies and disasters.[19] Further, the 2023 Ontario Emergency Management Strategy Action Plan focuses on enhanced provincial surge capacity through the Ontario Corps,[20] supported by the $110 million allocated by the province for emergency readiness for community organizations and municipalities.[21] The roles and responsibilities of the various governments and stakeholders involved in these initiatives are extremely multifarious – a topic of focus at a workshop that I recently led.[22]

Change

Domestic and international emergency management programs have undergone a paradigm shift, transitioning from response-oriented models to adaptation-based approaches that focus on preparedness, mitigation, and resilience building, which I have analysed and advocated for in several studies.[23] Similarly, the challenges of today – pandemics, climate change, conflicts, civil unrest, and cyberattacks – differ significantly from the emergencies of the past. As of 11 January 2024, for instance, COVID-19 has killed over 57,274 Canadians, exposed new socio-economic and health inequities and inequalities, and underlined both systemic deficiencies (as I argued in a 2019 study[24]) and weak links across entire sectors and their supply chains. Pandemics, for example, have existed since the beginning of time; however, economic and political globalization, growing income and wealth disparity, and disinformation campaigns on social media platforms are just some of the variables that are contributing to the complexities of managing today's pandemic risks. Prioritizing, identifying, and addressing the root causes of risk exposures and susceptibilities are certain to deliver the most effective measures, actions, and solutions.

Regarding Canada's changing climate, in 2021 alone, swathes of British Columbia were scorched by summer wildfires, and the floods affecting the province forced thousands of people from their homes and claimed five lives and over one million livestock animals. That same year, the Northwest Territories experienced chronic flooding, and Ontario witnessed several tornadoes, impacting unprepared populations. The Intergovernmental Panel on Climate Change's *Sixth Assessment Report* cautions Canadians to take heed and action (analysed by Harrison and Burch and McKenzie in chapters 9 and 10, respectively).[25]

With respect to cyberattacks, which are more frequent and far-reaching, such breaches threaten the safety of Canada and its citizenry by imperilling critical infrastructure, including the government and military, public health and education, energy and utilities, public transportation, and business and finance (see the detailed conversation by West in chapter 7). Additionally, potential threats due to unpatched smartphone vulnerabilities – for example, the September 2021 case of iPhones and distributed denial of service attacks – require urgent action and should sound the emergency alarm.

In order to confront these threats, a layered protective system is necessary – one that is comprised of built-in protections such as hazard zoning, risk-based development rules, measures for environmental and climate protection, early warning systems, risk transfer through insurance, multi-level governance, private-public partnerships, and, most importantly, community engagement.

As Canadian disasters and emergencies increase in frequency, intensity, and scope, it is necessary to re-evaluate, and possibly even redefine, the CAF's role in humanitarian assistance and disaster relief operations (HADR) operations, substituting or supplementing military response with a civilian response. Deploying the CAF for pandemic assistance is an inefficient use of human and financial resources. To echo an argument put forth by the non-partisan Conference of Defence Associations Institute, the time has come for Canada to establish a federal, non-military disaster response agency "akin to the United States' Federal Emergency Management Agency," an agency specifically designed to provide HADR.[26] By positioning HADR within the domain of emergency management, Canada will simultaneously preserve the CAF's bandwidth and build a range of national emergency management capabilities and competencies. The multifaceted puzzle of identifying gaps in the role of the CAF in domestic emergencies, the nature of civilian-military relations during non-combat natural disaster response, and the probe of the CAF in public administration is skillfully analysed in Johanu Botha's book *Boots on the Ground*.[27]

New thinking on disaster and emergency management also needs to emphasize community participation and engagement as a source of resilience building, with a particular focus on systemically under-represented and underserved groups, including women, Black communities, Indigenous peoples, visible minorities, people with disabilities, and members of the LGBTQ+ community (for more, see chapters in part 3 of this volume, "Inclusive Security"). Although Public Safety Canada is committed to community-based emergency management, the organization fails to outline concrete steps for advancing minority participation and engagement in disaster prevention, mitigation, preparedness, response, and recovery.[28]

Moreover, Canada must consider non-traditional solutions for disaster risk reduction and disaster resilience building, including machine-learning technologies, crowdsourced mobile applications, forest restoration methods like the Miyawaki method,[29] and the de-engineering and naturalization of rivers, watersheds, and coastal habitats. Toronto's Port Lands Flood Protection Project, for instance, will mitigate flood risk by naturalizing the outlet of the Don River.

Conclusion

Emergency management in Canada is designed to serve national and international commitments, meaning it is possible to strike a balance between a domestic disaster response unit and an overseas deployment unit, trained to operate in unison should the situation demand that.

Learning from the Colonial Pipeline cyberattack, which saw the United States issue emergency legislation, and the Russian attack on Ukraine, a non-NATO member but a strong ally of Canada (discussed by von Hlatky and Hollander in chapter 2), the federal government would be wise to develop tools and strategies to confront insecurities in critical systems that threaten social, economic, political, and environmental landscapes across Canada and that also threaten national and international security. Since Canada and the United States share the world's longest international land border (nearly 8,900 kilometres) and are similarly affected by complex disasters, it is critical for the two countries to cooperate on fronts such as digital security, net-zero economy, and next-generation technologies to foster future domestic and international security.

A timely, balanced, and whole-of-society approach to managing emergencies and disasters requires a comprehensive understanding of risks and their underlying root causes. An efficient emergency management program prioritizes lives before, during, and after disasters and also focuses on minimizing damage to physical and digital infrastructures while maintaining essential services. In the short term, government emergency assistance programs, such as Public Safety Canada's National Disaster Mitigation Program, aim to render immediate relief, recovery, and rehabilitation resources to affected regions. In the long term, however, strengthening resilience, coping, and adaptive capacities at the societal and systemic levels will allow for the delivery of the right resources at the right time in the right place. It has been established[30] that perceptions of risk and vulnerability are vital in accurately estimating threats and their impact – a critical aspect of effective emergency management and an overarching theme in the 2023 *National Adaptation Strategy*.[31] In conclusion, the key takeaways from Botha's brilliant book are relevant and fitting in this context – namely, the presence and quality of inter-organizational collaboration, and the need to break down the barriers to such collaboration.[32] Questions arising from these, if earnestly explored, will lead to a well-defined vision of the role and effectiveness of the CAF and ways to enrich civil-military relationships.

NOTES

1 The author thanks Tiana Putric, a York DEM alumna and Killam Fellow, for her incredible contribution as a research assistant on this project.
2 Lee Berthiaume, "Disaster Relief, a Threat to the Canadian Army's Fighting Edge, Commander Says," *National Post*, 20 January 2020, https://nationalpost.com/news/canada/disaster-relief-threatens-to-hinder-canadian-armys-readiness-for-combat-commander.
3 Christian Leuprecht and Peter Kasurak, "The Canadian Armed Forces and Humanitarian Assistance and Disaster Relief: Defining a Role," Centre for International Governance Innovation, 24 August 20202, https://www.cigionline.org/articles/canadian-armed-forces-and-humanitarian-assistance-and-disaster-relief-defining-role/.
4 Mary-Ann Russon, "US Fuel Pipeline Hackers' Didn't Mean to Create Problems," *BBC News*, 10 May 2021, https://www.bbc.com/news/business-57050690.
5 "Coronavirus Disease (COVID-19)," World Health Organization, accessed 19 March 2024, https://www.who.int/health-topics/coronavirus#tab=tab_1.
6 "Disasters Are 'Greatest Threats to Our National Security,'" United Nations Office for Disaster Risk Reduction, 29 October 2012, http://www.undrr.org/news/disasters-are-greatest-threats-our-national-security.
7 Canadian Centre for Cyber Security, "Cyber Threat Bulletin: The Cyber Threat to Canada's Electricity Sector," Government of Canada, last modified 30 November 2020, https://cyber.gc.ca/en/guidance/cyber-threat-bulletin-cyber-threat-canadas-electricity-sector.
8 Nicole Perlroth and Adam Satariano, "Ireland Health Cyberattack," *New York Times*, 20 May 2021.

9 Nirupama Agrawal, *Natural Disasters and Risk Management in Canada: An Introduction* (Dordrecht, Netherlands: Springer, 2018).
10 Ralph Goodale, *Public Safety Canada, 2017–18 Departmental Results Report* (Ottawa: Public Safety Canada, 2018), 18, https://www.publicsafety.gc.ca/cnt/rsrcs/pblctns/dprtmntl-rslts-rprt-2017-18/dprtmntl-rslts-rprt-2017-18-en.pdf.
11 Costas Armenakis and Nirupama Agrawal, "Estimating Spatial Disaster Risk in Urban Environments," *Geomatics, Natural Hazards and Risk* 4, no. 4 (2013): 289–98.
12 EM-DAT, International Disaster Database, CRED/UCLouvain, Brussels, Belgium, accessed 16 April 2024, https://public.emdat.be/data.
13 "Natural Hazards of Canada," Canadian Disaster Database, Public Safety Canada, accessed 16 April 2021, https://www.publicsafety.gc.ca/cnt/mrgnc-mngmnt/ntrl-hzrds/index-en.aspx.
14 Canadian Press, "Military Called in to Help Northwest Territories amid Surge of COVID-19 Cases," *Globe and Mail*, 21 August 2021, https://www.theglobeandmail.com/canada/article-military-called-in-to-help-northwest-territories-amid-surge-of-covid/.
15 Canada, Department of Finance, "Canada Commits $2 Billion in Additional Health Care Funding to Clear Backlogs and Support Hundreds of Thousands of Additional Surgeries," Government of Canada, 25 March 2022, https://www.canada.ca/en/department-finance/news/2022/03/canada-commits-2-billion-in-additional-health-care-funding-to-clear-surgery-and-diagnostics-backlogs.html.
16 Denis Smith, Richard Foot, Eli Yarhi, and Andrew McIntosh, "Emergencies Act," *Canadian Encyclopedia*, 18 March 2020, https://www.thecanadianencyclopedia.ca/en/article/emergencies-act.
17 "Proceedings of the Subcommittee on Canada's Emergency and Disaster Preparedness, Issue 1 – Evidence, Mar 4, 1999," Senate of Canada, accessed 19 March 2024, https://sencanada.ca/en/Content/Sen/committee/361/emer/01eva-e.
18 Public Safety Canada, "National Disaster Mitigation Program (NDMP)," Government of Canada, last modified 25 August 2023, https://www.publicsafety.gc.ca/cnt/mrgnc-mngmnt/dsstr-prvntn-mtgtn/ndmp/index-en.aspx.

19 Canadian Standards Association, *Emergency and Continuity Management Program* (Toronto: Canadian Standards Association, 2017), https://webstore.ansi.org/standards/csa/csaz16002017.
20 Government of Ontario, *A Safe, Practiced and Prepared Ontario: Provincial Emergency Management Strategy and Action Plan* (Toronto: King's Printer for Ontario, 2023), https://www.ontario.ca/page/a-safe-practiced-and-prepared-ontario
21 Government of Ontario, *2023 Ontario Budget: Building a Strong Ontario* (Toronto: King's Printer for Ontario, 2023), https://budget.ontario.ca/2023/chapter-1b.html.
22 "Nature-Triggered Extreme Events: Who Might/Could Respond," Canadian Defence and Security Network, 16–17 March 2023, Toronto, Ontario, https://www.cdsn-rcds.com/natural-disaster.
23 Nirupama Agrawal, Indra Adhikari, and Nathan Yiu, "Disaster Risk in Canada: A Data-Driven Discussion," *Canadian Journal of Emergency Management* 1, no. 2 (2021): 1–19, https://cdnjem.ca/v1n2i/.
24 Peter Tsasis, Nirupama Agrawal, and Natalie Guriel, "An Embedded Systems Perspective in Conceptualizing Canada's Healthcare Sustainability," *Sustainability* 11, no. 2 (2019): 531, https://doi.org/10.3390/su11020531.
25 Intergovernmental Panel on Climate Change, "Summary for Policy Makers," in *Climate Change 2021: The Physical Science Basis. Contribution of Working Group I to the Sixth Assessment Report of the Intergovernmental Panel on Climate Change* (Cambridge: Cambridge University Press, 2021), 3–32, https://www.ipcc.ch/report/ar6/wg1/downloads/report/IPCC_AR6_WGI_SPM.pdf.
26 Adam MacDonald and Carter Vance, "COVID-19 and the Canadian Armed Forces: Overview, Analysis, and Next Steps," *VIMY Paper 44*, Conference of Defence Associations Institute (April 2020), https://cdainstitute.ca/coivd-19-the-canadian-armed-forces-overview-analysis-and-next-steps/.
27 Johanu Botha, *Boots on the Ground: Disaster Response in Canada* (Toronto: University of Toronto Press, 2022).
28 Public Safety Canada, *Emergency Management Strategy for Canada: Toward a Resilient 2030* (Ottawa: Public Safety Canada, 2019), https://www.publicsafety.gc.ca/cnt/rsrcs/pblctns/mrgncy-mngmnt-strtgy/index-en.aspx.

29 "Miyawaki Method," Urban Forests, accessed 2 October 2021, http://urban-forests.com/miyawaki-method/.
30 Nirupama Agrawal, Mark Elliott, and Slobodan P. Simonovic, "Risk and Resilience: A Case of Perception versus Reality in Flood Management," *Water* 12, no. 5 (2020): 1254, https://doi.org/10.3390/w12051254.
31 Environment and Climate Change Canada, *Canada's National Adaptation Strategy: Building Resilient Communities and a Strong Economy* (Gatineau, QC: Government of Canada, 2023).
32 Botha, *Boots on the Ground*.

chapter nine

Climate Change and Canada's Economic Security

KATHRYN HARRISON[1]

Introduction

Climate change poses a grave threat to humanity. Although developing countries are most vulnerable, even a wealthy country like Canada is not immune to its devastating impacts. The 2021 "heat dome" in western Canada killed over six hundred people in British Columbia in a matter of days, and the town of Lytton, which experienced unprecedented temperatures, burned to the ground in just one of the hundreds of wildfires that followed. Five months later, an "atmospheric river" caused large-scale flooding that destroyed homes and infrastructure. Record-setting wildfires in 2023 prompted tens of thousands of Canadians to be evacuated from their homes and exposed millions of North Americans to unsafe air. The impacts of climate change on human well-being will only worsen, both in Canada and globally (see Burch and McKenzie in chapter 10 of this volume).

No country can fix climate change alone. Greenhouse gas emissions from anywhere in the world have an equal warming impact everywhere on the planet. Individual countries are thus reluctant to reduce their emissions unilaterally, lest they incur costs with negligible environmental benefit. That is why climate change has been a focus of international negotiations. Through the Paris Agreement, countries reassure each other that they will act together to reduce global emissions. However, wealthy nations like Canada, which has higher historical emissions per person than any other country,[2] have a disproportionate responsibility to act.

Against this background, this chapter focuses not on the need to reduce Canada's emissions, but on the less-acknowledged threat of climate action to Canada's *economic* security, or Canada's ability to sustain and ideally develop its economy in the face of internal and external challenges. As global action to mitigate climate change accelerates, Canada's carbon-intensive economy is especially vulnerable to both internal and external shifts. Actions to reduce Canada's own emissions impact the competitiveness of its emissions-intensive oil and gas exports, while other countries' efforts to reduce their emissions will reduce global demand for fossil fuels, disproportionately impacting high-cost producers like Canada.

International Climate Negotiations

The international community has negotiated several agreements to reduce greenhouse gas emissions over the past three decades. The 1992 UN Framework Convention on Climate Change (UNFCCC) set a broad goal to "stabilize greenhouse gas concentrations in the atmosphere at a level that will prevent dangerous human interference with the climate system," guided by a principle of "common but differentiated responsibilities."[3] Accordingly, the 1997 Kyoto Protocol focused on reducing emissions from wealthy countries. The protocol's impact was limited, however, by US non-ratification and by emissions growth in developing countries. Canada ratified both agreements but failed to implement the policies needed to meet its targets.[4]

The 2015 Paris Agreement built on these prior agreements by setting a specific goal to limit warming to well below 2°C, and ideally 1.5°C, and requiring all countries to submit emissions targets (though still informed by the principle of differentiated responsibility). Moreover, rather than one-off distant emissions targets, the agreement established an iterative process through which countries will revisit their goals every five years. Although the first set of national targets would only limit warming to between 3°C and 3.5°C, five-yearly "ratcheting" was intended to bend the trajectory towards 1.5°C.

The first ratchet year was 2021 at the twenty-sixth Conference of the Parties to the UNFCCC (COP26) in Glasgow. By then, the need for greater ambition had been reinforced by a 2018 Intergovernmental Panel on Climate Change (IPCC) report that anticipated severe and potentially irreversible impacts beyond 1.5°C. Going into COP26, emissions were still *increasing*. Although most countries submitted deeper reduction targets in advance of COP26, the collective effect would only limit warming to 2.7°C.[5] Modest progress was made by COP28 in 2023, yielding expectations that emissions will peak before 2030.[6] However, as long as greenhouse gases continue to be added to the atmosphere, the planet will continue to warm, and will likely surpass 1.5°C above pre-industrial levels by 2030.

Looking Ahead

Although fossil fuel combustion accounts for roughly 80 per cent of global greenhouse gas emissions, remarkably, the Paris Agreement does not mention fossil fuels. Still, whether stated or not, global climate goals have clear implications for fossil fuel consumption and, thus, production. The IPCC anticipates that in order to limit warming to 1.5°C, global emissions need to be reduced to net zero by 2050, a decade later for 2°C.[7] The International Energy Agency (IEA) projects that reaching net zero in 2050 demands that consumption of coal be reduced by 91 per cent, oil by 75 per cent, and fossil gas by 78 per cent relative to 2022 levels, with no new investments in fossil fuel infrastructure beyond projects already in progress.[8]

Under the UNFCCC, each country is responsible for emissions within its territory. This means that fossil fuel exporters are accountable only for emissions associated with the production of exported fuels, while the much greater emissions from the combustion of those exports are the responsibility of importing countries. While exporters thus evade responsibility for the full contribution to global emissions of their fossil fuel production, they are nonetheless economically vulnerable as global emissions decline for two reasons. First, exporters' efforts to reduce extraction emissions within their own borders will increase their costs of production and thus reduce demand for their products. Second, other countries' efforts to reduce their own territorial emissions will reduce global demand for fossil fuels.

How quickly that happens depends on global climate action. As noted above, the world is not on track to limit warming to between 1.5°C and 2°C. In addition to the 1.5°C scenario discussed above, the IEA analyses two other scenarios.[9] The "current policies" scenario assumes no policy changes after 2023, equivalent to 2.4°C of warming. The "advanced pledges" scenario would limit warming to 2.1°C *if* all national pledges are fulfilled without delay. However, coal, oil, and fossil gas consumption peak by 2030 and decline thereafter in all scenarios, though much more rapidly in the announced pledges and 1.5°C scenarios.

Implications for Canada

The economic implications of the transition away from fossil fuels are greatest for countries like Canada that produce fossil fuels on a large scale for export. Canada is the fourth-largest oil exporter globally,[10] with oil as its largest export. Between 1990 and 2019, Canada's oil production increased from 1.7 million barrels per day to 4.7 million barrels per day, while the share of production exported increased from 39 to 80 per cent.[11] Canada also is the sixth-largest global exporter of fossil gas,[12] with aspirations to significantly increase exports via marine shipping of liquified natural gas (LNG). Oil and gas contribute 5.3 per cent of direct GDP nationally, but 20 per cent in Saskatchewan and 30 per cent in Alberta and Newfoundland.[13] Canada also exports thermal and metallurgical coal, though in less economically significant quantities.

Canada is more vulnerable than most other oil and gas exporters due to both carbon intensity and the high costs of its production. Domestically, greenhouse gas emissions from oil and gas production almost doubled between 1990 and 2019, reflecting both increased volume and higher emissions per unit as production shifted from conventional oil to tar sands and from conventional to fracked gas. Oil and gas extraction contributes the largest share of Canada's emissions at 28 per cent of the national total. For decades, Canada's oil and gas industry was not threatened by domestic climate policies; however, that changed with the introduction of a national carbon price scheduled to increase the carbon price to $170/tonne of carbon dioxide emissions by 2030. Modelling in 2020 for the first time projected a reduction in oil and gas emissions.[14] Since then, Canada has passed legislation to make binding a more ambitious Paris Agreement target of a 40 to 45 per cent reduction by 2030, a target that cannot plausibly be met without significant emissions reductions from the oil and gas industry alongside other sectors. In 2022, the federal government announced its intention to require a 42 per cent reduction of current oil and gas production emissions by 2030, but it confirmed in 2023 that the target would be relaxed to a 35 to 38 per cent reduction.[15]

Efforts to reduce production emissions impact the cost of production for all global producers, but that is especially true for Canada's heavy oil, due to higher extraction emissions per barrel than most other global crude sources.[16] Canada's exports are thus expected to see a greater than average increase in production costs, with a resulting loss of global competitiveness. Although the Canadian industry has successfully lobbied for taxpayer subsidies to reduce extraction emissions via carbon capture and sequestration, and the option to pay for less-costly reductions in other sectors, other global producers have access to the same options, and with fewer emissions to offset.

In addition, just as Canada has announced that all new passenger vehicles and electricity generation will be mandated to achieve net zero emissions by 2035, so, too, can other countries. As such policies reduce global demand for fossil fuels, the price of those fuels will fall. A falling oil price disproportionately impacts those with relatively high production costs. Canada's heavy oil, which is more challenging to extract, thus will be among the first to be priced out of global markets.[17] This is why the IEA's comparison of oil production under its 2021 Announced Pledges Scenario anticipated that Canada would be the only major producer to experience a drop in production by 2030. Similarly, academic researchers have reported that Canada's unconventional oil reserves become economically "unburnable" almost overnight on a path to either 2°C or 1.5°C.[18]

Canada is unprepared for this transition. Before 2023, the annual reports of the Canadian Energy Regulator (CER) on Canada's energy future failed to consider the implications of meeting Canada's own climate goals, let alone global targets.[19] While successive federal governments have argued that downstream emissions from Canada's fossil fuel exports are the responsibility of destination countries, that convenient rationale ignores Canada's economic vulnerability, even under scenarios anticipating more than 2°C of warming. The result is a profound disconnect between Canada's climate and economic policies. Canada embraces ambitious domestic and global targets to limit warming to between 1.5°C and 2°C, even as it plans for fossil fuel exports entirely inconsistent with that goal. As a result, Canada faces a looming economic transition for which it is ill-prepared.

The Russian invasion of Ukraine (discussed by von Hlatky and Hollander in chapter 2 of this volume) and the resulting surge in oil and gas prices temporarily buoyed the fortunes of Canadian oil and gas exports. Europe's efforts to wean itself from Russian oil and gas imports prompted opportunistic declarations that "the world needs more Canadian oil and gas." The challenge, however, is that it takes years to build new LNG terminals and oil pipelines. In the meantime, the crisis in Ukraine prompted the European Union to hasten its already aggressive transition away from fossil fuels. Reflecting on Europe's response to the Ukraine war, the falling costs of renewables, and the United States' new climate law, the IEA's 2022 annual report concluded that "the era of rapid global growth in natural gas demand is drawing to a close." Canadian oil and gas exports saw a steeper decline than the global average in all IEA projections.[20]

Policy Recommendations

The world is not yet on a path to limit global warming to between 1.5°C and 2°C. Canada and other countries must adopt more aggressive policies to reduce their greenhouse gas emissions. Progress made since the negotiation of the Paris Agreement in 2015 must be accelerated.

However, Canada also faces a second challenge: preparing for a significant and potentially abrupt transition away from economic dependence on fossil fuel production. Canada's export-oriented oil and gas industry is disadvantaged in the global transition to a low-carbon economy by virtue of both emissions-intensive production and high production costs. To date, Canada has bet on the global failure to mitigate climate change, even as it has embraced global climate goals. However, recent analyses by the IEA reveal that a downturn in Canada's oil exports can be expected even at the insufficient current level of global commitment.

A number of policy reforms can help Canada better prepare for a looming economic transition. First, we must update our own national economic analysis. At the behest of the minister of natural resources, CER's annual report for the first time examined the economic prospects for Canada's energy industries given both Canada's commitment to reach net zero by 2050 and global climate goals. As climate policies rapidly evolve, it will be critical not only for CER to update its future scenarios annually, but to be transparent about the level of global warming implied by each – that is, about the degree to which our economic plans are predicated on an unsustainable global climate.

Second, we must invest in the economy of the future, rather than that of the past. Federal and provincial governments have dragged their feet on ending fossil fuel subsidies, clinging to a linguistic hedge to phase out only "inefficient" fossil fuel subsidies. Continued subsidies artificially prop up Canadian oil exports, and in so doing undermine global climate action. The commitment to ending subsidies also does not yet include a deadline to eliminate "public finance" through loans and equity, not least the expansion of the publicly owned Trans Mountain Pipeline. Governments should invest instead in the development of "wild card" technologies that will be needed to achieve net zero emissions in Canada, several of which hold the promise of comparative advantage.[21]

Third, Canada must end investment in new fossil fuel infrastructure that will lock in economic dependence on fossil fuels. In

2021, the IEA concluded that in a world moving to limit warming to between 1.5°C and 2°C, there would be no new fossil fuel projects. Since then, Canada has approved a new offshore oil field on the East Coast and another LNG terminal on the West Coast. Canada must reject new fossil fuel projects.

Fourth, the concentration of oil production in three provinces and gas production in two means that the necessary transition for workers and communities will be regionally concentrated. The federal government committed in the 2019 and 2021 elections to introduce just-transition legislation. The "Sustainable Jobs" bill introduced in Parliament in 2023 focuses on creating low-carbon jobs (a good thing) but sidesteps preparing for the decline of oil and gas in a carbon-constrained world.

Finally, Canada must collaborate with other global oil and gas producers to wind down fossil fuel production internationally. The UN's annual *Production Gap Reports* have revealed that planned fossil fuel production exceeds not only global climate goals but also predicted fossil fuel demand under current policies. Canada has not been alone in seeking to supply global markets for as long as it can,[22] but the collective effect is to undermine global efforts to mitigate climate change. Just as there is a need for collective action with respect to fossil fuel consumption, so, too, is there a need for coordination on fossil fuel supply. Canada should join the new Beyond Oil and Gas International Alliance launched at COP26 and support efforts to advance a fossil fuel non-proliferation treaty.

NOTES

1 I am grateful for research assistance from Meghan Wise, and for undergraduate students who year after year continue to inspire me with their commitment to making the world a more safe and just place.
2 Simon Evans, "Analysis: Which Countries Are Historically Responsible for Climate Change?," *Carbon Brief*, 10 May 2021, https://www.carbonbrief.org/analysis-which-countries-are-historically-responsible-for-climate-change/.
3 See articles 2 and 3 of UNCCC at https://unfccc.int/process-and-meetings/the-convention/history-of-the-convention/convention-documents.

4 Kathryn Harrison and Lisa McIntosh Sundstrom, eds., *Global Commons, Domestic Decisions: The Comparative Politics of Climate Change* (Cambridge, MA: MIT Press, 2010).
5 United Nations Environment Programme, *Emissions Gap Report 2021: The Heat Is On – a World of Climate Promises Not Yet Delivered* (Nairobi: UN Environment Programme, 2021), http://www.unep.org/resources/emissions-gap-report-2021.
6 "World Energy Outlook 2023: Executive Summary," IEA, accessed 11 January 2024, https://www.iea.org/reports/world-energy-outlook-2023/executive-summary.
7 Intergovernmental Panel on Climate Change, "Summary for Policy Makers," in *Climate Change 2021: The Physical Science Basis. Contribution of Working Group I to the Sixth Assessment Report of the Intergovernmental Panel on Climate Change* (Cambridge: Cambridge University Press, 2021), 3–32, https://www.ipcc.ch/report/ar6/wg1/downloads/report/IPCC_AR6_WGI_SPM.pdf.
8 IEA, "World Energy Outlook 2023: Executive Summary."
9 IEA.
10 "Petroleum and Other Liquids," US Energy Information Administration, accessed 19 March 2024, https://www.eia.gov/petroleum/.
11 "Canadian Crude Oil Exports: A 30 Year Review," Canada Energy Regulator, last modified 24 November 2023, https://www.cer-rec.gc.ca/en/data-analysis/energy-commodities/crude-oil-petroleum-products/report/canadian-crude-oil-exports-30-year-review/.
12 "Natural Gas," US Energy Information Administration, accessed 19 March 2024, https://www.eia.gov/international/data/world/natural-gas/.
13 Ramin Alahdad, Jai Hai, Guy Holburn, and Brian Rivard, "Energy in Canada: A Statistical Overview," Ivey Business School Energy Policy and Management Centre, December 2020, https://www.ivey.uwo.ca/media/3792944/iveyenergycentre_policybrief_dec2020_energyinca_overview_editedjan13.pdf.
14 Environment and Climate Change Canada, *A Healthy Environment and a Healthy Economy: Canada's Strengthened Climate Plan to Create Jobs and Support People, Communities and the Planet* (Gatineau, QC: Environment and Climate Change Canada, 2020), https://www.canada.ca/en

/services/environment/weather/climatechange/climate-plan/climate-plan-overview/healthy-environment-healthy-economy.html.
15 Environment and Climate Change Canada, *2030 Emissions Reduction Plan: Canada's Next Steps to Clean Air and a Strong Economy* (Gatineau, QC: Environment and Climate Change Canada, 2022), https://www.canada.ca/en/services/environment/weather/climatechange/climate-plan/climate-plan-overview/emissions-reduction-2030/plan.html.
16 Mohammad S. Masnadi et al., "Global Carbon Intensity of Crude Oil Production," *Science* 361, no. 6405 (2018): 851–3, https://doi.org/10.1126/science.aar6859.
17 Mark Jaccard, James Hoffele, and Torsten Jaccard, "Global Carbon Budgets and the Viability of New Fossil Fuel Projects," *Climatic Change* 150 (September 2018): 15–28, https://doi.org/10.1007/s10584-018-2206-2.
18 For the 2°C scenario, see Christophe McGlade and Paul Ekins, "The Geographical Distribution of Fossil Fuels Unused When Limiting Global Warming to 2°C," *Nature* 517 (2015): 187–90, https://doi.org/10.1038/nature14016. For 1.5°C, see Dan Welsby, James Price, Steve Pye, and Paul Ekins, "Unextractable Fossil Fuels in a 1.5 °C World," *Nature* 597 (2021): 230–34, https://doi.org/10.1038/s41586-021-03821-8.
19 Kathryn Harrison, Mark Jaccard, Nicholas Rivers, and Angela Carter, "Canada's Energy Regulator Turns a Blind Eye to Dangerous Global Warming," *Canada's National Observer*, 14 December 2021, https://www.nationalobserver.com/2021/12/14/opinion/canadas-energy-regulator-turns-blind-eye-dangerous-global-warming.
20 Simon Donner and Kathryn Harrison, "Opinion: Despite Calls for More Canadian Energy, the Sector Is Headed for Long-Term Decline," *Globe and Mail*, 7 November 2022, https://www.theglobeandmail.com/opinion/article-despite-calls-for-more-canadian-energy-the-sector-is-headed-for-long/.
21 "Canada's Net Zero Future: Finding Our Way in the Global Transition," Canadian Institute for Climate Choices, accessed 19 March 2024, https://climateinstitute.ca/reports/canadas-net-zero-future/.
22 Amy Janzwood and Kathryn Harrison, "The Political Economy of Fossil Fuel Production in the Post-Paris Era: Critically Evaluating Nationally Determined Contributions," *Energy Research & Social Science* 102 (August 2023): 103095, https://doi.org/10.1016/j.erss.2023.103095.

chapter ten

Knitting a Sweater with a Hammer: Tensions and Opportunities That Emerge from Securitizing Climate Change

SARAH BURCH AND JANETTA MCKENZIE

Introduction

The rampant combustion of fossil fuels over the last century and a half has pushed the planet along a warming trajectory with tragic human and ecological consequences. Climate change impacts encompass immediate (and increasingly frequent) extreme events, such as floods, wildfires, and heat waves, but also slow, chronic changes like melting permafrost, changing precipitation patterns, and rising sea levels. Taken together, these impacts on the natural environment carry profound consequences for humanity: around 40 per cent of the world's population lives near coastlines that may be inundated,[1] for instance, creating a growing number of likely "environmental refugees" and displaced people seeking safety. The imperative to transform towards more fundamentally sustainable, resilient, and equitable development paths is omnipresent and growing. Indeed, in 2023, the United Nations Intergovernmental Panel on Climate Change concluded its landmark *Sixth Assessment Report*, stating clearly that global greenhouse gas emissions are continuing to increase, and human-caused climate change is already affecting every region of the globe.[2] Furthermore, Canada's record on reducing greenhouse gas emissions means it ranks last among its G7 counterparts, according to a 2023 report by the federal environment commissioner.[3]

The process of responding to climate change – either by mitigation, by rapidly reducing greenhouse gas emissions, or by adaptation, protecting communities from the onslaught of impacts – is a political one, and as such comes up against competing priorities, pre-existing tensions, and limited resources. Fossil fuels are baked into our global infrastructure (as made evident by the enormous pressure on Germany in 2022 and 2023, in the wake of Russia's invasion of Ukraine, to reduce its dependency on Russian natural gas provided through the Nord Stream pipeline), supply chains, and lifestyles, creating enormous inertia behind a high-carbon development path, and similarly powerful resistance to the process of decarbonization. So, it is not only droughts, food shortages, and damaged infrastructure that might exacerbate conflict, but also the slow and complex process of decarbonization. As climate change impacts increasingly create a revolving door of emergencies that require rapidly mobilized disaster management (see the chapter by Agrawal in this volume), precious resources (financial, political, and social) are channelled away from the often invisible and longer-term project of greenhouse gas reduction. Yet, avoiding measures that tackle the root causes of climate change only ensures a future of insurmountable impacts. This vicious interplay between adaptation and mitigation priorities will only become more salient as we move into a warmer world.

A security framing of climate change attempts to better capture and communicate the human toll. The securitization of climate change, as we will discuss in this chapter, is a deeply contested issue embodying clear trade-offs. In Canada, the human security impacts of climate change are especially tricky to navigate due to our diversity of ecosystems and massive land area. Arctic communities are particularly vulnerable to climate impacts, such as melting permafrost and the attendant damage to roads and buildings, and the shifting distribution and richness of species that are central to Arctic communities' way of life. Extreme weather events are happening with increasing severity and frequency, exemplified by the extreme heat experienced in British Columbia in 2021, damaging wind and rainstorms (or *derechos*) in Ontario and Quebec in 2022, and record-setting wildfires in 2023, while critical infrastructure that connects Canadians to each other and the world is at risk of failure or disruption due to increasingly variable and extreme weather. Furthermore, our close economic and cultural connections to the United States (see the chapters by Norrlöf and von Hlatky and Hollander in this book) introduce added complexity to Canadian decisions about resource extraction, adaptation to climate change impacts, and decarbonization. These all constitute threats to human security – but is a national security response the most effective way to address these threats?

In this chapter, we explore the types of collaboration and resources that are required to successfully address the multifaceted and uncertain suite of climate change challenges, the trade-offs inherent in applying a traditional security lens, and the benefits that a more fulsome approach to human security might bring. We end by considering the necessity of a "just transition" approach to decarbonization, which is deeply relevant to the challenges Canada faces as it begins to reconcile its robust oil and gas industry with a potentially decarbonized future, so that full attention is paid to the unequal distribution of the costs and consequences of the transition.

Should We Frame Climate Change as a Security Issue?

The debate over the expansion of "national security" to include a broad definition of risk, including climate change, is not settled, although there is increasing acceptance of new and more complex dimensions of security.[4] Canada's Department of National Defence (DND) identifies climate change as a threat multiplier, emphasizing the potential climate impacts on infrastructure, personnel safety, and the frequency and severity of disasters and conflicts.[5] Additionally, DND acknowledges its role as a significant emitter of greenhouse gases, as it is responsible for just under half of the federal government's fleet and facilities emissions.[6] Other countries, like the United Kingdom, Australia, and the United States, have also integrated climate change into their strategic plans, partially in response to changing definitions of security – in particular, the idea of human security.[7]

By the mid-1990s, as the Cold War ended, scholars began to question if we should be broadening our definition of "national security," positing that security and conflict were linked more to underlying structures like the rapidly globalizing economy, class/racial/gender inequality, and interstate relationships.[8] In response, some proposed the notion of "human security," which quickly gained traction in the international community and eventually became embedded in the United Nations Framework Convention on Climate Change with the release of the United Nations Development Programme's *Human Development Report 1994: New Dimensions of Human Security.*[9]

The United Nations describes human security as "an approach to assist Member States in identifying and addressing widespread and cross-cutting challenges to the survival, livelihood and dignity of their people."[10] It calls for "people-centred, comprehensive, context-specific and prevention-oriented responses that strengthen the protection and empowerment of all people."[11] The central arguments for including climate change in studies of human security are (1) that violence and conflict are affected by a greater web of interconnected factors, and climate change exacerbates the conditions that lead to security risks,[12] and (2) that appealing to security frameworks may increase the attention and resources committed to sustainable development and climate change mitigation.[13]

We should be wary of framing climate change through a security lens, however, in part because it risks fitting large-scale, complex, and deeply uncertain challenges into a narrow zero-sum game. Responding to climate change can deliver multiple benefits that accrue along different temporal and spatial scales, wherein the resilience of one nation (or its progress towards decarbonization) enhances the resilience of another. Additionally, security challenges tend to be dealt with by institutions with a great deal of military power and resources at their disposal, often meant for short-term deployment. Many national security institutions deal with climate change mainly in terms of increased risk of natural disasters (particularly to their facilities), or in the context of "climate refugees" fleeing changing global conditions.[14]

But these are not the resources needed to tackle the root causes of climate change.[15] Climate change is neither a brief, violent skirmish, nor even a protracted, multi-year conflict with clear alliances (such as the unfolding invasion of Ukraine by Russia, which took on renewed intensity in mid-2022, the takeover of the government in Afghanistan by the Taliban in 2021, or the eruption of violence in Israel and Palestine in October 2023). Instead, climate change mitigation and adaptation require deep, sustained, inclusive, and flexible effort across all sectors and facets of human life over the course of many decades. Technological innovation is required, along with collaboration on a societal level, and deep structural changes in the way we work, live, eat, travel, and consume.

Ultimately, the resources available as a result of securitizing climate change are at odds with this type of transformation.[16] This is not to say that this broader view of human security and climate security has no value: it does, particularly as we further our understanding of structural and systemic risks; moreover, a people-centred approach to security prioritizes human well-being. However, this security framework has limited value as a tool to encourage climate action, which requires cross-sectoral and cross-jurisdictional solutions that stimulate systemic transformation. It is akin to using a hammer to knit a sweater: to knit a sweater requires time, learning, effort, the correct tools, and the willingness to correct mistakes as they become apparent.

Significant challenges are emerging, however, that stymie efforts to cultivate this type of adaptable, whole-of-society approach to climate change. In particular, the rise of right-wing populism in the late 2010s and early 2020s indicates problematic socio-political currents that may fly in the face of coordinated efforts to address climate risks.

The Rise of Right-Wing Populism and the Consequences for Collaboration

It is clear that a constellation of challenges confronts a democratic, inclusive, and evidence-based approach to the super wicked problem of climate change.[17] Right-wing populism (and the nostalgic anti-science and anti-media rhetoric that go along with it), nationalism, and the rise of anti-government actors (e.g., the 2022 "Freedom Convoy," which began in opposition to COVID-19 vaccine mandates but at its core rejected the sort of collectivism, trust in science, and effective democratic governance that is integral to progress on climate change) is one such cluster of challenges that may directly undercut the ability to meaningfully address climate change.[18]

For some, populism is viewed as a general force for good, an emancipatory movement by which aggrieved members of the general population challenge dominant power structures. It relies on a shared definition of the "people" versus the "elites" (or "the establishment"). Where elites were once those with extreme wealth, in many places where populism is taking hold, a different definition is being cultivated. Scientists, the media, and those in support of international organizations like the United Nations or global treaty-making processes are coming under fire from right-wing populists, such as the president of Argentina, Javier Milei (a self-described anarcho-capitalist), former president of Brazil Jair Bolsonaro, former president of the United States Donald Trump, and the current prime minister of Italy, Giorgia Meloni.[19]

Populism is an indication of the alienation of large swathes of society, distrust of elites, and the concentration of wealth, influence, and power.[20] In some cases it may be a symptom of anxiety and dissatisfaction with the complexity and imbalances of the past. It often gives rise to a charismatic leader who claims to be a voice for the people, expressing their grievances and alienation. In liberal democracies, populism is a force behind democratic backsliding,[21] as it may undermine independent institutions, such as the media or judiciary, that are viewed as serving establishment interests. Right-wing populism in particular is an impassioned manifestation of the tensions between individual liberty and pluralism, on the one hand, and popular sovereignty and equality, on the other, revealing antagonisms between the liberal and democratic traditions.[22]

International security has typically been relatively fertile ground for global collaboration, but some contemporary right-wing populist leaders have brought isolationist rhetoric to the fore, often communicating deep scepticism of this type of collaboration as well as international organizations like the World Health Organization and treaties like the Paris Agreement on climate change. So, while the risks of climate change are shared (although unevenly distributed), and trust building and protracted collaboration may be key ingredients of successful progress towards minimizing these risks, reinvigorated political tensions frequently challenge such efforts.

Populist leaders tend to focus on short-term policies that provide immediate benefits to people close to home, which (especially when it comes to the long-term and fundamentally global task of greenhouse gas reductions) may be in direct tension with good climate policy.[23] This is in contrast to nature-based solutions to climate change, for instance, which seek to enrich the capacity of ecosystems to provide important carbon-sinking services, while also offering shade, enhanced biodiversity, improved public health, and more. Nowhere is the collision of climate change and populism more evident than in the backlash against carbon pricing. If there is limited trust in the government to spend money wisely, then its decisions may seem opaque and contradictory. Moreover, if there is suspicion that science has been compromised as well, then there is little reason for populist-leaning citizens to support making additional payments to counteract climate change, which, they feel, may or may not even happen, and which may or may not harm someone else in some distant future.

Challenging the Trade-offs Associated with a Security Lens on Climate

It is not clear that securitization leads to more and better action on climate change. However, the role of climate change as a "threat multiplier" – causing more resource scarcities, mass migration, and exacerbating instability in the decades to come – suggests that there is a need to address the security implications of climate change, without fully securitizing the issue.[24] But we should be cautious about the implications of this "threat multiplier" discourse.

Often the causal chain from climate change to drought/famine/resource scarcity can be indirect and tenuous.[25] Violent conflict, mass displacement of refugees, and natural resource scarcities are influenced by a variety of interconnected variables and contextual factors, and climate change may be one of these factors in some circumstances.[26] In the sections that follow, we explore the intersection between climate change and security, exploring ways to highlight the full range of threats that climate change creates without descending into an unyielding securitization of the issue.

Climate Change and Human Security

The debate among scholars regarding the relationship between climate change and national security has raged for decades, and it has also been taken up by several defence ministries globally, including in the United States, Australia, and the United Kingdom.[27] But outside of these official bodies, the climate-security discourse has rarely percolated through to other ministries and organizations. Indeed, this narrative may have little utility for a finance ministry setting a carbon tax, or a research and development policy meant to stimulate innovation in renewable energies.

Human security challenges the pre-1990 state-centric approach to security and proposes that we instead emphasize systemic issues (like poverty, inequality, and climate change) as opposed to security against a physical threat (like direct military action). This emphasis on individuals at risk and structural barriers to well-being is in line with the post–Cold War security landscape, as these types of risks are much more common and pervasive than interstate military conflict, especially in the twenty-first century.[28] This is not to diminish the immediate and severe impacts of military conflicts, such as that in Ukraine, Afghanistan, and Israel and Gaza; rather, it is to emphasize that poverty, wealth inequality, hunger, and water insecurity (to name a few) tend to pose a greater risk to more people than conventional warfare (while also planting the seeds for further violent conflict).

So how do we articulate the full range of risks to human security without crossing the line into the full securitization of climate change, which typically is not associated with the long-term, societal responses that are needed? Perhaps we should leverage the financial and political resources of defence institutions to support those that actually coordinate climate change mitigation: environment departments, finance ministries, and others. But must climate change be framed as a security issue to bring those institutions on board? At this stage, there are few countries in the world that do not at least recognize the need to mitigate climate change to some extent, and most have already committed to long-term, systematic decarbonization initiatives. At the twenty-eighth Conference of the Parties to the United Nations Framework Convention on Climate Change, which featured the first global stock taking of progress towards the goals laid out in the Partis Agreement, it was evident that clear progress had been made on climate policy in most high-emitting countries. Many state-level plans (including Canada's), however, remain inadequate to limit warming to less than 2°C above pre-industrial average global temperatures, and nonetheless are consistently under fire from right-wing populist groups.

Future Directions

Climate change is a collective action problem of great urgency, and collaboration is required to address it in a rapid and meaningful way. Civil society groups, academics producing rigorous social science, and people engaged in politics are important voices on solutions, not least because this is fundamentally a social and political problem, not a technical one. A crucial aspect of the path moving forward is a sincere consideration of the ways that we will continue to fail on climate change if we don't focus enormous effort on a just transition that provides dignity to those who are finding their livelihoods shifting beneath them. This requires legitimate and iterative efforts to engage a diverse swathe of Canadians in the process of envisioning a sustainable future for the country, as well as the development of policies and plans (such as Canada's first *National Adaptation Strategy*, which proposes responses to the extreme weather, disrupted supply chains, and depleted biodiversity that result from a changing climate) that directly address the deep structural drivers of both vulnerability and high-carbon development pathways.

Ultimately, transformations are already occurring, from the rapid escalation of solar power production and sustainable urban design to the rise of right-wing populism and fractured, polarizing politics. The convoy of truckers that converged on the Canadian capital, protesting COVID-19-related restrictions and vaccine mandates, while also harassing journalists and health-care workers,[29] is evidence of the unrest and distrust that is taking on a new face in the wake of the pandemic. Climate change is increasingly a partisan and polarizing issue in Canada, generating powerful pushback, especially from provinces that have historically relied most on fossil fuel extraction to generate wealth and employment. Simultaneously, climate change impacts threaten the security and resilience of Indigenous communities, and decarbonization presents the possibility of advancing meaningful reconciliation, or, in contrast, bringing about a new brand of colonialism. The trends are contradictory, pushing and pulling at each other to gain dominance. New, flexible, and inclusive forms of governance will be required to meet the challenge of climate change, requiring the mobilization and leveraging of resources that have not traditionally targeted the intersections between human and ecological systems. A just transition will address the unequal distribution of both the impacts of climate change and the costs and benefits of decarbonization, but it rests upon robust processes for making these costs transparent and co-producing the necessary solutions. Ultimately, viewing climate change through the more nuanced lens of human security may reveal new opportunities for collaboration and policy innovation.

NOTES

1 "Factsheet: Percentage of Total Populations Living in Coastal Areas," United Nations, accessed 20 March 2024, https://www.un.org/esa/sustdev/natlinfo/indicators/methodology_sheets/oceans_seas_coasts/pop_coastal_areas.pdf.
2 Intergovernmental Panel on Climate Change, *Synthesis Report of the IPCC Sixth Assessment Report: Summary for Policymakers* (Geneva: IPCC, 2023), https://report.ipcc.ch/ar6syr/pdf/IPCC_AR6_SYR_SPM.pdf.

3 Office of the Auditor General of Canada, *Reports of the Commissioner of the Environment and Sustainable Development to the Parliament of Canada. Report 5: Emissions Reductions through Greenhouse Gas Emissions Regulations* (Ottawa: Office of the Auditor General of Canada, 2023), https://www.oag-bvg.gc.ca/internet/English/parl_cesd_202304_05_e_44243.html.
4 For a discussion of the evolution of environmental security discourse, see Maria Julia Trombetta, "Environmental Security and Climate Change: Analysing the Discourse," *Cambridge Review of International Affairs* 21, no. 4 (2008): 585–602, https://doi.org/10.1080/09557570802452920.
5 Canada, Department of National Defence, *Defence Energy and Environment Strategy: Harnessing Energy Efficiency and Sustainability: Defence and the Road to the Future, 2020–2023* (Ottawa: Department of National Defence, 2020), https://www.canada.ca/en/department-national-defence/corporate/reports-publications/dees.html.
6 "Government of Canada's Greenhouse Gas Emissions Inventory," Government of Canada, accessed 20 March 2024, https://open.canada.ca/data/en/dataset/6bed41cd-9816-4912-a2b8-b0b224909396.
7 Australian Government and Department of Defence, *Defending Australia in the Asia Pacific Century: Force 2030: Defence White Paper 2009* (Canberra: Department of Defence, 2009); UK Ministry of Defence, *Global Strategic Trends: The Future Starts Today* (London: Ministry of Defence, 2018), https://www.gov.uk/government/publications/global-strategic-trends; US Department of Defense, *Quadrennial Defense Review Report* (Washington, DC: Department of Defense, 2010), https://dod.defense.gov/Portals/1/features/defenseReviews/QDR/QDR_as_of_29JAN10_1600.pdf.
8 Trombetta, "Environmental Security and Climate Change."
9 United Nations Development Programme, *Human Development Report 1994: New Dimensions of Human Security* (New York: Oxford University Press, 1994), http://hdr.undp.org/en/content/human-development-report-1994.
10 UN General Assembly, Resolution 66/290, A/RES/66/290 (10 September 2012), https://documents.un.org/doc/undoc/gen/n11/476/22/pdf/n1147622.pdf?token=mWhw65gLW01eYXaplT&fe=true.
11 UN General Assembly, Resolution 66/290.
12 Thomas Homer-Dixon, *Environment, Scarcity, and Violence* (Princeton, NJ: Princeton University Press, 1999).

Richard A. Matthew, "Is Climate Change a National Security Issue?" *Issues in Science & Technology* 27, no. 3 (2011): 49–60.

13 Jaap de Wilde, "Environmental Security Deconstructed," in *Globalization and Environmental Challenges: Reconceptualizing Security in the 21st Century*, ed. Hans G. Brauch (Berlin: Springer, 2008), 595–602.

14 Daniel H. Deudney and Richard A. Matthew, eds., *Contested Grounds: Security and c-Conflict in the New Environmental Politics* (Albany: State University of New York Press, 1999).

15 Simon Dalby, "Climate Change," *RUSI Journal* 158, no. 3 (2013): 34–43, https://doi.org/10.1080/03071847.2013.807583; Daniel Deudney, "The Case against Linking Environmental Degradation and National Security," *Millennium* 19, no. 3 (1990): 461–76, https://doi.org/10.1177/03058298900190031001.

16 Rita Floyd, "The Environmental Security Debate and Its Significance for Climate Change," *International Spectator* 43, no. 3 (2008): 51–65, https://doi.org/10.1080/03932720802280602.

17 A "super wicked problem" is a global environmental issue with four characteristics: "time is running out; those who cause the problem also seek to provide a solution; the central authority needed to address them is weak or non-existent; and irrational discounting occurs that pushes responses into the future." Kelly Levin, Benjamin Cashore, Steven Bernstein, and Graeme Auld, "Overcoming the Tragedy of Super Wicked Problems: Constraining Our Future Selves to Ameliorate Global Climate Change," *Policy Sciences* 45, no. 2 (2012): 123.

18 Matthew Lockwood, "Right-Wing Populism and the Climate Change Agenda: Exploring the Linkages," *Environmental Politics* 27 no. 4 (2018): 712–32.

19 Ed Atkins and Filippo Menga, "Populist Ecologies," *Area* 54, no. 2, (2021): 224–32; Katja Freistein, Frank Gadinger, and Christine Unrau, "From the Global to the Everyday: Anti-globalization Metaphors in Trump's and Salvini's Political Language," Global Cooperation Research Papers 24 (Duisburg, Germany: Centre for Global Cooperation Research, 2020), https://doi.org/10.14282/2198-0411-GCRP-24.

20 Karl Aiginger, "Populism: Root Causes, Power Grabbing and Counter Strategy," *Intereconomics* 55, no. 1 (2020): 38–42.

21 Valeriya Mechkova, Anna Lührmann, and Staffan I. Lindberg, "How Much Democratic Backsliding?," *Journal of Democracy* 28, no. 4 (2017): 162–9.

22 Chantal Mouffe, "The 'End Of Politics' and the Challenge of Right-Wing Populism," in *Populism and the Mirror of Democracy*, ed. Francisco Pannizza (London: Verso, 2005), 72–98.
23 See Emmanuelle Cohen-Shacham, Gretchen Walters, Christine Janzen, and Stewart Maginnis, eds., *Nature-Based Solutions to Address Global Societal Challenges* (Gland, Switzerland: International Union for Conservation of Nature and Natural Resources, 2016).
24 Patrick Huntjens and Katharina Nachbar, "Climate Change as a Threat Multiplier for Human Disaster and Conflict," *Working Paper 9*, The Hague Institute for Global Justice (May 2015), https://thehagueinstitute forglobaljustice.org/portfolio/climate-change-as-a-threat-multiplier-for-human-disaster-and-conflict/; Matthew, "Is Climate Change a National Security Issue?"
25 Floyd, "The Environmental Security Debate"; Jan Selby, Omar S. Dahi, Christiane Fröhlich, and Mike Hulme, "Climate Change and the Syrian Civil War Revisited," *Political Geography* 60 (September 2017): 232–44, https://doi.org/10.1016/j.polgeo.2017.05.007.
26 Jon Barnett and W. Neil Adger, "Climate Change, Human Security and Violent Conflict," *Climate Change and Conflict* 26, no. 6 (2007): 639–55, https://doi.org/10.1016/j.polgeo.2007.03.003; Simon Dalby, "Threats from the South? Geopolitics, Equity, and Environmental Security," in *Contested Grounds: Security and Conflict in the New Environmental Politics*, ed. Daniel Deudney and Richard Matthew (Albany: State University of New York Press, 1999), 187–219.
27 U.S. Department of Defense, *Quadrennial Defense Review Report*; Australian Government and Department of Defence, *Defending Australia in the Asia Pacific Century*; United Kingdom, Ministry of Defence, *Global Strategic Trends*.
28 Mary Kaldor, *Human Security: Reflections on Globalization and Intervention* (Cambridge: Polity Press, 2007).
29 Salmaan Farooqui, "Some Journalists Face Harassment, Assault While Reporting on Convoy Protests, Group Says," *Globe and Mail*, 20 February 2022, https://www.theglobeandmail.com/canada/article-some-journalists-face-harassment-assault-while-reporting-on-convoy/.

PART 3

Inclusive Security

chapter eleven

Leveraging Diversity to Mitigate Groupthink

AISHA AHMAD

In August 2021, the world witnessed the decisive victory of the Taliban across Afghanistan, a miserable end to a twenty-year international intervention in that country. Afghanistan was Canada's longest-ever military mission, and its failure will take years to process. Yet, the hard truth is that after decades of bloody war fighting, Canada and its allies lost. How could a multi-billion-dollar US, NATO, and UN intervention be defeated by a profoundly ignorant, small-scale insurgent group? Why was the outcome of the war so abysmal? What was wrong with the Afghan mission, and why did no one in the policy community identify and address these problems before it was too late?

There are many explanations for the failure of the mission that warrant investigation.[1] In this chapter, I address one essential factor: the lack of intellectual diversity among leaders and decision makers at critical junctures in the conflict, resulting in dangerous echo chambers and tragic mistakes. I contend not only that the exclusion of diverse perspectives caused Canadian and other allied decision makers to believe delusional ideas about the Afghan mission, but that even their later efforts to include "Afghan voices" were designed to confirm their pre-existing beliefs about the conflict. As a result, Canadian and other allied decision makers ignored hard truths about the Afghan war, silenced dissenting voices, jeopardized operational effectiveness, and undermined their chances of achieving a better resolution. The results were dire.

The Afghan conflict took the lives of 158 members of the Canadian Armed Forces, killed an estimated 241,000 people in Afghanistan and neighbouring Pakistan,[2] cost Canadian taxpayers at least $18 billion, and ultimately ended in total defeat.

Looking to the future, Canada and its allies would do well to proactively develop practices and systems that address echo chambers and other biases in its defence and security institutions, with the goal of improving strategic analysis. One simple and effective way to achieve this is to ensure that there is adequate diversity among leaders, decision makers, and task forces. There is ample research showing that diverse teams are more innovative, effective, and better at solving problems than teams comprised of members who are more similar.[3] It is therefore advantageous to ensure that decision-making teams in Canadian security and defence institutions are diverse – both in terms of identity and intellectual perspective – to mitigate the risk of dangerous cognitive biases.

Considering the many complex threats ahead, it is imperative Canada address the vulnerabilities created by a lack of inclusivity in our security and defence institutions. In this chapter, I propose that Canada's existing diversity is an untapped strategic asset and that our country can easily cultivate experts with a wide range of backgrounds, skills, and perspectives. If used effectively, this latent diversity and expert talent can help reduce the risk of echo chambers, improve situational awareness, challenge dangerous misconceptions, and enhance operational effectiveness.

Echo Chambers and Mission Failure

Psychologists and neuroscientists alike have uncovered how cognitive biases – systematic mental errors caused by the brain's desire to simplify complex information – can lead to suboptimal decision making.[4] Since the 1960s, security scholars have applied these important insights to the study of foreign policy, revealing how psychological factors such as stress, information shortcuts, and historical analogies can all affect decision making in times of crisis.[5] There is extensive research showing how cognitive psychological factors shape how human beings interpret signals and make strategic choices in wartime.[6] Robert Jervis's foundational work identified fourteen hypotheses on these types of cognitive misperceptions, including "Decision-makers tend to fit incoming information into their existing theories and images."[7] Jervis's sharp insights spurred a wave of cognitivist research in security studies, which proved highly relevant during the Cold War and thereafter.

One particularly important contribution was the concept of "groupthink," developed in 1972 by social psychologist Irving Janis. Through his extensive study of foreign policy decisions during the Pearl Harbor attacks, the Bay of Pigs disaster, and the Cuban Missile Crisis, Janis discovered that when leaders and decision-making teams had shared biases, homogenous backgrounds, and an absence of internal dissent, they inevitably created dangerous echo chambers that led to perilous outcomes.[8] According to Janis, the "symptoms" of groupthink include an illusion of invulnerability, belief in one's own moral rightness, negative stereotyping of opponents, and silencing of dissenters.[9] His theory has had an extremely wide impact in multiple areas of study, from business management to health care.[10]

Janis's foundational work shows that insular, homogenous teams are more likely to underestimate their rivals, overlook or misunderstand important information, and make costly blunders.[11] Much research has since been done on the pernicious effects of this groupthink phenomenon in the field of security and defence, including recent studies analysing the disastrous American invasion of Iraq.[12] Other studies suggest that diversifying teams and encouraging dissenting perspectives can mitigate the problem of groupthink.[13]

None of that good advice was heeded by the United States or NATO during critical periods of the Afghan war. Rather, homogenous and insular teams of political decision makers – rendered overconfident by their ignorance of the Afghan theatre – put forward a mission and political narrative that fit their world view. Even a decade after 9/11, security agencies in the United States and other allied nations still lacked essential language competencies in

Pashto.[14] This was not simply a matter of needing "translators"; rather, it was indicative of a profound socio-cultural and political ignorance of Afghanistan, and a fundamental inability among elite decision makers to understand basic signals communicated in the theatre. Although Canada and other allied nations scrambled to find translators to assist them in the field, the big decisions about the overall war effort were made by ill-qualified leaders and experts who had little local or regional knowledge.

The outcomes were absurd. On the one hand, Canadian politicians boasted that the Afghan mission would advance women's rights; on the other hand, they partnered with and empowered warlords who had records of perpetrating ethno-genocidal rape campaigns.[15] While Canadian leaders made lofty speeches about supporting Afghan girls, women in rural Kandahar Province told me that their daughters were being grabbed off the streets and raped by local militias working alongside NATO.[16] By the early to mid-2000s, it was clear that the United States, Canada, and other NATO allies were dealing with problematic local partners who were making it easier for the Taliban to win local support. In fact, many Canadian soldiers were horrified that they were working alongside Afghan militiamen turned soldiers who regularly engaged in sexual violence against children.[17]

The official narrative and the ground reality were worlds apart, and sometimes exact opposites. NATO allies burned the fields of poor opium farmers, boasting of a crackdown on illicit drugs; meanwhile, Canada worked with strongman Ahmed Wali Karzai, the brother of then Afghan president Hamid Karzai, even though the CIA had accused him of being deeply involved in the heroin trade.[18] In 2005, poor farmers who lost their opium crops swore to me they would switch sides and support the Taliban if it meant saving their livelihoods.[19] Yet, while there was early evidence that many aspects of the Afghan mission were self-defeating, neither Liberal nor Conservative governments in Canada welcomed critical feedback that challenged their predetermined notions about the conflict. It was a quintessential case of groupthink, resulting in disastrous foreign policy outcomes.

This was especially true on the matter of negotiating with the Taliban. Although the Afghan war eventually concluded with a negotiated agreement, the opportunity to settle the conflict through peace talks existed long before. In fact, on 4 December 2001, President Karzai negotiated a deal with the senior leadership of the Taliban, known as the Shah Wali Kot agreement, in which the Taliban agreed to surrender and stop fighting in exchange for amnesty and dignity.[20] This deal would have ended the war in Afghanistan with the Taliban in a losing position. Unfortunately, US secretary of defence Donald Rumsfeld interjected and forced Karzai to retract the deal with the Taliban, disallowing a negotiated settlement among the Afghan parties to the conflict.[21] The Americans demanded that the war continue.

The American veto of the Shah Wali Kot surrender meant that the Taliban were forced to continue fighting, long after they wanted to lay down their arms. By 2005, the Taliban were still fighting, but from the nadir of their power; they had been pushed back from their territorial holdings and had not yet built the momentum for a long and drawn-out insurgency. The original Taliban leadership was intact and had maintained close ties to Pakistan's Inter-Services Intelligence (ISI) Agency. At this time, I personally met with elite members of the ISI who could securely bring top Taliban decision makers to the bargaining table.[22] I identified channels for potential negotiations, as well as some baseline criteria for initiating direct talks. At this time, the Taliban were still open to talks, and would have been negotiating from a position of relative weakness.

Having intimately witnessed this critical juncture first-hand, I can attest that the political climate between 2005 and 2008 – in both Canada and the United States – was deeply opposed to negotiations with the Taliban, including quiet Track II deliberations. A few bold leaders from within the Liberal Party dared to publicly suggest the possibility of talks with the Taliban, only to encounter severe censure for doing so.[23] When the Conservative government of Stephen Harper took power in 2006, it further stonewalled critical perspectives and silenced any discussion of talks. Only the NDP, under the leadership of Jack Layton, asked to be briefed about these issues and advocated for opening talks at this critical juncture.[24] For daring to raise these issues, other Canadian leaders then derisively gave Mr. Layton the infamous nickname "Taliban Jack" and called him a terrorist sympathizer.[25]

Although I did not work in the American context at this time, I was in touch with a small cohort of scholars and practitioners who were also working to open a channel for talks. Yet, despite the fact that al-Qaeda had long ago separated from the Taliban,[26] during this critical period, the American government continued to insist that "we don't negotiate with terrorists." By the time the Americans changed their position on negotiations, the opportunity to achieve a favourable deal had passed. As Dr. Barnett Rubin, who was deeply involved in the American process, explains, "By 2009 ... the idea of negotiation with the Taliban began to gain traction. The U.S. military argued for postponing negotiations until the U.S. was in a 'position of strength.' But it was too late. The U.S. had already squandered its position of strength."[27]

Hoping to regain an advantageous bargaining position, in 2009 the Obama administration then authorized a massive troop surge and drone campaign to push back the Taliban.[28] However, by this point, the Taliban had built a robust and resilient insurgency and were well prepared to wait out the Americans. When the Trump administration finally signed a deal in 2020,[29] its terms and implications were the opposite of what the 2001 Shah Wali Kot deal achieved, essentially handing the Taliban the basis for a decisive military victory. This outcome was significantly better for the Taliban than what they may have accepted in 2005 (i.e., harder guarantees on minority and women's rights, and possibly even power sharing with some other Afghan political actors), and was very close to the Taliban's perceived best-negotiated outcome (i.e., foreign troop withdrawal and total military victory). This means it was possible that the exact same deal – and arguably a much better one – could have been signed over fifteen years prior, thus sparing all the lives lost through the continued fighting. Bravado and slogans will not bring those lives back.

The Afghanistan case is not unique in its tragedy. For example, during the disastrous 1992–5 UN mission in Somalia, Canada believed it was championing a purely humanitarian cause. In reality, Canada, the United States, and other allied nations had accidentally taken sides in a complex clan conflict and ended up worsening the civil war.[30] Not only did those decision makers fail to realize that they were unintentionally empowering the Abgal sub-clan over the Habr-Gidir, but they also did not connect these clan dynamics to the spike in violence. As a result, Canada's intervention in Somalia ended in murder, horror, and total mission failure.[31] Could this crucial knowledge have been acquired during the operational planning process? Absolutely, if the right voices had been included in briefings and deliberations.

When it comes to security, many crucial observations simply cannot be made from the sidelines. I have personally witnessed academics present statistical data about the rise in jihadist violence in West Africa, yet draw dangerously misleading conclusions from these data. While there certainly has been a spike in jihadist violence in the Sahel region, some colleagues have suggested to senior members of the defence and intelligence community that global "epicentres of extremism are moving" to Africa.[32] With no insight into local environmental conflicts between Fulani pastoralists and Dogon farmers in the Sahel, these analysts fundamentally misunderstood the jihadist threat in the Sahel region and overplayed the international angle. Unless experts with local knowledge and differing perspectives are in the room to challenge such assertions, it can be all too easy to misread conflict dynamics from afar.

Inclusive Excellence and Mission Success

Canada's Afghanistan mission ended in total failure and a decisive military victory for the Taliban. Its operation in Somalia was a disaster and a scandal and helped perpetuate enduring state failure. Its dangerous deployment to Mali ended miserably in 2023, when the Malian government expelled UN peacekeepers for failing in their mission. In all these cases, there were ample opportunities to change course before these situations spiralled out of control. Canadian policy makers missed those opportunities.

While there is no silver bullet for mission success, increasing diversity can help reduce the risk of groupthink and other cognitive errors, and thus improve decision making in our defence and foreign affairs institutions. For example, looking to the future, a task force working on Canada's mission to Haiti should include diverse methodological expertise, welcoming statisticians and ethnographers alike. Moreover, it ought not be comprised of only French Canadian peacekeeping veterans, nor only leaders from the Haitian diaspora, but of a diverse mix of experts with different positions and experiences of the conflict. Most importantly, experts who are highly critical of Canada's role in Haiti should be given the opportunity to present evidence and contrary arguments. The goal should be increased diversification of backgrounds, expertise, and perspectives among experts and leaders, especially those involved in mission design. Such diversity might make it harder to achieve harmonious decisions, but it will also help to avoid the false comfort of group conformity on matters of global security.

Canada has the advantage of having a highly diverse and educated citizenry, which is a significant untapped strategic asset. Unfortunately, Canadian defence and security institutions have not yet made good use of this asset. Rather, there have been serious allegations of gender and racial discrimination in the Canadian Armed Forces and the Canadian Security and Intelligence Services. The chapter by MacKenzie and Wegner in this volume presents a sharp analysis of the effects of gender and racial violence within the Canadian military, whereas Zine's chapter looks at Islamophobia within Canada's security and intelligence agencies. This discriminatory conduct is not only abhorrent in any civilized society, but it is also a poor way to retain valuable staff. To address this problem, Canada should conduct an equity audit of key security and defence institutions to identify where it is undermining its own success. One example of this type of audit is the 2022 Arbour Report, which presented a full review of sexual misconduct in the Canadian Armed Forces and concrete recommendations to address these problems.[33] However, not all equity-focused audits need to be public facing; internal reviews can also provide Canada's defence and security institutions with valuable information on where to make needed improvements, and also enhance training, recruitment, and promotion opportunities for Canadian experts from a wide range of backgrounds.

Substantive efforts to improve diversity in defence and security should not be mistaken for lip service initiatives that aim merely to check a box. For example, many efforts to include "Afghan voices" in Canada drew from a small contingent of elites from Kabul who shared many of the same views as their NATO allies. Since the Taliban takeover in 2021, many of my Afghan colleagues have come to the painful realization that their experiences inside the "Kabul bubble" were worlds apart from those of Afghans living in rural Ghazni or Nimroz. It takes work to cultivate a larger and more diverse network of contacts to avoid these biases, but it can and must be done.[34] Indeed, research shows that diasporas can be biased about conflicts in their home countries, and such biases must be considered when seeking out "local" perspectives.[35]

Finally, it is not enough to simply increase diversity among our leaders and decision makers. Experts and practitioners who are tasked with working together on security problems will naturally build a spirit of camaraderie. While that in-group harmony can be productive, it can also make it harder for individual members to present alternative perspectives or dissent from the group. To avoid the pitfalls of groupthink and other cognitive biases, it is therefore imperative that the Canadian defence and security community create systems to regularly challenge its teams to wrestle with opposing perspectives.

Special branches of the military already know the value of these practices and have incorporated "challenge sessions" into their planning processes. I have personally advised senior military leaders from over a dozen allied nations through these types of challenge sessions. These elite military branches know that if you cannot access and understand your enemy's perspective, there is a fair chance you will misperceive the conflict and make dangerous miscalculations. They have even trained specialized practitioners to play the role of the enemy in "red team" war-gaming exercises.

Unfortunately, the majority of Canada's civilian political decision makers and security experts have yet to learn this important lesson, with dire consequences. Unable to differentiate between empathy and sympathy, they often miss the chance to benefit from empathetic learning about the enemy. Academics can be just as guilty of this groupthink mentality as political leaders.[36] Naturally, the Russian invasion of Ukraine sparked a strong reaction across Western nations (see von Hlatky and Hollander's chapter in this volume). However, it is quite revealing that feelings about Russian aggression ran so hot that some scholars and analysts censured prestigious American academics who had – years prior to the 2022 invasion – uncovered evidence that supported some of Russia's claims on NATO enlargement.[37] This unprofessional behaviour has further escalated after the eruption of war in Israel and Palestine in October 2023, as universities across North America face serious allegations of censure, silencing, and bias.

It is imperative that this plague of groupthink be eradicated in academic and policy circles alike. Good scholars and practitioners are comfortable with discomfort. They do not just welcome dissenting perspectives – they seek them out. They push themselves to access "enemy perspectives" and try to assess the strategic environment from those angles. They root out groupthink and are mindful of their internal preference for confirming information. And the absolute best will clear everything off the table and ask, "How are we the bad guys in this story?" Because everyone is the protagonist in their own minds, and that, too, is a cognitive error.

Since the 1960s, researchers have explained how groupthink and other psychological biases can worsen global security crises. Canada has repeatedly experienced the consequences of these biases in its own security and defence community, resulting in missed opportunities and failed missions. These failures should burn into our national psyche and make clear that increased diversity and inclusion within our security institutions is not a matter of progressive politics. It is a matter of success or failure, life or death. It is therefore imperative that Canada scrub out any lingering and debilitating biases in our defence and security institutions that could undermine the national interest. It is high time to call up the best minds, from all walks of life, to address the new challenges ahead.

NOTES

1 I have addressed some of these explanations for jihadist success in other publications, including Aisha Ahmad, *Jihad & Co.: Black Markets and Islamist Power* (Oxford: Oxford University Press, 2017), and Aisha Ahmad, "The Long Jihad: The Boom-Bust Cycle behind Jihadist Durability," *Journal of Global Security Studies* 6, no. 4 (2021): ogaa048, https://doi.org/10.1093/jogss/ogaa048.
2 Neta C. Crawford, "Calculating the Costs of the Afghanistan War in Lives, Dollars and Years," *The Conversation*, 21 September 2021, http://theconversation.com/calculating-the-costs-of-the-afghanistan-war-in-lives-dollars-and-years-164588.
3 David Rock and Heidi Grant, "Why Diverse Teams Are Smarter," *Harvard Business Review*, 4 November 2016, https://hbr.org/2016/11/why-diverse-teams-are-smarter; Khalil Smith, "How Diversity Defeats Groupthink," *Rotman Management Magazine*, 4 November 2016, https://www.rotman.utoronto.ca/Connect/Rotman-MAG/Issues/2020/Back-Issues---2020/Fall2020-ToolkitforLeaders/Fall2020-FreeFeatureArticle-HowDiversityDefeatsGroupthink; Akshaya Kamalnath, "Gender Diversity as the Antidote to 'Groupthink' on Corporate Boards," *Deakin Law Review* 22, no. 1 (2017): 85–106, https://dx.doi.org/10.2139/ssrn.3097396.
4 Martin Hilbert, "Toward a Synthesis of Cognitive Biases: How Noisy Information Processing Can Bias Human Decision Making," *Psychological Bulletin* 138, no. 2 (2012): 211–37, https://doi.org/10.1037/a0025940; J. Ehrlinger, W.O. Readinger, and B. Kim, "Decision-Making and Cognitive Biases," in *Encyclopedia of Mental Health*, 2nd ed., ed. Howard S. Friedman (Oxford: Academic Press, 2016), 5–12, https://doi.org/10.1016/B978-0-12-397045-9.00206-8; Johan E. Korteling, Anne-Marie Brouwer, and Alexander Toet, "A Neural Network Framework for Cognitive Bias," *Frontiers in Psychology* 9 (September 2018), https://www.frontiersin.org/article/10.3389/fpsyg.2018.01561.
5 Christer Pursiainen and Tuomas Forsberg, "Biased Decisions," in *The Psychology of Foreign Policy*, ed. Christer Pursiainen and Tuomas Forsberg

(Cham, Switzerland: Springer International, 2021), 163–207, https://doi.org/10.1007/978-3-030-79887-1_5; Jan Angstrom, "Mapping the Competing Historical Analogies of the War on Terrorism: The Bush Presidency," *International Relations* 25, no. 2 (2011): 224–42, https://doi.org/10.1177/0047117811404448; Yuen Foong Khong, *Analogies at War: Korea, Munich, Dien Bien Phu, and the Vietnam Decisions of 1965* (Princeton, NJ: Princeton University Press, 2020), https://www.degruyter.com/document/doi/10.1515/9780691212913/html; Steve A. Yetiv, *National Security through a Cockeyed Lens: How Cognitive Bias Impacts U.S. Foreign Policy* (Baltimore: Johns Hopkins University Press, 2013).

6 Ole R. Holsti, *Crisis Escalation War* (Montreal: McGill-Queen's University Press, 1972); Robert Jervis, "Hypotheses on Misperception," *World Politics* 20, no. 3 (1968): 454–79, https://doi.org/10.2307/2009777; Geoffrey Blainey, *The Causes of War*, 3rd ed. (London: Macmillan Press, 1988); Stephen Van Evera, *Causes of War: Power and the Roots of Conflict* (Ithaca, NY: Cornell University Press, 1999); Rose McDermott, "The Feeling of Rationality: The Meaning of Neuroscientific Advances for Political Science," *Perspectives on Politics* 2, no. 4 (2004): 691–706, https://doi.org/10.1017/S1537592704040459; Jonathan Mercer, "Rationality and Psychology in International Politics," *International Organization* 59, no. 1 (2005): 77–106.

7 Jervis, "Hypotheses on Misperception."

8 Irving Lester Janis, *Groupthink: Psychological Studies of Policy Decisions and Fiascoes*, 2nd ed. (Boston: Houghton Mifflin, 1982).

9 Janis, *Groupthink*.

10 Marlene E. Turner and Anthony R. Pratkanis, "Twenty-Five Years of Groupthink Theory and Research: Lessons from the Evaluation of a Theory," *Organizational Behavior and Human Decision Processes* 73, no. 2 (1998): 105–15, https://doi.org/10.1006/obhd.1998.2756.

11 Janis, *Groupthink*; Turner and Pratkanis, "Twenty-Five Years of Groupthink Theory and Research."

12 Dina Badie, "Groupthink, Iraq, and the War on Terror: Explaining US Policy Shift toward Iraq," *Foreign Policy Analysis* 6, no. 4 (2010): 277–96; Brandon Kennedy, "The Hijacking of Foreign Policy Decision Making: Groupthink and Presidential Power in the Post 9/11 World," *Southern California Interdisciplinary Law Journal* 21, no. 3 (2012): 633–80; Franz Eder, "Making Concurrence-Seeking Visible: Groupthink, Discourse Networks,

and the 2003 Iraq War," *Foreign Policy Analysis* 15, no. 1 (2019): 21–42, https://doi.org/10.1093/fpa/orx009.
13 Taylor H. Cox and Stacy Blake, "Managing Cultural Diversity: Implications for Organizational Competitiveness," *The Executive* 5, no. 3 (1991): 45–56; Smith, "How Diversity Defeats Groupthink"; Kamalnath, "Gender Diversity as the Antidote to 'Groupthink' on Corporate Boards"; Rebecca Reid, Susanne Schorpp, and Susan W. Johnson, "Trading Liberties for Security: Groupthink, Gender, and 9/11 Effects on U.S. Appellate Decision-Making," *American Politics Research* 48, no. 3 (2020): 402–13, https://doi.org/10.1177/1532673X19881627.
14 Tabassum Zakaria, "U.S. Spy Agencies Struggle with Post-9/11 Languages," Reuters, 19 September 2011, https://www.reuters.com/article/us-usa-intelligence-language-idUSTRE78I4P820110919.
15 Aisha Ahmad, "Afghan Women: The State of Legal Rights and Security," *Policy Perspectives* 3, no. 1 (2006): 25–41.
16 Author interview, Kandahar Province, Afghanistan, 2005.
17 David Pugliese, "'Man Love Thursdays' Returns," *Ottawa Citizen*, 6 October 2008, https://ottawacitizen.com/news/national/defence-watch/man-love-thursdays-returns.
18 James Risen, "Reports Link Karzai's Brother to Afghanistan Heroin Trade," *New York Times*, 4 October 2008, https://www.nytimes.com/2008/10/05/world/asia/05afghan.html; Max Fisher, "Ahmed Wali Karzai Was Symbol of Afghan War's Complexity," *The Atlantic*, 12 July 2011, https://www.theatlantic.com/international/archive/2011/07/ahmed-wali-karzai-was-symbol-of-afghan-wars-complexity/241810/.
19 Author interview, Kandahar Province, Afghanistan, 2005.
20 "Taliban Agree to Surrender Kandahar: Power Transfer Begins Today," *Dawn*, 7 December 2001, http://beta.dawn.com/news/9630/taliban-agree-to-surrender-kandahar-power-transfer-begins-today.
21 Michael R. Gordon with Norimitsu Onishi, "A Nation Challenged: Talks Continuing; Offer Is Made to Surrender Taliban's Last Stronghold; Deal May Hinge on Amnesty," *New York Times*, 7 December 2001, https://www.nytimes.com/2001/12/07/world/nation-challenged-talks-continuing-offer-made-surrender-taliban-s-last.html.
22 Author interviews, Peshawar, Rawalpindi, and Islamabad, Pakistan, 2006, 2009.

23 Gordon Smith, *Canada in Afghanistan: Is It Working?* (Calgary: Canadian Defence and Foreign Affairs Institute, March 2007), https://www.uvic.ca/research/centres/globalstudies/publications/publicationsdb/pubs/canada-in-afghanistan-is-it-workin-id-358.php; "NATO Should Talk to Taliban Because Military Victory Impossible: Report," *CBC News*, 1 March 2007, https://www.cbc.ca/news/canada/nato-should-talk-to-taliban-because-military-victory-impossible-report-1.680359.
24 Author's direct observations.
25 "Layton Calls on Harper to Support Taliban Talks," *CBC News*, 30 October 2008, https://www.cbc.ca/news/canada/layton-calls-on-harper-to-support-taliban-talks-1.761635; Scott Taylor, "'Taliban Jack' Was Right All Along," *Hill Times*, 13 February 2019, https://www.hilltimes.com/2019/02/13/taliban-jack-right-along/188135.
26 Personal communication, Dr. Barnett Rubin, 2024.
27 Barnett Rubin, "The Two Trillion Dollar Misunderstanding" (unpublished manuscript in the author's possession).
28 Kevin Marsh, "Obama's Surge: A Bureaucratic Politics Analysis of the Decision to Order a Troop Surge in the Afghanistan War," *Foreign Policy Analysis* 10, no. 3 (2014): 265–88.
29 For more on US decline, see Norrlöf's chapter in this volume.
30 Aisha Ahmad, "Agenda for Peace or Budget for War?," *International Journal* 67, no. 2 (2012): 313–31.
31 Sherene Razack, *Dark Threats and White Knights: The Somalia Affair, Peacekeeping, and the New Imperialism* (Toronto: University of Toronto Press, 2004).
32 Direct author observations, Defence Intelligence Agency, Pentagon, 2019.
33 Louise Arbour, *Report of the Independent External Comprehensive Review of the Department of National Defence and the Canadian Armed Forces* (Ottawa: Department of National Defence, 2022), https://www.canada.ca/en/department-national-defence/corporate/reports-publications/report-of-the-independent-external-comprehensive-review.html.
34 A prime example is Anand Gopal, *No Good Men among the Living: America, the Taliban, and the War through Afghan Eyes* (New York: Henry Holt and Company, 2014).
35 Yossi Shain and Aharon Barth, "Diasporas and International Relations Theory," *International Organization* 57, no. 3 (2003): 449–79, https://doi.org/10.1017/S0020818303573015; Terrence Lyons, "Conflict-Generated

Diasporas and Transnational Politics in Ethiopia," *Conflict, Security & Development* 7, no. 4 (2007): 529–49, https://doi.org/10.1080/14678800 701692951; Amanda Roth, "The Role of Diasporas in Conflict," *Journal of International Affairs* 68, no. 2 (2015): 289–301.

36 David B. Resnik and Elise M. Smith, "Bias and Groupthink in Science's Peer-Review System," in *Groupthink in Science: Greed, Pathological Altruism, Ideology, Competition, and Culture*, ed. David M. Allen and James W. Howell (Cham, Switzerland: Springer International Publishing, 2020), 99–113, https://doi.org/10.1007/978-3-030-36822-7_9.

37 Two examples of solid scholarship on NATO and Russia that received such backlash are John J. Mearsheimer, "Why the Ukraine Crisis Is the West's Fault: The Liberal Delusions That Provoked Putin Essays," *Foreign Affairs* 93, no. 5 (2014): [i]–89; Joshua R. Itzkowitz Shifrinson, "Deal or No Deal? The End of the Cold War and the U.S. Offer to Limit NATO Expansion," *International Security* 40, no. 4 (2016): 7–44, https://doi.org/10.1162/ISEC_a_00236.

chapter twelve

Gender and Security: Tackling Insecurity Inside the Canadian Military

MEGAN MACKENZIE AND NICOLE WEGNER

Military institutions have long been considered agents of state security. Yet, within these institutions, gendered and racialized insecurities are rampant. Feminist scholars have expressed concern about the prevalence of racist, ableist, sexist, violent, and misogynist practices within militaries, from unsuccessful attempts to integrate women into the armed forces,[1] routine scandals and illicit behaviours,[2] sexualized hazing,[3] racialized hazing,[4] as well as the ways that these practices extend outward in forms of unsanctioned racialized violence[5] and sexualized violence[6] towards communities that the armed forces are meant to serve. Contemporary issues, from unsuccessful attempts to integrate women into the armed forces, high levels of intra-service sexual assault and harassment, and ongoing mental health crises – including post-traumatic stress disorder (PTSD) and veteran suicide rates – demonstrate that militaries themselves are sources of insecurity, particularly for their employees. The Canadian Armed Forces (CAF) has not been immune to these problems. In 2021, a series of high-profile cases and a class action lawsuit related to internal sexual misconduct put a spotlight on a toxic military culture. At the same time, military suicide rates continue to climb, and the CAF is struggling to recruit due, in part, to the sexist and hostile work culture within the organization.

Members of the public historically resist reflecting on or criticizing the ways that militaries themselves can be sources of insecurity, both for service members and the public they are meant to serve. We argue that military exceptionalism – or the series of beliefs about the unique nature of the military, its history, and the type of work required of service members – has influenced this resistance and limited debate on the ways that military institutions can be sources of insecurity. We argue that internal military dynamics and culture should be treated as a national security concern. We use the concept of *military exceptionalism* to frame this analysis, and we focus specifically on the CAF. Military exceptionalism is a term that tends to be loosely associated with the unique nature of military service, and the revered place that the military holds within society and the public imagination. While military exceptionalism is often only broadly defined, it is readily associated with the assumption that members of the military are and should be subject to different standards and forms of accountability compared to civilians. We argue that ideas about military exceptionalism are strongly gendered and can inhibit the public's ability to critically reflect on weaknesses or the need for institutional change.

Internal military dynamics matter because the military is the most trusted public institution in most Western countries.[7] In Canada, the CAF has a historical reputation as a globally helpful institution, particularly involving nostalgia for Canada's peacekeeping history. This history, combined with national ideals and myths about Canada's global role as a "helpful hero," has facilitated long-standing public support for the forces.[8] Yet, in 2021, an internal survey among CAF members showed that 38.5 per cent of respondents did not have confidence in the military's leadership.[9] A critical examination of the internal dynamics of military institutions can help us reflect upon and problematize assumptions that militaries are central tools for providing security. We begin the chapter by highlighting instances of gendered insecurity within the CAF – military suicide and military sexual violence – before outlining the broader implications of these issues for the Canadian public.

Understanding PTSD and Suicide in the Military

Over the past two decades, post-traumatic stress disorder and military suicide have represented an increasing concern for many Western militaries. In Canada, since 2010, more veterans have died from suicide than were killed during the War in Afghanistan between 2001 and 2014. PTSD has become incredibly costly for contemporary militaries in both human and financial terms.[10] In their research focused on the United States, the RAND Corporation concluded that "post-deployment costs to society resulting from PTSD and major depression for 1.64 million deployed servicemembers could range from $4.0 to $6.2 billion (in 2007 dollars), depending on how we account for the costs of lives lost to suicide."[11] Between 2014 and 2018, the Canadian government topped up the military's disability insurance spending by $1.2 billion in response to a significant increase in the number of annual claims.[12] Despite these financial investments, there has been growing concern that militaries are inadequately providing veterans with mental health services, as well as an increasing awareness of the community effects of this issue, such as high levels of intimate-partner violence in military families.[13] There is a misconception that the main "cause" of military suicide is overseas deployment and exposure to combat trauma.[14] While service member and veteran suicides have been regularly linked to overseas deployments and PTSD, medical and psychology scholarship show how other elements of service are associated with suicide rates, including military sexual trauma,[15] sexualized violence,[16] addictions,[17] broader mental health issues,[18] long deployments,[19] employment precarity or "churn,"[20] and institutional practices and stigma.[21]

The problem with misunderstanding military suicide as primarily an expected yet tragic outcome of military deployments and service is that it serves to depoliticize the problem as a policy issue requiring an increasingly medicalized response.[22] Calls for more medical services do not address the root cause of military traumas, many of which are acquired in the barracks, in the bedroom, or in homes on bases. Framing military suicide as an outcome of deployment or combat trauma also reinforces "resilience" discourses that treat PTSD and trauma as preventable through mental and physical resilience training. Resilience narratives individualize trauma and ignore wider trends among service members, in which veteran suicide has been associated with phenomena not connected to deployments, including domestic violence, gender-based and sexual violence, and poverty. These narratives are also gendered and reinforce ableist ideals of "good soldiers" as strong, "macho," and physically and mentally fit. Alison Howell has pointed out how PTSD often comes to be characterized as an individual disorder that must be treated on an individual basis. This understanding of PTSD disconnects the diagnosis from broader questions about war and militarization and manages to both generalize the impacts of war and individualize people's recovery needs. As Howell writes, "Treating trauma as a medical problem has meant that it is approached as something to be cured, safely sequestering the experiences of ... war, in the private realm, and removing them from political scrutiny and action."[23] Because of the tenuous association of PTSD and military suicide with deployment (rather than understanding these to be multi-causal phenomena), these security crises have been understood as military (rather than socio-political) problems. This attitude reflects military exceptionalism and fails to recognize the ways that the military itself may be unequipped to rectify such complex problems. In turn, solutions to military suicide and PTSD may be inadequately applied due to internal, gendered military expectations about how to produce "good soldiers" at the expense of individual security and health.

Within militaries, feminists have also expressed concerns about military sexual violence. Military sexual violence (MSV), or unwanted sexual activity perpetrated by a service member against another service member, is an international problem. The CAF first established policies related to sexual harassment in 1988 but did not begin training on this issue until 1998, and only began collecting consistent data on MSV in 2015. Survey data shows that 27 per cent of women in the CAF have been sexually assaulted in their careers, and members of the CAF were twice as likely to be sexually assaulted compared to the general population.[24] It was also found that female regular force members are four times more likely than males to report, and were more likely to identify their supervisor or other higher-ranking personnel as the perpetrator. Another survey released in 2018 conveyed similar findings; a notable difference was that 30 per cent of regular force members reported fearing the negative consequences of reporting MSV.[25]

Attention to MSV in Canada has alternated between periodic though significant coverage of sensational or salacious cases in the media and relative silence and inaction on the issue. While MSV impacts men and women, women are over-represented as victims and most of the high-profile cases of MSV in Canada have involved senior male service members assaulting women of a lower rank. Given the ways that the military works to foster a "band of brothers" environment, defined by camaraderie, trust, and loyalty,[26] there have been historic concerns about the ability of the internal military justice system to address MSV cases and hold perpetrators accountable. There is strong evidence that the band of brother culture can lead to "codes of silence," with service members protecting each other and encouraging victims to stay silent in order to protect their careers.

Data supports these concerns. While legal trials for sexual assault within the CAF have been happening since at least the 1990s, there has been no external audit and little information is available on conviction rates. Elaine Craig found that, for cases of sexual assault, conviction rates were much lower in the military and acquittal rates much higher than in the civilian sphere.[27] Craig also found that other mechanisms, like plea bargains and pleading guilty to other offences like "drunkenness" and "disgraceful conduct," have led to a lack of conviction on sexually specific charges. Military exceptionalism – or the belief that these "internal" problems should be handled from within the military legal system and chain of command – is a significant component explaining why there has been widespread failure to rectify MSV, and how these issues continue to be positioned as ongoing scandals rather than *security* or policy failures.

However, a number of recent developments related to MSV in Canada indicate that systemic change may finally be possible. In 2019, the Federal Court signed off on a $900 million class action lawsuit settlement for victims of sexual assault employed by the Canadian military or the Department of National Defence. The settlement provides victims with payments of between $5,000 and $55,000. The period for victims to come forward with claims ran from 25 May 2020 to 24 November 2021; over 4,600 individuals filed claims dating as far back as the 1980s. In April 2021, former Supreme Court justice Louise Arbour was tasked with leading an external review into MSV. While some criticized this endeavour as yet another delay tactic to avoid making systemic changes, others were hopeful that Arbour's expertise and reputation would lead to a series of robust, concrete recommendations. In October 2021, Anita Anand was sworn in as minister of defence. In her first day on the job, she made explicit commitments to addressing MSV and acknowledged the complexity of the problem and the need for a multi-pronged and long-term plan. Less than a month later, Anand announced that sexual misconduct cases would be taken outside of the military justice system as a short-term measure to address the issue. In 2022, Justice Arbour released her report, which included forty-eight recommendations designed to help the CAF address its systemic sexual violence problem. Defence Minister Anand responded with a commitment to treat the report as a "road map" and implement all recommendations over time. There is no doubt that the national attention paid to MSV in 2020 and 2021 pushed military and political leaders to acknowledge the systemic nature of the problem and commit to addressing it. Time will tell if these commitments translate into long-term change.

Looking Forward

Many other chapters in this book identify external security challenges for Canada: the decline of American influence in international affairs (Norrlöf), the future of NATO-Russia relations (von Hlatky and Hollander), emergency management (Agrawal), climate change (Burch and McKenzie), future peacekeeping responsibilities (Coleman and Pingeot), and cybersecurity threats (West). By contrast, we seek to draw attention to an internal security challenge, though one with implications for the many issues discussed by our colleagues in proceeding chapters. Addressing external security challenges assumes a competent and reliable defence force, and this poses a problem for the CAF, which is historically lacking in inclusivity and responsiveness to diverse perspectives (see chapter by Ahmad). Sexual misconduct and a crisis of mental health support in the CAF pose obvious challenges for recruitment (and this has its own operational security implications for the forces). Routine exploitative behaviour by senior leadership also hinders institutional effectiveness and responsiveness. However, we wish to conclude by challenging the assumption that the future of Canadian security should involve the military as a primary tool for solving the complex challenges raised by our colleagues. Our chapter shows that militaries themselves can be sources of great insecurity, especially for their employees. We suggest that the security issues that exist within the CAF are not inevitable by-products of a unique institutional and work environment, but rather the consequence of what Aisha Ahmad calls "suboptimal decision making" and "groupthink" in chapter 11 of this volume, enabled by widespread impunity for exploitative senior leaders in a stringently hierarchical organization hostile to diversity and accountability. Militaries are given a wide berth to do as they please, public memories are short, and the belief that militaries are capable of making ethical and political choices without oversight has resulted in soldiers being treated as disposable, and senior leaders committing scandalous illicit behaviour with impunity.

How will PTSD, veteran suicide, and military sexual violence be prioritized in Canada moving forward? In the wake of the sexual misconduct scandals involving an extraordinary number of senior military leaders in 2021, newly appointed minister of defence Anita Anand made firm commitments to address this issue and ensure broad culture change in the CAF. But what remains unclear is whether this can be enacted by existing senior members of the CAF, whose entire professional careers have taken place within an institution described as toxic. Can cultural change be led from within? And can the CAF's culture change enough to shift deeply rooted problems like toxic masculinity? This is not simply a matter for human resources; rather, it is a matter of human security and should be prioritized as such.

NOTES

1 Megan MacKenzie, *Beyond the Band of Brothers: The US Military and the Myth That Women Can't Fight* (Cambridge: Cambridge University Press, 2015), https://doi.org/10.1017/CBO9781107279155.
2 Megan MacKenzie, Eda Gunaydin, and Umeya Chaudhuri, "Illicit Military Behavior as Exceptional and Inevitable: Media Coverage of Military Sexual Violence and the 'Bad Apples' Paradox," *International Studies Quarterly* 64, no. 1 (2020): 45–56, https://doi.org/10.1093/isq/sqz093.
3 Cynthia Enloe, *The Morning After: Sexual Politics at the End of the Cold War* (Berkeley: University of California Press, 1993); Josh Ceretti, "Rape as a Weapon of War(riors): The Militarisation of Sexual Violence in the United States, 1990–2000," *Gender and History* 28, no. 3 (2016): 794–812, https://doi.org/10.1111/1468-0424.12250.
4 Sandra Whitworth, *Men, Militarism and UN Peacekeeping: A Gendered Analysis* (Boulder, CO: Lynne Rienner, 2004).
5 Sherene Razack, *Dark Threats and White Knights: The Somalia Affair, Peacekeeping, and the New Imperialism* (Toronto: University of Toronto Press, 2004); Melanie Richter-Montpetit, "Empire, Desire and Violence: A Queer Transnational Feminist Reading of the Prisoner 'Abuse' in Abu Ghraib and the Question of 'Gender Equality,'" *International Feminist Journal of Politics* 9, no. 1 (2007): 38–59, https://doi.org/10.1080/14616740601066366.
6 Jasmine-Kim Westendoff, *Violating Peace: Sex, Aid, and Peacekeeping* (Ithaca, NY: Cornell University Press, 2020).
7 Courtney Johnson, "Trust in the Military Exceeds Trust in Other Institutions in Western Europe and U.S.," Pew Research Center, 4 September 2018, https://www.pewresearch.org/short-reads/2018/09/04/trust-in-the-military-exceeds-trust-in-other-institutions-in-western-europe-and-u-s/.
8 Nicole Wegner, "Helpful Heroes and the Political Utility of Militarized Masculinities," *International Feminist Journal of Politics* 23, no. 1 (2021): 5–26, https://doi.org/10.1080/14616742.2020.1855079.

9 Paul Wells, "A Crisis of Confidence in the Canadian Armed Forces," *Maclean's*, 14 May 2021, https://macleans.ca/politics/ottawa/a-crisis-of-confidence-in-the-canadian-armed-forces/.
10 Ken MacLeish, "Churn: Mobilization–Demobilization and the Fungibility of American Military Life," *Security Dialogue* 51, nos. 2–3 (2020): 194–210, https://doi.org/10.1177/0967010619889469.
11 Christine Eibner, *Invisible Wounds of War: Quantifying the Societal Costs of Psychological and Cognitive Injuries* (Santa Monica, CA: RAND Corporation, 2008), https://www.rand.org/content/dam/rand/pubs/testimonies/2008/RAND_CT309.pdf.
12 Sharon Adams, "At What Price?," *Legion Magazine*, 12 July 2019, https://legionmagazine.com/at-what-price/.
13 Alysha D. Jones, "Intimate Partner Violence in Military Couples: A Review of the Literature," *Aggression and Violent Behavior* 17, no. 2 (2012): 147–57, https://doi.org/10.1016/j.avb.2011.12.002.
14 Megan MacKenzie and Nicole Wegner, "War Myths and the Normalization of PTSD and Military Suicide: The Military Suicide Equation," *International Political Sociology* 16, no. 2 (2022): olab033, https://doi.org/10.1093/ips/olab033.
15 Irene Williams and Kunsook Bernstein, "Military Sexual Trauma among U.S. Female Veterans," *Archives of Psychiatric Nursing* 25, no. 2 (2011): 138–47, https://doi.org/10.1016/j.apnu.2010.07.003.
16 Rebecca K. Blais and Lindsey L. Monteith, "Suicide Ideation in Female Survivors of Military Sexual Trauma: The Trauma Source Matters," *Suicide & Life-Threatening Behavior* 49, no. 3 (2019): 643–52, https://doi.org/10.1111/sltb.12464; Rebecca K. Blais and Christian Geiser, "Depression and PTSD-Related Anhedonia Mediate the Association of Military Sexual Trauma and Suicidal Ideation in Female Service Members/Veterans," *Psychiatry Research* 279 (September 2019): 148–54, https://doi.org/10.1016/j.psychres.2018.12.148; Whitney S. Livingston, Jamison D. Fargo, Adi V. Gundlapalli, Emily Brignone, and Rebecca K. Blais, "Comorbid PTSD and Depression Diagnoses Mediate the Association of Military Sexual Trauma and Suicide and Intentional Self-Inflicted Injury in VHA-Enrolled Iraq/Afghanistan Veterans, 2004–2014," *Journal of Affective Disorders* 274 (September 2020): 1184–90, https://doi.org/10.1016/j.jad.2020.05.024.

17 Gursimran Thandi et al., "Alcohol Misuse in the United Kingdom Armed Forces: A Longitudinal Study," *Drug and Alcohol Dependence* 156 (November 2015): 78–83, https://doi.org/10.1016/j.drugalcdep.2015.08.033.
18 Mark A. Ilgen et al., "Psychiatric Diagnoses and Risk of Suicide in Veterans," *Archives of General Psychiatry* 67, no. 11 (2010): 1152–58, https://doi.org/10.1001/archgenpsychiatry.2010.129.
19 Mark A. Reger, Raymond P. Tucker, Sarah P. Carter, and Brooke A. Ammerman, "Military Deployments and Suicide: A Critical Examination," *Perspectives on Psychological Science: A Journal of the Association for Psychological Science* 13, no. 6 (2018): 688–99, https://doi.org/10.1177/1745691618785366.
20 MacLeish, "Churn.".
21 Magdalena Kulesza, Eric R. Pedersen, Patrick W. Corrigan, and Grant N. Marshall, "Help-Seeking Stigma and Mental Health Treatment Seeking among Young Adult Veterans," *Military Behavioral Health* 3, no. 4 (2015): 230–9, https://doi.org/10.1080/21635781.2015.1055866.
22 Allison Howell, "The Art of Governing Trauma: Treating PTSD in the Canadian Military as a Foreign Policy Practice," in *Canadian Foreign Policy in Critical Perspective*, ed. J.M. Beier and L. Wylie (Oxford: Oxford University Press, 2009), 125–33.
23 Alison Howell, "The Demise of PTSD: From Governing through Trauma to Governing Resilience," *Alternatives: Global, Local, Political* 37, no. 3 (2012): 216, http://www.jstor.org/stable/23412509.
24 "Sexual Misconduct in the Canadian Armed Forces, 2016," Statistics Canada, 28 November 2016, https://www150.statcan.gc.ca/n1/pub/85-603-x/85-603-x2016001-eng.htm.
25 "2018 Survey on Sexual Misconduct in the Canadian Armed Forces Backgrounder," Government of Canada, last modified 4 November 2021, https://www.canada.ca/en/department-national-defence/services/benefits-military/conflict-misconduct/sexual-misconduct/research-data-analysis/2018-survey-backgrounder.html.
26 MacKenzie, *Beyond the Band of Brothers*.
27 Elaine Craig, "An Examination of How the Canadian Military's Legal System Responds to Sexual Assault," *Dalhousie Law Journal* 43, no. 1 (2020), https://digitalcommons.schulichlaw.dal.ca/dlj/vol43/iss1/1/.

chapter thirteen

Indigenous Security

CHELSEA PARKER AND SHERYL LIGHTFOOT

Introduction

On the global stage, Canada aims to be perceived as a leader in promoting and upholding human rights. Domestically and internationally, Canadian political and legal systems claim to emphasize human rights and the integration of difference into a single, cohesive polity grounded in the country's particular rendering of multiculturalism. Yet, Canada's international reputation works to obscure the fact that Canada is constructed upon a two-tiered system of human rights: one tier for settler Canada, and a second, lower tier for Indigenous peoples, who have yet to see their human rights realized in Canada. Canada's efforts to establish its international reputation as a steward of human rights are compromised by the ambiguity of Indigenous human rights. Political rhetoric supports the universality of human rights, but domestic policy reflects a significant gap where Indigenous peoples are concerned. As this disparity becomes more apparent at home and abroad, Canada faces mounting pressure from the human rights community to reconcile its relationship with Indigenous peoples by recognizing and upholding Indigenous human rights equally with other peoples in Canada.[1] Consequently, the two-tiered system has generated a human rights gap within Canada that gives rise to economic and political security risks. That is, when these two tiers come into conflict with one another, the discrepancies inherent in the Canadian political and legal status quo are exposed to international and domestic audiences, resulting in reputational damage.

This chapter begins by taking a look at Canada's precarious human rights record to shed light on salient contradictions that impugn the legitimacy of Canada's claims to international leadership in the protection of human rights. Canada's failure to live up to its reputation is exposed in its relationship with Indigenous peoples, where resource extraction projects and land rights disputes lead to conflict and human rights abuses that put Canada's economic and political security at risk. Further, this chapter shows how Canada's two-tiered rights system was entrenched through Confederation and despite constitutional amendments geared towards establishing equal rights in Canada, persisting systemic barriers often inhibit Indigenous peoples from being able to exercise their rights. Subsequently, analyses of the 2020 Mi'kmaq fishing crisis, government responses to blockades and protests, as well as the discovery of unmarked graves at former Indian residential schools not only exemplify the various human rights violations faced by Indigenous peoples in and by Canada, but also reveal the risks these flashpoints pose to Canada's political and economic security. This chapter closes with an overview of the ways in which regulatory and policymaking structures developed in alignment with the United Nations Declaration on the Rights of Indigenous Peoples and the Declaration on the Rights of Indigenous Peoples Act, providing a way forward by offering a framework to rectify Canada's human rights gap.

Canadian Human Rights in Context

Canada endeavoured to build its reputation as a leader in human rights on the international stage by producing, signing, and ratifying the international order's earliest human rights–based agreements and advocating for their adoption both domestically and internationally.[2] However, Indigenous human rights stand in contradiction to Canada's attempt to project leadership on human rights. Indigenous human rights are far from respected domestically, compromising Canada's credibility as an authoritative voice on international human rights matters.[3] While progress can be observed in the areas of language and cultural rights, efforts to bring Canadian law and policy into alignment with Indigenous human rights, and to realize Indigenous rights to land and self-determination, have seriously lagged behind international standards.

Canada's reluctance to advance Indigenous rights to land and self-determination stems from its dependency on extractivism from unceded Indigenous lands and territories. This economic context is critical to understanding why and how the Canadian government has an abysmal Indigenous human rights record. As a fundamental component of Canada's economic model, resource extraction and development on Indigenous peoples' traditional lands are pursued vigorously by both the Canadian government and private investors. Resource-extractive industries rely on the attraction of foreign direct investment. It is in part the predictability and stability of Canada's economic landscape that attracts investors.[4] The failure to build Indigenous rights and title – the inherent Aboriginal[5] right to land and territory – into Canadian investment policy has left investors uncertain as they observe costly and lengthy conflicts over unsettled Indigenous rights in Canada,[6] thereby put Canada's economic and political security at risk. Where Canada's progressive rhetoric ends, the political reality of an inadequate and often contradictory two-tiered rights system begins, and the international and business community may begin to doubt Canada's stability and authority as a partner in politics and business.[7] Domestic policies and actions have a substantial influence on a nation's global reputation and its capacity to exercise influence internationally, a topic covered in depth by Norrlöf earlier in the volume. Flashpoint events in Canada have garnered international attention in addition to generating on-the-ground turmoil, alienating political allies and potential investors on whom Canada depends for its reputation of progress and stability.

Indigenous Human Rights in Legal Context

In the late twentieth century, a series of Supreme Court cases increasingly recognized underlying Indigenous rights that require reconciliation with the prevailing Canadian legal system. For example, section 35 of the Constitution Act, 1982, affirms the "Aboriginal and treaty rights of Aboriginal peoples,"[8] while not clearly defining them, embedding Indigenous rights as rights that still must be litigated. The two-tiered rights system in Canada not only persists in contemporary policy and law but was also baked into the pre-Confederation legal treatment of Indigenous peoples by the British Crown. The Royal Proclamation of 1763 states that only the British Crown, not individual settlers, can receive land via treaty from Indigenous peoples; at the same time, it is often cited as an early acknowledgment of the pre-existing Indigenous title to land now claimed by Canada.[9] The proclamation also positions Aboriginal title as existing solely when recognized by the British Crown and establishes a distinction between title – by which Indigenous peoples preside over land until it is ceded – and sovereignty.

While the government could own and exercise sovereignty over land, Indigenous governments were relegated to titular oversight, setting the stage for the appropriation of Indigenous nations as a domestic area of administrative grievance. The Indian Act of 1876 established Indian status and Canadian citizenship as mutually exclusive. Therefore, managing the rights of citizens and managing the rights of status Indians became the administrative duty of different governing institutions, thereby cementing two streams of rights and protections in Canada.[10] While Indian status and Canadian citizenship are no longer mutually exclusive, the bifurcated rights system remains ingrained in the Canadian polity. The Canadian Charter of Rights and Freedoms might seek to establish equal rights in Canada across the board; however, pre-existing and new sociopolitical systemic barriers prevent Indigenous peoples from being able to use and apply these rights.

Risks to Political Security: Mi'kmaq Lobster Fishing and Canada's Reputation

The 2020 Mi'kmaq fishing crisis illustrates how Canada's poor record on Indigenous rights can culminate in threats to political security. In the 1999 decision in *R v. Marshall*, the Supreme Court of Canada upheld and recognized the Aboriginal treaty right to harvest and profit to an indeterminate threshold of "moderate livelihood."[11] Departing from the demands of commercial fishers that their Mi'kmaq counterparts be subject to the same regulations, the court determined that Mi'kmaq treaty rights do indeed *exist*, but are limited to moderation.[12] Without the jurisdiction to create federally sanctioned fishing regulations, Mi'kmaq fishers have been subjugated to the undefined financial maximum of moderation established in the 1999 Marshall decision. Working within these regulations, the Sipekne'katik First Nation established a self-regulated lobster fishery in 2020, which operated outside of the federally regulated fishing season. Commercial fishers cited concerns that their commercial profits would be endangered when Sipekne'katik launched their fishery, and the Department of Fisheries and Oceans (DFO) followed up by insisting the Mi'kmaq adhere to seasonal restrictions on lobster fishing.[13] In recognition of their treaty rights, the Sipekne'katik Nation pushed back by calling for a set of regulations to be established on a nation-to-nation basis.[14]

Assurances from the federal government of a forthcoming nation-to-nation relationship have yet to create meaningful development through which self-regulation for Mi'kmaq fishers becomes a reality. Instead, the Canadian government's response favours commercial fisheries' federally regulated fishing rights and demands that Sipekne'katik desist or adhere to the DFO's federally regulated fishing season. Despite enduring vandalism, arson, and assault, the Sipekne'katik held to their treaty rights, did not heed the DFO's order, and continued to fish before the DFO season began.

This flashpoint event has gone from being solely a domestic issue to a concern of the international community. Condemnation directed at Canada's domestic response to the issue, including the RCMP's failure to respond adequately, has garnered international criticism. Transposing Canada's purported role as an advocate and influencer of human rights at the international level, the United Nations Committee on the Elimination of Racial Discrimination called on Canada to account for its lacklustre response to racism against Mi'kmaq fishers and its role in protecting Mi'kmaq treaty rights.[15] These rights, as affirmed by subsequent court decisions, date back to before Confederation, when the Peace and Friendship Treaties established the Mi'kmaq right to fish and trade freely.[16]

In April of 2021, Chief Mike Sack of the Sipekne'katik First Nation announced that the fishery would continue to operate according its self-determined season and requested that the United Nations send peacekeepers to keep band members safe where the federal government had assumedly fallen short in doing so the previous year. In positioning Canada as a site where an outside actor must keep the peace, Chief Sack's request exposes the civic disorder produced by the two-tiered rights system and invites intervention where that system has proven inadequate for Indigenous peoples. Beyond raising the potential for immediate intervention in Canadian affairs, this request is a hit to Canada's reputation: Canada's treatment of Indigenous peoples has positioned it as subject to – rather than directing – United Nations human rights advocacy. Indeed, many contemporary United Nations reports call on Canada to work with First Nations to make changes to Canadian law based on Canada's failure to live up to its commitments to the International Covenant on Civil and Political Rights and the International Covenant on the Elimination of Racial Discrimination. Specifically, the United Nations Human Rights Committee called on Canada to report its progress on addressing land rights violations and violence against Indigenous women, prompting Assembly of First Nations national chief Perry Bellegarde to call for "action now on our collective agenda for closing the human rights gap."[17]

Risks to Economic Security

In addition to compromising Canada's reputation as a reliable partner in international politics and human rights, Canada's noncommittal approach to Indigenous human rights endangers the stable inflow of foreign investment in Canada. Opposition to the

Coastal GasLink Pipeline – a 670-kilometre-long, $6.6 billion project in the works since 2012 – erupted in part over the pipeline project itself, but the pipeline also became a flashpoint for broader and more complex issues like Indigenous governance and land rights.[18] The police cleared camps erected in opposition to the pipeline's use of traditional Wet'suwet'en land over which hereditary chiefs were denied influence. In response, blockades and protests sprung up across Canada in solidarity. One such blockade established by the Mohawks in Tyendinaga, Ontario – more than three thousand kilometres east of Wet'suwet'en territory – pledged to remain in place until police left Wet'suwet'en territory, notably sidestepping questions of whether the pipeline project *should* go forward, and instead focusing on unsettled Indigenous rights to land and security.[19]

As a result, CP Rail was forced to shut down its entire eastern network, halting all cross-country freight trains. This impacted supply chains, leaving investors and project managers scrambling to transport their products across the country. It was assessed that the Canadian government had no legitimate power to tear down blockades and arrest protestors, nor would this strategy be effective at preventing other blockades from springing up. Officials claimed that the blockades cost millions of dollars in lost profits, and thousands of passengers were unable to travel between Ontario and Quebec. However, in overseeing the blockades, hereditary chiefs are "exercising [their] jurisdiction" over land, water, air, and the inherent Indigenous rights held by First Nations.[20] In addition to the costs imposed by this flashpoint event, Canadian economic security was jeopardized by the signals sent to potential investors abroad. With the increasing frequency of contentious legal battles, drawn out by negotiation and contestation over free, prior, and informed consent (FPIC), Canada risks losing the reputation it has previously built with foreign investors.

Unmarked Graves at Former Indian Residential Schools

Canada's international reputation took further hits as its two-tiered rights system became even more evident abroad when the human rights abuses committed through the Canadian residential schooling over more than a century system came under the international spotlight. Residential schools were constructed and run by the Canadian government and churches with the core objective of indoctrinating and assimilating Indigenous children into Christian settler-colonial society. Children were forcibly separated from their parents, families, culture, and language, and made to suffer unthinkable physical, sexual, and mental abuse at the hands of school staff.[21] Canada's residential schools garnered international attention after the discovery in May 2021 of 215 unmarked graves on the grounds of the former Kamloops Indian Residential School. In response, a panel of United Nations experts condemned the "large scale human rights violations" and "heinous crimes" committed against Indigenous children.[22] Subsequent discoveries at St. Eugene's Mission School in Cranbrook, British Columbia, and Marieval Indian Residential School in Marieval, Saskatchewan, prompted the United Nations to call for criminal charges to be brought against perpetrators wherever possible. Experts now estimate that over ten thousand Indigenous children died or went missing from Canada's residential schools.[23]

United Nations experts encouraged transparency from the Catholic Church. Further, they urged the Canadian government to conduct forensic exams to identify remains and "conduct criminal investigations [to] prosecute and sanction the perpetrators and concealers who may still be alive."[24] Despite the clear allocation of responsibility to the federal government, Ottawa's calls on the Catholic Church to voluntarily provide information have not rendered results as the federal government cannot compel the church to cooperate. With significant international attention on the increasing number of remains discovered at the former sites of Indian residential schools, and the ongoing refusal of the federal government to heed the advice of the United Nations, Canada's already precarious reputation as a leader in human rights continues to deteriorate. As Burch and McKenzie highlight in chapter 10 of this volume, interstate relationships that foster collaborative solutions are increasingly necessary for solving contemporary global issues. As Canada's international reputation is brought into question by its contestation of Indigenous rights, the country's capacity to participate in collaborative forms of interstate trust building is limited.

In combination with Mi'kmaq calls for UN peacekeepers in Canada and the international business community's scepticism of Canadian policies aimed at upholding FPIC, global expectations in advancing human rights have surpassed what Canada has been willing to do domestically. International fora such as the Organization of American States have called on Canada to do more in investigating and pursuing justice for Indigenous peoples and the rights they are frequently promised, but which rarely enumerated or defended.[25] Though often framed as an issue of domestic policy, Indigenous rights contestations have bled into the international sphere and continue to impact Canadian policymaking at all levels of government.

A Way Forward

Canada was one of only four countries that initially voted against the United Nations Declaration on the Rights of Indigenous Peoples (UNDRIP). Still, it has since become the first to pass legislation that aims to align Canadian laws, policies, and practices with UNDRIP.[26] The Declaration on the Rights of Indigenous Peoples Act (DRIPA, previously known as Bill C-15) seeks to rectify the lack of domestic accountability, leaving Indigenous peoples to pursue international lines of redress.[27] An opportunity to bolster Indigenous self-determination and ensure that resource projects benefit Indigenous communities, article 32 of DRIPA affirms the rights of Indigenous peoples to "determine and develop priorities and strategies for the development or use of their lands or territories and other resources."[28]

In creating a regulatory and policy framework that aligns Canadian industry with UNDRIP, DRIPA provides an opportunity for Canada to uphold Indigenous human rights and reconcile its discriminatory, two-tiered human rights system. Because DRIPA embeds principles of FPIC resource management, there are fewer opportunities for further uncertainty and negotiations surrounding Indigenous treaties and human rights. Allowing for swifter decision making and respecting Indigenous human rights would mitigate the uncertainty that discourages foreign direct investment *and* provide the potential for First Nations to be partners in Canadian economic growth, rather than subject to encroachments on their rights to land and treaty. As such, DRIPA provides the potential for a legal framework that can prevent conflict and discord and foster productive arrangements.[29] In the absence of DRIPA's legal framework, Canada's human rights gap becomes increasingly glaring. In Ontario, the provincial government and private corporations disregarded FPIC in the mineral-rich Ring of Fire region, which prompted five First Nations leaders to visit the Ontario legislature to ask whether the government planned to seek consent from First Nations before plans were made for development.[30] The legislation seeking to enshrine provincial autonomy over resource use in Saskatchewan led Indigenous leaders to threaten blockades.[31] Additionally, the arrest of Wet'suwet'en land defenders and their subsequent removal from blockades drew criticism from domestic and international organizations alike, thereby further jeopardizing Canada's fiscal and reputational well-being as a result of the state's failure to adhere to UNDRIP.[32]

Furthermore, flashpoints of conflict in the two-tiered human rights system – at Wet'suwet'en or Kanesatake, for example – frequently result in violent altercations. UNDRIP, however, provides Canada with an opportunity to peacefully recognize Aboriginal rights and avoid treating Indigenous resistance as a threat to domestic security. Rather, in affirming the right to Indigenous political self-determination, DRIPA encourages engagement with Indigenous peoples as full holders of human rights.[33] It is important to recognize, then, that the threat Canada faces is not strictly a domestic one: circumventing the principles of UNDRIP serves to compromise Canada's economic and political security.

Requiring the government to win informed consent from Indigenous communities for relevant policies, as per DRIPA, is now commonplace when doing business with foreign direct investors; in other words, the government's prior threshold of consultation has been superseded by a consent threshold with Indigenous peoples. Thus, the passage of DRIPA increases the reliability of Canada's investment portfolio by re-engaging in the corporation-to-nation relationship. With measures for dealing with resistance and redress, DRIPA helps to mitigate the likelihood that altercations between participants will turn violent and disruptive by providing alternative means for resolution instead of the current norm of extensive and expensive legal battles.[34] Similarly, DRIPA serves to guarantee that the exercise of treaty rights is consistent with existing Canadian public policy, allowing the pursuance of Indigenous rights within a pan-Canadian framework.[35] With a lower likelihood of violent escalation, and a path for redress beyond lobbying international fora to push Canada forward,[36] DRIPA has the potential to greatly improve the nation-to-nation relationship both parties seek in a demonstrable way.

Aligning Canada's legal and political framework with the principles outlined in UNDRIP is difficult and time-consuming, but it ultimately rectifies a system in which the rights of settlers and commercial industry are guaranteed, while those of Indigenous peoples and communities are in flux and secondary. Building certainty into a system currently plagued with ambiguity not only allows for greater domestic stability, it also improves the security of Canada's foreign investment and allows for predictability in Canada's human rights regime at home and abroad. Failing to commit to UNDRIP in a meaningful way and instead adhering to the status quo poses a greater risk to Canadian security than making the changes demanded by DRIPA. If Canada is interested in retaining or regaining its international reputation as a paragon of human rights, it must credibly search for and commit to solutions that end the uncertainty created by a two-tiered human rights system. In this respect, DRIPA and the larger movement to end this uncertainty should be politically and economically marketable, creating long-term positive opportunities for Canada in partnership with Indigenous peoples.

NOTES

1 Sheryl Lightfoot, *Global Indigenous Politics: A Subtle Revolution* (Abingdon, UK: Taylor and Francis, 2016), 176.
2 David Petrasek, "Liberals' Vague 'Values' Talk Undermines Rights Promotion," Centre for International Policy Studies, 2 February 2018, https://www.cips-cepi.ca/2018/02/02/liberals-vague-values-talk-undermines-rights-promotion/.
3 Sheryl Lightfoot, "A Promise Too Far? The Justin Trudeau Government and Indigenous Rights," in *Justin Trudeau and Canadian Foreign Policy*, ed. Norman Hillmeer and Philippe Lagasssé (New York: Palgrave Macmillan, 2018), 166.
4 "Key Facts about Canada's Competitiveness for Foreign Direct Investment," Government of Canada, last modified 14 June 2021, https://www.international.gc.ca/trade-commerce/economist-economiste/analysis-analyse/key_facts-2020-12-faits_saillants.aspx?lang=eng.
5 "Aboriginal" is an umbrella term used to collectively refer to First Nations, Inuit, and Métis that is found in the Canadian Constitution and most often used in legal contexts and for government policy in Canada. See Linc Kesler, *Indigenous Peoples: Language Guidelines*, version 3.0 (Vancouver: University of British Columbia, 2021), https://assets.brand.ubc.ca/downloads/ubc_indigenous_peoples_language_guide.pdf.
6 John Borrows, "Indigenous Diversities in International Investment and Trade," in *Indigenous Peoples and International Trade*, ed. John Borrows and Risa Schwartz (Cambridge: Cambridge University Press, 2020), 28.
7 Lightfoot, "A Promise Too Far?," 166.
8 "Constitution Act, 1982 Section 35," Indigenous Foundations, accessed 22 March 2024, https://indigenousfoundations.arts.ubc.ca/constitution_act_1982_section_35/.
9 John Borrows, "Wampum at Niagara: The Royal Proclamation, Canadian Legal History, and Self-Government," in *Aboriginal and Treaty Rights in Canada*, ed. Michael Asch (Vancouver: UBC Press, 1997), 160.
10 Sheryl Lightfoot, "Indigenous Peoples and Canadian Defence," in *Canadian Defence Policy in Theory and Practice*, ed. Thomas Juneau, Philippe Lagassé, and Srdjan Vucetic (Cham, Switzerland: Palgrave Macmillan, 2020), 217–31.

11 "The Facts behind Mi'kmaw Fishing Rights," *APTN National News*, 22 September 2020, https://www.aptnnews.ca/national-news/the-facts-behind-mikmaw-fishing-rights/.
12 Graham Slaughter, "Mi'kmaq Lobster Dispute: A Conflict Brewing since the 1700s," *CTV News*, 20 October 2020, https://www.ctvnews.ca/canada/mi-kmaq-lobster-dispute-a-conflict-brewing-since-the-1700s-1.5153568.
13 Michael MacDonald, "The Dispute over Nova Scotia's Indigenous Lobster Fishery, Explained," *Canada's National Observer*, 20 October 2020, https://www.nationalobserver.com/2020/10/20/news/nova-scotia-indigenous-lobster-fishery-dispute-explained.
14 MacDonald, "The Dispute over Nova Scotia's Indigenous Lobster Fishery."
15 Taryn Grant, "UN Committee Calls on Canada to Respond to Claims of Racist Violence against Mi'kmaw Fishers," *CBC News*, 10 May 2021, https://www.cbc.ca/news/canada/nova-scotia/united-nations-committee-mi-kmaw-moderate-livelihood-lobster-fishery-1.6020492.
16 APTN, "The Facts Behind Mi'kmaw Fishing Rights."
17 Coalition for the Human Rights of Indigenous Peoples, "UN Human Rights Report Shows That Canada Is Failing Indigenous Peoples," Union of British Columbia Indian Chiefs, accessed 22 March 2024, https://www.ubcic.bc.ca/canadafailingindigenouspeoples.
18 "The Wet'suwet'en Conflict Disrupting Canada's Rail System," *BBC News*, 20 February 2020, https://www.bbc.com/news/world-us-canada-51550821.
19 Ian Austen, "Who and What's behind the Blockades Disrupting Canada's Rails," *New York Times*, 29 February 2020, https://www.nytimes.com/2020/02/21/world/canada/pipeline-blockades-explainer.html.
20 Scott Neuman, "Canadian Pipeline Protest Forces Closure of Major Rail Link," *NPR*, 14 February 2020, https://www.npr.org/2020/02/14/805940471/canadian-pipeline-protest-forces-closure-of-major-rail-link.
21 Erin Hanson, Daniel P. Games, and Alexa Manuel. "The Residential School System," Indigenous Foundations, accessed 22 March 2024, https://indigenousfoundations.arts.ubc.ca/residential-school-system-2020/.

22 "UN Experts Call on Canada, Holy See to Investigate Mass Grave at Indigenous School," Office of the High Commissioner on Human Rights, 4 June 2021, https://www.ohchr.org/en/press-releases/2021/06/un-experts-call-canada-holy-see-investigate-mass-grave-indigenous-school.
23 Ian Austen, "How Thousands of Indigenous Children Vanished in Canada," *New York Times*, 28 March 2022, https://www.nytimes.com/2021/06/07/world/canada/mass-graves-residential-schools.html.
24 Office of the High Commissioner on Human Rights, "UN Experts Call on Canada, Holy See."
25 Sheryl Lightfoot and David MacDonald, "Yes, Canada Is Guilty of Genocide. Now It's Time to Act," *The Tyee*, 10 June 2019, https://thetyee.ca/Opinion/2019/06/10/Yes-Canada-Is-Guilty-Genocide-Missing-Women-Inquiry/.
26 Rachele Aiello, "Bill to Align Canadian Law with UN Indigenous Rights Declaration Passes to Become Law," *CTV News*, 16 June 2021, https://www.ctvnews.ca/politics/bill-to-align-canadian-law-with-un-indigenous-rights-declaration-passes-to-become-law-1.5473285.
27 Sara King-Abadi, "Industry and First Nations Groups Are Hopeful for the Nationwide Adoption of UNDRIP after Seeing the Results in British Columbia," *CIM Magazine*, 25 February 2021, https://magazine.cim.org/en/news/2021/undrip-legislation-could-spell-more-certainty-for-resource-development-en/.
28 King-Abadi, "Industry and First Nations Groups Are Hopeful."
29 Terry Teegee, "Bill C-15 Brings Economic Stability to Canada," *Toronto Star*, 28 May 2021, https://www.thestar.com/opinion/contributors/2021/05/28/bill-c-15-brings-economic-stability-to-canada.html.
30 Sarah Law, "First Nations Leaders Walk Out of Queen's Park after Heated Exchange over Mining Proposals," *CBC News*, 29 March 2023, https://www.cbc.ca/news/canada/thunder-bay/firstnations-queenspark-mining-1.6794907.
31 Keenan Sorokan, "'We Will Blockade': FSIN Chiefs Threaten Action in Response to Saskatchewan First Act," *CTV News*, 16 December 2022, https://saskatoon.ctvnews.ca/we-will-blockade-fsin-chiefs-threaten-action-in-response-to-saskatchewan-first-act-1.6198799.
32 Kathleen Martens, "Amnesty Condemns RCMP Attack on Wet'suwet'en Territory," *APTN National News*, 30 March 2023, https://www.aptn

news.ca/national-news/amnesty-condemns-rcmp-attack-on-wetsuweten-territory/.
33 Sheryl Lightfoot, "Indigenous Disruptions: How Indigenous Self-Determination Practices Can Deepen and Expand International Theory," in *Globalizing International Theory: The Problem with Western IR Theory and How to Overcome It*, ed. Allan Layug and John M. Hobson (London: Routledge, 2022), 200–18.
34 Max Fisher, "Indigenous People Advance a Dramatic Goal: Reversing Colonialism," *New York Times*, 17 June 2021, https://www.nytimes.com/2021/06/17/world/canada/indigenous-kamloops-graves.html.
35 Fisher, "Indigenous People Advance a Dramatic Goal."
36 Fisher.

chapter fourteen

Islamophobia in Canada: The Security-Industrial Complex

JASMIN ZINE

Islamophobia is best captured as "a fear and hatred of Islam and Muslims (and those perceived as Muslims) that translates into individual actions and ideological and systemic forms of oppression that support the logic and rationale of specific power relations."[1] This definition moves beyond reducing Islamophobia to fear or hatred on the part of individuals and instead situates it as a system of oppression that operates within ideological and systemic structures of power that are expressed through various manifestations of anti-Muslim racism.

In Canada, these Islamophobic effects have manifested in anti-Muslim hate crimes, including the 2017 terror attack at a Quebec City mosque that killed six Muslim men and the mowing down by truck of four members of a Pakistani Muslim family in London, Ontario, during an evening stroll in 2021. The assailants in both attacks were inspired by white nationalist ideologies. Yet Muslims have been of far more interest to security agencies as potential threats to national security than as the victims of terror attacks.

Islamophobia has become inextricably linked to contemporary security discourses, policies, and practices in ways that target and vilify Muslim communities in Western nations as well as globally (China, Myanmar, India, Kashmir, and Palestine are cases in point). Since the attacks of 11 September 2001, right-wing populism has been gaining traction in many Western nations, including the United States, where Donald Trump's presidency was built on a platform of anti-Muslim policies and xenophobia (see Norrlöf's chapter in this volume). In Canada and elsewhere, Muslim youth have been identified as security threats and potential jihadists, which has led to practices of racial and religious profiling.

The recirculation of Islamophobic tropes also carries more dire consequences. For instance, Israel has leveraged the "violent terrorist Muslim" stereotype in its war against Gaza, using the dehumanizing characterization of Palestinians as "bloodthirsty monsters" and "human animals" as political cover for unbridled military violence. This deadly campaign strategically relies upon ingrained anti-Muslim narratives and Orientalist tropes popularized after 9/11 to authorize a wholesale genocidal war against Palestinian people under the guise of fighting terrorists.

Contemporary refugee policies and practices are also an example of the differential treatment of Muslim migrants (see Mourad's chapter in this volume). For example, Europe's welcoming of white Ukrainian refugees fleeing the Russian invasion is in stark contrast to the cages and border encampments built for the influx of Syrian refugees over the past several years and the treatment of current asylum-seekers from Afghanistan. Instead of a welcome mat, Muslim refugees have been met with xenophobic gatekeeping and deplorable conditions at many fortified European borders.[2]

Islamophobic ideologies have material consequences in the way they shape, inform, and authorize global militarism as well as domestic policies relating to immigration, security, and religious freedom. In this way, Islamophobia provides a rationale for systemic practices such as racial and religious profiling and surveillance, state policies governing religious attire (e.g., hijab/niqab bans), as well as authorizing institutional discrimination in education, employment, social services, health care, and law enforcement. Canadian security policies targeting Muslims include, for example, the Anti-terrorism Act,[3] the use of security certificates,[4] and the Passenger Protect Program or "No Fly List."[5] Under the banner of public safety, even children have been falsely flagged as security threats and placed on the No Fly List. A six-year-old Muslim boy, Adam Ahmad, made headlines in 2016 when he was stopped at Toronto's Pearson International Airport and flagged as a possible security threat. He was travelling with his father to see his favourite hockey team, the Montreal Canadiens, when he was prevented from boarding his flight.[6] The securitization of Muslim children is another example of a troubling pattern of racial profiling that reinforces stereotypes of Muslims as potential threats to national safety and security. While the federal government has recently implemented measures to prevent people from being wrongly added to the No Fly List,[7] these systemic practices have already caused harm and have unfairly stigmatized Muslim children.

Another example of systemic Islamophobia is the undue surveillance of Muslim charities by the Canada Revenue Agency (CRA). According to a report by the International Civil Liberties Monitoring Group, the "faulty and unsubstantiated national security 'risk assessment' approach to the monitoring of terrorism financing in the charitable sector has led to Muslim charities in Canada being unduly targeted for surveillance, audits, and revocation of their charitable status."[8] Another investigation revealed that "the CRA's allegations of terrorism financing against Muslim charities often rely on biased opinions from terrorism experts, policies from right-wing think tanks, and distorted facts from Islamophobic media sources."[9] Kutty and Bhabha argue that because of the biased sources used by the CRA, "Muslim charities are placed under the disproportionate burden of having to demonstrate that they are not connected to terrorism or extremism."[10] The Islamophobic conflation of Muslims with terrorism allows these state practices to appear justified rather than biased and discriminatory. Pushing back against this undue scrutiny, the Muslim Association of Canada has mounted a Charter of Rights challenge against the CRA, claiming targeted charities were subject to audits tainted by Islamophobic bias that jeopardized their ability to provide charitable services to thousands of Canadian Muslims.[11]

Islamophobia and the Security-Industrial Complex

Contemporary techniques of governance operate through a "security-industrial complex" (SIC), which I define as a network of interconnected institutions, technologies, economies, and policies through which state and non-state actors operate within contemporary surveillance regimes.[12] The SIC constitutes the apparatus through which post-9/11 governmentality and exceptionalism operate. Hayes identifies the SIC as a process by which "the boundaries between internal and external security, policing and military operations, have been eroded," and argues that new forms of surveillance of "public and private places, of communications and of groups of individuals" have been accelerated by the "war on terror."[13] In the post-9/11 state of exception, military and security communities,[14] along with academics and the media, function as part of the SIC by which Muslims are profiled, studied, policed, disciplined, and indefinitely detained.

These targeted practices do not occur without consequences. There is a well-documented nexus between Islamophobia and youth radicalization.[15] It is important to address the counterproductive consequences of surveillant practices based on the problematic racial coding of Muslims as terrorists, radicals, and jihadists, and how security policies and practices informed by these stereotypes create the very conditions and responses they aim to challenge.

To better understand how Islamophobia and the SIC converge and impact what I call "the 9/11 generation of Muslim youth," I present three related concerns for examination. The first relates to how "racial securitization" operates within a post-9/11 "state of exception." The second involves the impact of the SIC on the 9/11 generation of Canadian Muslim youth, and the third addresses the nexus between Islamophobic securitization and recruitment to radical associations.

Racial Securitization and the Post-9/11 State of Exception

Securitizing Muslims as contemporary racial folk devils relies upon specific logics and tactics. Political and ideological categories such as the "radical" and the "jihadist" are coded into an index of suspicion that informs the practices of racial and religious profiling. These practices are underwritten by the war on terror, in which Orientalist representations of Muslims are politically redeployed as signifiers of deviance and moral panic during times when exceptional state security measures have been normalized.

"Racial securitization" operates through sets of regulatory ideologies, policies, strategies, and techniques employed by the state (as well as some non-state actors) that are constituted and enacted through conflating racial and religious identities with the assessment of risk and public safety.[16] This form of securitization links race and the racialization of religion to the SIC as the basis upon which threats to public safety are determined and guarded against.[17]

Giorgio Agamben argues that a "state of exception" is created when securitized conditions are introduced under limited and extraordinary circumstances.[18] He contends that such measures are no longer exceptional and have become normalized as the dominant paradigm of governance. Hallmarks of the state of exception include anti-terrorism policies, the practice of extraordinary rendition (in both Canada and the United States), and the use of security certificates as part of the Canadian Immigration and Refugee Protection Act, which has effectively led to the dismantling of the rights of non-citizens through indefinite detention along with the reliance of secret trials and evidence.[19]

Increasingly, non-state institutions, organizations, and actors are conscripted into fulfilling the mission of securing the safety of the nation and exercising control over all areas of social life. Public servants and private citizens are asked to profile and identify deviant individuals and groups that may pose risks to public safety and civility. For example, security agencies have called upon mosques and religious organizations to be partners in public safety and help weed out extremists in their midst. Civil society participates in the supervisory networks conducting profiling and surveillance. Schools, universities, and community organizations are recruited to perform surveilling practices in ways that further extend the disciplinary function of the state.[20] For example, programs developed for the purposes of Countering Violent Extremism (CVE), such as the Prevent policy in the United Kingdom, have enlisted preschool teachers to help identify "potential radicals" among the toddlers in their care.[21]

In the United States, the American Civil Liberties Association documented how the American government is recruiting businesses and individuals in the construction of a surveillance society.[22] A security program dubbed "Eagle Eyes" was billed as "an anti-terrorism initiative that enlists the eyes and ears of Air Force members and citizens in the war on terror."[23] The program offers training in how to detect terrorist activity and a telephone tip line. According to its web page, "Anyone can recognize elements of potential terror planning when they see it."[24] This messaging secures the public's role in a security apparatus that seeks to identify suspicious activity and individuals, including "People who don't seem to belong in the workplace, neighbourhood, business establishment or anywhere else ... If a person just doesn't seem like he or she belongs, there's probably a reason for that."[25] These programs widen the reach of the security industry by asking for the public's assistance in profiling their neighbours, reporting who they deem to be "out of place," and identifying potential threats. Racial biases are deeply embedded in the judgments and assumptions underlying the practices that distinguish between good (safe) and bad (dangerous) citizens. Those distinctions are a driving force shaping public policy and security practices.

In Canada, a "National Strategy on Countering Radicalization to Violence" involves training nurses, school counsellors, psychologists, social workers, youth workers, and parole and probation officers to identify and assess cases of violent radicalization.[26] Expanding state surveillance through civil society agents has been shown to lead to problematic outcomes, as the previous examples show. Given that CVE agendas in other "Five Eyes" jurisdictions are underpinned by Islamophobia and racial angst, if Canada's security agencies follow the same trajectory, their attempts to build bridges with Muslim communities will ring hollow and the consequences will be equally counterproductive.

Securitized Subjects: The 9/11 Generation of Muslim Youth

The backlash Muslims faced after 9/11 has had a profound effect on young Muslims. The radical, the terrorist, the extremist, and the jihadist are the new ontologies ascribed to Muslim youth who, according to this view, are violent, degenerate fanatics hell-bent on the destruction of the West. While a very small minority of Muslim youth engage in ideologically driven violence, these constructs nevertheless inform the dominant paradigm through which the majority are viewed. The prevalence of these archetypes leaves little room for Muslims to locate themselves outside of these constrictive typologies. These derogatory categories underscoring the global jihadi threat are purveyed without reference to the histories and complex geopolitical struggles that shape these terms, and without acknowledging the role of US foreign policies and the war on terror in creating the conditions for reactionary ideologies to give rise to violent movements abroad.[27] These new taxonomies of difference tell us who is to be watched, punished, and exiled for fear they may disrupt "our freedom," "our values," and "our nation." The boundaries of belonging and citizenship and those separating the desirable from undesirable immigrants are anchored in these distinctions. Nationhood, citizenship, and civil and human rights hang in the delicate balance between the fear and moral panic generated among "good citizens" towards the Muslim "anti-citizen."[28]

The security-industrial complex and its archipelago of interconnected disciplinary networks shape the experiences of the 9/11 generation of Muslim youth and govern their actions and choices in a post-9/11 state of exception. For example, the University of Toronto's Muslim Students' Association (MSA) reported that its executives had been receiving unannounced visits from both the Canadian Security and Intelligence Service (CSIS) and the Royal Canadian Mounted Police (RCMP) from 2016 onward. These visits occurred on campus as well as at the executives' homes.[29] At Toronto Metropolitan University (formerly Ryerson University), Muslim students found recording devices behind the curtains of their prayer room.[30]

Muslim youth report looking over their shoulder, self-censoring, and modifying behaviours, speech, comportment, and clothing to avoid undue scrutiny in a post-9/11 context.[31] The panoptic gaze reinforces feelings of alterity and fuels the trauma that Muslim youth experience growing up under the spectre of suspicion.

The surveillance Muslims have endured since 9/11 has led to self-surveillance, whereby individuals try to avoid suspicion by second-guessing and curtailing otherwise innocent actions for fear they might be misread as subversive.[32] Maira observes that the "surveillance stories" the 9/11 generation of Muslim youth tell "help to do the regulatory work of surveillance in deepening anxieties and producing self-regulation among those who are objects of surveillance by virtue of their race, religion, nationality, citizenship status or political activities."[33] Michel Foucault describes this effect within a "panoptic society" where individuals are objectified as subjects under constant surveillance and in turn begin to regulate their own behaviour and actions in accordance with dominant norms.[34] He outlines how the regulatory gaze is inverted and interiorized so that the subjects themselves perform the work of governmental surveillance: "There is no need for arms, physical violence, material constraints. Just a gaze. An inspecting gaze, a gaze which each individual under its weight will end by interiorizing to the point that he is his own overseer, each individual thus exercising this surveillance over and against himself."[35]

I refer to this phenomenon as a "panopticon of self-surveillance" in which the external regulatory gaze is internalized, thereby leading to self-policing. For example, in my ethnographic study of the 9/11 generation,[36] youth participants were asked about how 9/11 impacted them since they all experienced this event and the Islamophobic backlash that ensued during their formative years. To my surprise, many stated that "9/11 didn't affect them." However, when I would then ask them questions about the kind of activities their youth groups were doing, I would hear examples explaining how their MSA decided not to go up north to play paintball because they did not want to appear as if they were running a jihadi training camp. But "9/11 didn't affect them." Some said that they stopped playing violent video games on their laptops when sitting in public spaces so that people would not fear they were engaging in a rehearsal for a violent attack. But "9/11 didn't affect them." It became clear that for the 9/11 generation, self-surveillance was a normative practice. These youth were not aware of a world where securitization didn't impact their lives, and they were socialized into accommodating these conditions.

The Nexus between Islamophobic Securitization and Recruitment to Extremist Groups

The nexus between Islamophobia and radicalization has been well-documented.[37] Racial and religious profiling as a strategy of CVE programs is counterproductive and has been shown to fuel a dialectic between Islamophobia and violent forms of Islamism and radicalization. Jihadist groups and the rhetoric and ideologies they promote operate in a symbiotic relationship with far-right extremism. Islamophobia fuels extremist logic on both sides (be it religious extremism or far-right political ideologies) and should be viewed as a threat to civil liberties and democratic values. The nexus between Islamophobia and radicalism (whether jihadist or far right) cannot be ignored and must be acknowledged by security agencies to work against this unintended consequence.

While there have been some cases of Canadian Muslim youth being drawn into reactionary extremist movements, such as with the arrest of the so-called Toronto 18 in 2006, the Parliament Hill shooting in 2014, as well as some cases where youth have been recruited as foreign fighters,[38] a wholesale focus on young Canadian Muslims as potential radicals can become a self-fulfilling prophecy. Islamophobic narratives that cast "dangerous Muslim men" as potential jihadis result in undue forms of targeting and racial and religious profiling.[39] These practices exacerbate the problems they aim to prevent. According to McKenzie, current security approaches to dealing with radicalization involve surveilling youth until they cross the line and then arresting them.[40] He asserts that with such tactics, "[it] is not inconceivable that an alienating CVE agenda could in fact create the very problem it sets out to solve."[41]

As a result of these securitized conditions, Muslims feel more reticent to report situations of Islamophobic bias they face when crossing borders.[42] The RCMP, Public Safety Canada, and CSIS have been reaching out to Muslim communities to be "partners in public safety," engaging in community roundtables as well as actively recruiting Muslims into their ranks. These initiatives speak to an interest in winning the "hearts and minds" of young Muslims to make sure they do not end up on a path of radicalization, and yet these community forums are led by the very agencies policing and surveilling Muslims, which undermines the trust they hope to gain.

Ending the vicious cycle between Islamophobia and radicalization involves security agencies taking seriously the notion that by focusing their attention disproportionately on Muslim communities, post-9/11 security measures are reproducing the conditions that heighten tensions and create unintended and counterproductive consequences. As a result of these short-sighted tactics, the 9/11 generation of Canadian Muslim youth feel themselves "under siege" having come of age in an era where anti-Muslim racism has been normalized by state policies and practices. Twenty years after the 9/11 attacks, it is important to take stock of Islamophobia and its impact on Muslim communities who are rendered suspect. It is also imperative that we remain attentive to how resurgent anti-Muslim narratives provide the ideological underpinning for state violence, ethnic cleansing, and genocide against Muslims globally. Security agencies must dismantle practices that rely on racial and religious profiling or else they will continue to fuel the pernicious effects and consequences that foment anti-Muslim hate and violence.

NOTES

1 Jasmin Zine, *Under Siege: Islamophobia and the 9/11 Generation* (Montreal: McGill-Queen's University Press, 2022), 14. See also Jasmin Zine, ed., *Islam in the Hinterlands: Muslim Cultural Politics in Canada* (Vancouver:

UBC Press, 2012). The aftermath of the 9/11 phase of Islamophobic history has made "Muslimness" salient for those who would otherwise not identify with the category due to a lack of religiosity or more secular lifestyle preferences. For these more culturally affiliated Muslims (i.e., those who acknowledge a cultural connection to Islam but eschew religious practice), or even those who identify as atheists and distance themselves from Islam, they are nonetheless still affected by Islamophobia by virtue of racial affiliation with and origins in Muslim countries, or by their Muslim-sounding names. People misidentified and perceived to be Muslim have also suffered the impact and violence of Islamophobia. For example, Balbir Singh Sodhi, a Sikh man mistaken for an Arab Muslim because of his turban, was killed in reprisal for the 9/11 attacks.

2 Haley Ott, "As Afghanistan Crisis Worsens, Europe Adopts Less Welcoming Stance towards Refugees," *CBS News*, 13 September 2021, https://www.cbsnews.com/news/afghanistan-taliban-crisis-europe-less-welcoming-stance-refugees/.

3 Shaista Patel, "The Anti-terrorism Act and National Security: Safeguarding the Nation against Uncivilized Muslims," in Zine, *Islam in The Hinterlands*, 272–98.

4 Jacqueline Flatt, "The Security Certificate Exception: A Media Analysis of Human Rights and Security Discourses in Canada's *Globe and Mail* and *National Post*," in Zine, *Islam in the Hinterlands*, 239–71.

5 Uzma Jamil, "Can Muslims Fly? The No-Fly List as a Tool of the 'War on Terror,'" *Islamophobia Studies Journal* 4, no. 1 (2017): 72–86, https://doi.org/10.13169/islastudj.4.1.0072.

6 The #NoFlyListKids website documents stories of children like Adam who are flagged as security threats. See "#NoFlyListKids – Canadian Children Falsely Flagged as Security Threats," accessed 25 March 2024, https://noflylistkids.ca/en/home/.

7 The federal government has proposed changes to rectify the passenger-screening processes that have resulted in people being falsely named on the No Fly List. See for example Jim Bronskill, "Families with Kids Ensnared by No-Fly List Invited to Test Federal Remedy," *CTV News*, 11 February 2020, https://www.ctvnews.ca/canada/families-with-kids-ensnared-by-no-fly-list-invited-to-test-federal-remedy-1.4806375. These measures came through the advocacy of members of #NoFlyListKids,

8 Tim McSorley, *The CRA's Prejudiced Audits: Counter-Terrorism and the Targeting of Muslim Charities in Canada* (Toronto: Canadian Civil Liberties Monitoring Group, 2021), 3, https://iclmg.ca/wp-content/uploads/2021/06/Prejudiced-Audits-ICLMG-2021.pdf.
9 Faisal Kutty and Faisal Bhabha, "The Problem of Systemic Bias in CRA Audits," *Philanthropist Journal*, 27 March 2023, https://thephilanthropist.ca/2023/03/the-problem-of-systemic-bias-in-cra-audits/.
10 Kutty and Bhabha, "The Problem of Systemic Bias in CRA Audits."
11 Roger Boisvert, "National Muslim Charity Launching Legal Challenge of CRA Audit, Calling It Islamophobic," *CBC News*, 13 April 2022, https://www.cbc.ca/news/politics/mac-cra-charter-challenge-1.6417684.
12 Zine, *Under Siege*.
13 Ben Hayes, *Arming Big Brother: The EU's Security Research Programme* (Amsterdam: Transnational Institute, April 2006), https://www.statewatch.org/publications/reports-and-books/arming-big-brother-the-eu-s-security-research-programme/.
14 Military organizations dominate research and development in these areas under the banner of "security research" and "dual-use" technology, avoiding both the constraints and controversies of the arms trade.
15 Tahir Abbas, *Islamophobia and Radicalization: A Vicious Cycle* (London: Hurst & Co., 2019); Tahir Abbas and Imran Awan, "Limits of UK Counterterrorism Policy and Its Implications for Islamophobia and Far Right Extremism," *International Journal for Crime, Justice and Social Democracy* 4, no. 3 (2015): 16–29, https://doi.org/10.5204/ijcjsd.v4i3.241.
16 Zine, *Under Siege*.
17 Khyati Y. Joshi, *New Roots in America's Sacred Ground: Religion, Race, and Ethnicity in Indian America* (New Brunswick, NJ: Rutgers University Press, 2006).
18 Giorgio Agamben, *State of Exception* (Chicago: University of Chicago Press, 2005).
19 See Robert Diab, *Guantánamo North: Terrorism and the Administration of Justice in Canada* (Black Point, NS: Fernwood, 2008); Flatt, "The Security Certificate Exception"; Patel, "The Anti-Terrorism Act and National Security."

who have been pressing the government for several years to change this discriminatory system.

20 See also Nadia Fadil, Martijn de Koning, and Francesco Ragazzi, *Radicalization in Belgium and the Netherlands: Critical Perspectives on Violence and Security* (London: I.B. Tauris, 2019).
21 The UK Counter-Terrorism and Security Act (2015) places a Prevent duty on early years settings "to have due regard to the need to prevent people from being drawn into terrorism." To demonstrate conformity, the act outlines the following: staff are encouraged to identify children who may be vulnerable to radicalization and know what to do when they are identified; assess the risk of children being drawn into terrorism; and work with local partners such as the police, Prevent coordinators, Channel police practitioners, and their Local Safeguarding Children Board to take account of local risks and respond appropriately. See also Katy Pal Sian, "Spies, Surveillance and Stakeouts: Monitoring Muslim Moves in British State Schools," *Race Ethnicity and Education* 18, no. 2 (2015): 183–201.
22 Jay Stanley, *The Surveillance Industrial Complex: How the American Government Is Conscripting Businesses and Individuals in the Construction of a Surveillance Society* (New York: American Civil Liberties Union, 2004).
23 See also "Eagle Eyes Program Urges People to Say Something If They See Something," Joint Base San Antonio, 9 December 2019, www.jbsa.mil/News/News/Article/2035476/eagle-eyes-program-urges-people-to-say-something-if-they-see-something/.
24 "Eagle Eyes Program Urges People to Say Something."
25 Stanley, *The Surveillance Industrial Complex*, 4.
26 See Canada Centre for Community Engagement and Prevention of Violence, *National Strategy on Countering Radicalization to Violence* (Ottawa: Canada Centre for Community Engagement and Prevention of Violence, 2018, https://www.publicsafety.gc.ca/cnt/rsrcs/pblctns/ntnl-strtg-cntrng-rdclztn-vlnc/index-en.aspx#s82.
27 Tahir Abbas, *Islamic Radicalism and Multicultural Politics: The British Experience* (London: Routledge, 2011); Abbas, *Islamophobia and Radicalization*; Deepa Kumar, *Islamophobia and the Politics of Empire* (Chicago: Haymarket Books, 2012).
28 Zine, *Islam in the Hinterlands*.
29 Josie Kao, "Muslim Students' Association Says Executives Receiving Surprise Visits from Law Enforcement," *The Varsity*, 13 November 2018,

https://thevarsity.ca/2018/11/12/muslim-students-association-says-executives-receiving-surprise-visits-from-law-enforcement/.
30 Baljit Nagra, *Securitized Citizens: Canadian Muslims' Experiences of Race Relations and Identity Formation Post-9/11* (Toronto: University of Toronto Press, 2017).
31 Zine, *Under Siege*.
32 Zine.
33 Sunaina Marr Maira, *The 9/11 Generation: Youth, Rights, and Solidarity in the War on Terror* (New York: New York University Press, 2016), 201.
34 Michel Foucault, "The Subject and Power," in *Power: Essential Works of Foucault, 1954–1984*, ed. James D. Faubion (New York: New Press, 1994).
35 Foucault, "The Subject and Power," 155.
36 Zine, *Under Siege*.
37 Abbas, *Islamophobia and Radicalization*; Abbas and Awan, "Limits of UK Counterterrorism Policy."
38 John Monahan, Rima Berns-McGown, and Michael Morden. *The Perception and Reality of "Imported Conflict" in Canada* (Toronto: Mosaic Institute, 2014).
39 Sherene Razack, *Casting Out: The Eviction of Muslims from Western Law and Politics* (Toronto: University of Toronto Press), 2008.
40 Robert L. McKenzie, "Day 2 Keynote Address," in *Youth Resiliency: Hate, Racism and Youth Radicalization Report: Midaynta Community Services 3rd Annual Conference Report* (Toronto: Midaynta Community Services, 2018), 11.
41 McKenzie, "Day 2 Keynote Address," 11.
42 Nagra, *Securitized Citizens*.

chapter fifteen

Refugees and Security in Canada: Invisibility, Crisis, and Discretion

LAMA MOURAD[1]

The idea that refugees and migrants pose potential threats to states and their citizens has become deeply entrenched in contemporary understandings of state security, both in the media and in scholarly work.[2] By all accounts, this is a relatively novel development in our collective understanding of "security,"[3] and, as the response to the displacement of millions of Ukrainians across Europe and to Canada starting in 2022 shows, not a necessary one. While Canada was a relative "latecomer to the securitarian world,"[4] it has quickly "caught up" with other countries in the Global North in its response to asylum-seekers. Unlike the United States and much of Europe, it continues nonetheless to benefit from significant reputational power – in the words of the UN high commissioner for refugees – as a country with "extraordinary generosity" towards refugees.[5]

This chapter demonstrates how Canada's policies related to asylum-seekers and refugees are built on a duality that can only be understood holistically: on the one hand, Canada has relatively strong protections for the refugees and asylum-seekers who make it to Canada either following an exacting selection process or by overcoming significant and growing hurdles; on the other hand, it adopts a highly securitized approach that aims to keep the majority of refugees and asylum-seekers from reaching Canadian territory in the first place. In addition to the extensive geographic "buffers" that Canada already possesses, it has long-established legal and bureaucratic hurdles – which, in fact, continue to expand – to accessing its territory and claiming asylum. This dual trend was further reinforced in 2023 with the Trudeau-Biden agreement that extended the scope of the Safe Third Country Agreement (STCA) to the entirety of the Canada-US border and water crossings, in exchange for Canada's provision of fifteen thousand additional spots "on a humanitarian basis" for migrants from South and Central America, whom the state will have much discretion in selecting. Only days after this agreement came into force, its effect in pushing migrants and asylum-seekers to more dangerous crossings was made all too apparent with the death of eight people attempting to cross into the United States via the St. Lawrence River.[6] The special program for South and Central American migrants is emblematic of a growing practice of ad hoc responses to specific humanitarian crises that provide pathways – increasingly differentiated – for civilians in need of protection, only further reinforcing the discretionary nature of Canada's response to displacement worldwide.

The turn towards securitized policies on a global scale has occurred during a period of large-scale displacement, with the number of displaced persons worldwide more than doubling over the last decade, reaching a high of over 117 million by the end of 2023. While this increase speaks in part to our ability to track and measure displacement more accurately, it is undoubtable that the world's displaced population has continued to grow due to the intensity and intractability of conflicts around the globe. In 2023, the resurgence of conflict in Sudan and the Israel-Hamas war in Gaza resulted yet again in massive numbers of forcibly displaced people. Throughout this period, some overall patterns of displacement have remained the same – in particular the fact that the majority of forcibly displaced persons live in the Global South, either as internally displaced persons within their own states or in neighbouring countries. Refugees from the Global South face very limited safe and legal pathways to access protection in countries in the Global North. Canada's asylum and refugee policies, and their possible future incarnations, should be read against this important backdrop. It bears mentioning that while Canada's so-called generosity is often heralded relative to other countries in the Global North, it pales in comparison to the differential hosting responsibility that countries in the Global South, such as Lebanon, Uganda, and Colombia, have taken on.[7]

By the late 1990s, and especially after 9/11, Canada began to make its most profound shift towards a clear "security-control" paradigm, drawing on policy ideas from allies, in what has been termed a "European turn" in Canada's immigration and refugee policy.[8] The attacks of 9/11 aligned Canadian and US interests in "securing the border" and galvanized the adoption of the STCA, which became a cornerstone of Canada's securitized asylum framework.[9] As Zine discusses in this volume, policies and narratives of securitization during this period also had significant consequences on domestic populations, particularly on Muslim youth within the country. However, Canada continued to benefit from its reputation as a hospitable country for immigrants and refugees. This reputation is built on both historic and contemporary episodes. For instance, the Nansen Refugee Award, given by the Office of the United Nations High Commissioner for Refugees (UNHCR) to honour "individuals, groups and organizations who go above and beyond the call of duty to protect refugees," was granted to the Canadian people in 1986 for their response to the plight of Indochinese refugees, in the first and only instance so far of an entire nation being recognized.[10] In 2016, UNHCR applauded Canada's remarkable efforts in resettling 25,000 Syrian refugees, a notable departure from the lower refugee quotas of the years prior. By comparison, the United States, which historically has been the country with the largest resettlement program in the world, accepted approximately 12,500 Syrian refugees that year, a number that plummeted after the passage of President Trump's notorious 2017 executive orders known colloquially as the "Muslim Ban."[11]

The unparalleled speed and scope of Canada's response to displaced Ukrainians in 2022 casts further light on its relatively limited response to refugees displaced by conflicts in the Global South, even those "remarkable" examples such as the case of 25,000 Syrian refugees cited above. Within a month of Russia's invasion of Ukraine in February 2022, Canada announced that an "unlimited" number of Ukrainians would be eligible for a free, fast-tracked temporary residence visa that would provide them with open work permits (three years) and an "expedited path" towards permanent residency.¹² By November 2023, over 200,000 Ukrainians had arrived in Canada under this program. Both the breadth and speed of this program were quickly juxtaposed with stalled efforts to bring in 40,000 Afghan refugees, as per the Canadian government's commitment in 2021 after the Taliban seized power, whose arrivals were delayed by both logistical as well as bureaucratic hurdles.¹³

From a humanitarian and rights perspective, Canada's refugee and asylum policy is notable on a global level in at least three respects. First, Canada has been and continues to be among the world's largest recipients of resettled refugees, briefly even overtaking the United States as the largest resettlement country from 2018 to 2019.¹⁴ Second, Canada is considered a "pioneer" of private sponsorship–based resettlement, whereby individuals or community groups and organizations can sponsor (through financial support) individuals or families. It has the world's longest-standing program of private sponsorship, one that has served as an increasingly popular model for other states.¹⁵ Third, Canada's refugee-determination process is among the most robust in the world, providing asylum-seekers with access to an appeals process and a pre-removal risk assessment, and it benefits from relatively strong insulation from partisan politics.¹⁶ Nonetheless, important critiques of the Canadian system include the arbitrariness of adjudicator decisions at the Immigration and Refugee Board and the process by which judges review appeals at the Federal Court, as well as the privileging of "efficiency" over "fairness" in this process.¹⁷

Simultaneously, Canada is among the world's leaders in extraterritorial controls on migration,¹⁸ being the first country to develop a network of immigration control officers in the 1990s, which served to make it increasingly difficult for asylum-seekers to access Canadian territory through activities such as training airline personnel and local officials abroad on identifying improper travel documents and adopting carrier sanctions against airlines that allow travellers with improper documentation to arrive to Canada.¹⁹ As Mountz argues, for the most part, these policies "ha[ve] happened quietly, under the radar of otherwise well-informed international audiences and the Canadian public."[20] While it is often argued that Canada's public discourse remains largely devoid of securitized fears of refugees and asylum-seekers, the alarmist rhetoric that emerged as a result of the increase between 2017 and 2020 in the number of "irregular arrivals"[21] (i.e., asylum-seekers entering Canada outside recognized ports of entry) may be explained in part by the country having one of the most managed flows of refugees and asylum-seekers globally.

Arguably, the most effective strategy of interdiction has been the adoption of the STCA with the United States in 2002 (and which went into effect in 2004). Until March 2023, the STCA effectively barred asylum-seekers and refugees coming from the United States, with limited exceptions, from lodging a refugee recognition claim at land-based ports of entry. Prior to the adoption of the STCA, between 1995 and 2001, around one-third of refugee claimants in Canada entered at the US-Canada border.[22] The STCA thus had the near-immediate effect of more than halving the number of asylum claims made at the border the following year. As a report published by the Wilson Center states, "[w]hile some of the reduced claims at ports of entry may be the result of claimants heading inland, the overall trend is clear: the STCA caused total asylum claims (inland + port of entry) to decrease."[23] The agreement has been the subject of numerous legal challenges and appeals, the first lodged in 2006. Most recently, in October 2022, the Supreme Court of Canada heard arguments on the constitutionality of the STCA, following the appeal of a Federal Court decision in July 2020 that struck the agreement down for violating the Canadian Charter of Rights and Freedoms.[24] In reaching a decision in 2023, the Supreme Court ultimately did not settle definitively the constitutionality of the STCA, but sent the section 15 challenge (related to equality) back to the lower courts. The matter will undoubtedly continue to be of major importance in the near future, particularly as asylum and border policy in the United States continues to be a subject of major political debate and volatility.

The STCA was brought back into the limelight with the election of Donald Trump in 2016. As the United States restricted the arrival of refugees, asylum-seekers, and others who benefited from temporary protection (like Haitian migrants), Canada was faced with increased demands for protection as many of these groups were targets of Trump's rhetoric and eventually his policies. This drove a rapid spike in the number of people who crossed into Canada outside "regular ports of entry" in order to avoid activating the STCA.[25] Historically, so-called spontaneous arrivals – in particular, those arriving by boat – have served to mobilize support for the adoption of policies and legislation that further criminalize asylum-seekers in Canada. With the arrival in 2009 and 2010 of Tamil refugees by boat, suspected (though ultimately unfounded) ties between the refugees and the Liberation Tigers of Tamil Eelam were leveraged as justification for the adoption of new legislation that targeted, among other things, so-called irregular maritime arrivals (defined as a group numbering two or more arriving by boat).[26] Those found to have been "smuggled" faced mandatory detention and severe restrictions, such as a five-year bar from applying for permanent residence or sponsoring family members, even if later recognized as refugees.[27] The fact that these arrivals represented a remarkably small percentage of asylum-seekers in the country (less than 2 per cent in 2010), coupled with the stark "lack of evidence tying the passengers with terrorist organizations,"[28] reveals Canada's pattern of never "let[ting] a good crisis go to waste."[29]

The election of Trump as US president set off one such crisis, as it also affected other critical aspects of Canadian security and the international order (see Norrlöf in this volume). While undoubtedly not the only driver, the election was followed by a relatively significant increase in the number of asylum-seekers crossing at "irregular" border crossings, most notably at the unofficial border crossing of Roxham Road in Quebec.[30] In response, Canada adopted provisions that barred access to the regular refugee system to anyone who had previously "made a claim" in any of the Five Eyes nations.[31] Going further, at the outset of COVID-19, the Canadian government designated Roxham Road as a "port of entry" for the purposes of the STCA and coordinated with the United States to "direct back" any asylum-seekers who attempted to cross.[32] While this designation was repealed in November 2021 when the

US-Canadian border reopened,³³ and following significant pressure from refugee advocates, an additional protocol rendered it irrelevant. Signed in March 2023, the new regulation extends the applicability of the STCA to the entirety of the US-Canada border, including water crossings, and prohibits asylum-seekers crossing the US-Canada border from making a refugee claim within fourteen days of crossing.³⁴ This effectively pushes asylum-seekers to take more dangerous and remote routes where they are less likely to encounter police or border officers, and grants significant discretion to the Canada Border Services Agency or the Royal Canadian Mounted Police in determining whether or not a person has crossed within that time period.

Critically, two of Canada's most-heralded policies in support of refugees – namely, its commitment to global resettlement and its path-breaking sponsorship programs – provide the state with a great deal of control and discretion and raise important concerns about the future of state-funded refugee protection. Canada's focus on resettlement as the main pillar of its refugee program has allowed it to be highly selective when determining which refugees it brings to its territory. Canada is not unique in this regard. Indeed, this forms part of a pattern in the Global North, where states have aimed to blur the boundaries between refugees and asylum-seekers, on the one hand, and economic migrants on the other – providing governments with both greater control over refugees and the possibility of using resettlement as yet another immigration track.³⁵ One of the most notable examples of this in Canada is the inclusion of an additional criterion – namely, a refugee's ability to "successfully integrate" – in its selection of refugees eligible for resettlement. UNHCR, for its part, has taken issue with these provisions, stating in 2000 that it

> believes that "integration potential" should not be a determining factor in the selection of refugees for resettlement ... If Canada's refugee resettlement program is definitively to disentangle itself from Canada's immigration program, then, in UNHCR's view, *it must distance itself as much as possible from immigration criteria.*³⁶

At times, the use of additional criteria in the resettlement process has led to accusations of discrimination against certain groups of refugees, such as Muslims. For instance, in October 2015, then Conservative Party leader and prime minister Stephen Harper admitted to having placed a priority on resettling "primarily Christians and other religious minorities" from Syria, despite the fact that the vast majority of Syrian refugees were Muslim.[37] While the language used for this criterion has changed over the last few years from "successfully integrate" to the applicant's "ability to establish" themselves in the country, it remains unclear whether its application has shifted; guidelines for determining this criteria include the applicant's "potential for being resourceful," "potential for employment," as well as their potential to learn one of Canada's official languages.[38] Its ambiguity continues to allow the Canadian government to prioritize refugees for resettlement that are more "attractive" vis-à-vis the country's stated priorities, whether they be economic or otherwise.[39]

Canada's private sponsorship model also raises important concerns regarding the long-term support for state-funded refugee protection. First formalized and introduced into legislation as part of the 1976 Immigration Act, the program itself is composed of two main streams: a purely private stream, and a "blended" stream in which private individuals split the costs of sponsorship with the state.[40] Both the Indochinese and Syrian experiences demonstrate that in times characterized by high levels of civil society mobilization and government interest, the program can bring in large numbers of refugees with a great deal of public support.[41] Between 1979 and 1981, Canadians sponsored nearly thirty-five thousand refugees from Vietnam, Cambodia, and Laos – more than those brought in through the government-assisted resettlement program.[42] As mentioned above, it was on this basis that Canada (and Canadians) were awarded the Nansen Award. Similarly, between 2015 and 2018, over twenty-five thousand Syrians were resettled through a form of private sponsorship.[43]

While public support for private sponsorship remains high in Canada, advocates and sponsors fear that reliance on the program may allow governments to de-prioritize state-funded resettlement and shift responsibility onto private citizens. If private sponsors do not pick up this responsibility in turn, governments can rely on this reluctance as "evidence" of a lack of appetite on the part of the Canadian public for further resettlement. The principle of "additionality" – whereby private sponsorship should be in addition to, and separate from, government commitments – is considered a key pillar of the Canadian model. However, it has been threatened in practice numerous times. For instance, an over-reliance on private sponsors was undeniably the backbone of the Conservative government's response to calls for resettling Syrian refugees. Up until 2015, the overwhelming majority of the nearly 1,300 Syrians approved for resettlement to Canada were privately sponsored, with the government only supporting 360. In 2015, following calls from UNHCR, the government committed to an additional 10,000 Syrian refugee spots but held that 60 per cent of those would be brought in through the private system – with no prior consultation with private sponsorship agreement holders.[44]

In addition to the concern that private sponsorship may serve as a smokescreen for the de-funding of government-led resettlement, resettlement more broadly can serve to render more palatable restrictions in other areas of refugee and asylum policy that the state may be more invested in limiting. This was particularly apparent in 2010 when the Canadian government announced a package of legislation aimed at "reforming" Canada's refugee and asylum system, which included a number of provisions that concerned advocates as they were prefaced with mention of an increase to Canada's resettlement program of up to 2,500 spaces per year.[45] Notably, 80 per cent of these new allotments would also have to be filled by private sponsors.[46]

As this chapter has demonstrated, Canada's refugee and asylum policies can only be understood as bifurcated, relying on "generosity" in areas where the state has substantial discretion, alongside (and serving to justify) highly securitized and restrictive measures in those areas where it faces the potential of "uncontrolled" displacement. What is also clear is that Canada is not alone in this regard – it learns from peer countries in the Global North, and its own models are emulated by these same countries.

For instance, as Ukrainians began fleeing the Russian invasion in February 2022, the European Union activated the 2001 Temporary Protection Directive (TPD) for the first time since its enactment, despite numerous calls for its use in the cases of migrants and refugees arriving in the European Union from countries such as Syria, whose citizens were also fleeing war. The TPD, much like Canada's policy towards Ukrainians, allows Ukrainians to work in addition to granting them the possibility of applying for asylum. While these responses are laudable, they remain the exception to the existing trend of interdiction and deterrence – what Fitzgerald calls "the architecture of repulsion"[47] – that dominates the approach of countries in the Global North to asylum, which up until recently was directed primarily at populations from the Global South. This "unequal solidarity" makes a powerful case for how the securitization of asylum in the Global North is at least in part an institutionalized manifestation of racism.[48] In Canada, while there are likely a number of drivers explaining the unprecedented nature of the response to Ukrainian refugees, including the strength of Ukrainian diaspora networks, many have also identified the racialization of Afghans and systemic racism as undeniable factors in contrasting the response to the needs of civilians in both contexts.[49]

The proliferation of ad hoc "humanitarian pathways" only raises further questions regarding the inconsistency between different responses to crises and concerns with a splintering of the country's response to displaced populations worldwide. Canada has a long history of resettling refugees through special programs, with the responses to Indochinese and Syrian refugees being perhaps the most noteworthy examples. Unlike the latter, however, these new pathways have been separated from traditional resettlement processes and include different rights as well as conditions.

Most recently, major concerns have been raised by advocates regarding the government's programs for Palestinians fleeing the war in Gaza and for Sudanese fleeing the conflict in their country. In both cases, the programs developed require applicants to have family members in Canada who can help support them, are capped at relatively low numbers, particularly given the overwhelming need, and include significant processing hurdles. In the case of the measures for Palestinians from Gaza, the government plan, announced nearly three months after the outbreak of the war, provides temporary (a maximum of three years) residency for up to a thousand Palestinians currently in Gaza who have Canadian family members capable of supporting them during their time in Canada. While the temporary nature of the program may be tied to concerns that such efforts could potentially facilitate the permanent forced displacement of Gazans from the Gaza Strip,[50] the temporary pathway for Ukrainians included a provision of eligibility for permanent residency at a later point, which was notably absent in the Gaza program. In addition, other conditions, including the eligibility criteria, fees, financial support required, and the extensive background information and biometric testing, as well as technical hurdles required in the visa process itself, means that the Gaza program is subject to claims of unequal treatment in comparison to the Ukrainian response.[51] As of April 2024, despite the nearly one thousand applications submitted within weeks of the program being announced, very few applications had been approved, and not a single Palestinian from Gaza had arrived to Canada under the program. Family members of Canadians are reported to have died while waiting for their files to be processed.[52] Some of the requirements of the program, including invasive and unprecedented disclosure of personal information, such as explaining scars and/or injuries, are particularly reflective of the "security-control" paradigm highlighted above. The expanding use of special programs may herald an increased disconnection between refugee resettlement, on the one hand, and "humanitarian pathways," on the other, with the latter providing the state with even greater discretion and less established rights.

Nonetheless, the need for protection for refugees and other migrants is unlikely to diminish – and more refugees are likely to need safe refuge in the years to come, which may ultimately require additional mechanisms and pathways. A lesson to be learned from the Canadian context is that sustained and engaged public pressure and the work of strong civil society advocacy groups – the kind of work that maintains the principle of "additionality" in private sponsorship, for instance, and that continues to highlight the inconsistencies across different "humanitarian pathways" – can help transform government policy in this arena. Canada, as Mountz highlights, relies in part on the public invisibility of its restrictive measures.[53] More recently, civil society pushed for and ultimately succeeded in getting the Canadian government to include a refugee adviser in Canada's delegation to the Global Refugee Forum in 2019; this was subsequently made official policy in June 2020 for future delegations to meetings of the global refugee regime. While still in its early days, this practice has already been emulated by other countries of the Global North, like Germany and the United States in 2021.[54]

As evidenced by the continued challenges against the STCA and the success in undoing the Designated Countries of Origin list, public advocacy is perhaps most effective when coupled with legal challenges. Similar strategies have shown some success in challenging the "architecture of repulsion," not just in Canada but across the Global North, thereby linking legal challenges with transnational advocacy. In a landmark case, *Hirsi Jamaa and Others v. Italy*, which concerned the interception by Italian authorities of Somali and Eritrean nationals who were then handed over to Libyan authorities in the port of Tripoli, the European Court of Human Rights unanimously found the Italian state in violation of the European Convention of Human Rights. In making its decision, the court relied on testimony and reports from a wide array of actors, including UNHCR, Human Rights Watch, the Columbia Law School Human Rights Clinic, the Aire Centre, Amnesty International, the International Federation for Human Rights, and the Council of Europe's Committee for the Prevention of Torture.[55]

While the intertwining of security and forced displacement may appear firmly entrenched, the widespread political and social mobilization for the protection of displaced Ukrainians has shown that it is not inevitable. Rather, this may open space for greater advocacy and legal challenges that help ensure that access to asylum is maintained and strengthened alongside, and not in contrast with, generosity in other areas of refugee protection. The effectiveness of legal challenges, however, may be more limited in areas where existing rights are not established for those seeking protection, such as in the case of ad hoc programs that do not categorize applicants as refugees or asylum-seekers. For that reason, greater public scrutiny and pressure to harmonize these approaches remain the primary bulwark against making refugee and asylum response in Canada subject to even higher levels of political opportunism and governmental discretion.

NOTES

1 The author would like to thank Alison Gondosch for her research assistance on this chapter, as well as Dr. Rawan Arar, Emilio Rodriguez Romero, and Fatima Mourad, and the anonymous reviewers for their comments. Any mistakes remain the author's own.
2 For examples from the media, see Franco Ordoñez, "Authoritarians Are Using Migrants as Weapons. The White House Frets It's on the Rise," *NPR*, 13 December 2021, https://www.npr.org/2021/12/13/1062794948/authoritarians-migrants-weapons-white-house-worries; "Why Is Belarus Using Migrants as 'Weapons' against the EU?," *Al Jazeera*, 18 November 2021, https://www.aljazeera.com/program/the-stream/2021/11/18/is-belarus-using-migrants-as-weapons-against-the-eu. Scholarly accounts include Myron Weiner, "Security, Stability, and International Migration," *International Security* 17, no. 3 (1992–3): 91–126; Kelly M. Greenhill, *Weapons of Mass Migration: Forced Displacement, Coercion, and Foreign Policy* (Ithaca, NY: Cornell University Press, 2010); Idean Salehyan and Kristian Skrede Gleditsch, "Refugees and the Spread of Civil War," *International Organization* 60, no. 02 (2006), https://doi.org/10.1017/S0020818306060103.
3 Anne Hammerstadt, "The Securitization of Forced Migration," in *The Oxford Handbook of Refugee and Forced Migration Studies*, ed. Elena Fiddian-Qasmiyeh, Gil Loescher, Katy Long, and Nando Sigona (Oxford: Oxford University Press, 2014), 265–77.
4 Dagmar Soennecken, "Shifting Up and Back: The European Turn in Canadian Refugee Policy," *Comparative Migration Studies* 2, no. 1 (2014): 103, https://doi.org/10.5117/CMS2014.1.SOEN.
5 Lauren La Rose, "UN High Commissioner for Refugees Praises Canada for 'Extraordinary Generosity,'" UN Refugee Agency, 26 February 2018,

https://www.unhcr.ca/news/un-high-commissioner-refugees-praises-canada-extraordinary-generosity/.

6   Jay Heisler, "US-Canada Border Deal Faces Criticism after River Deaths," *VoA News*, 6 April 2023, https://www.voanews.com/a/us-canada-border-deal-faces-criticism-after-river-deaths/7039846.html.

7   For an analysis of the situation in Lebanon, see Lama Mourad, "Open Borders, Local Closures: Decentralization and the Politics of Local Responses to the Syrian Refugee Influx in Lebanon" (PhD diss., University of Toronto, 2019).

8   Idil Atak and François Crépeau, "The Securitization of Asylum and Human Rights in Canada and the European Union," in *Contemporary Issues in Refugee Law*, ed. Satvinder Singh Juss and Colin Harvey (Cheltenham, UK: Edward Elgar, 2013), 227–57; Soennecken, "Shifting Up and Back"; J.A. Sandy Irvine, "Canadian Refugee Policy: Understanding the Role of International Bureaucratic Networks in Domestic Paradigm Change," in *Policy Paradigms, Transnationalism, and Domestic Politics*, ed. Grace Skogstad (Toronto: University of Toronto Press, 2011), 171–201.

9   Audrey Macklin, "Disappearing Refugees: Reflections on the Canada-U.S. Safe Third Country Agreement," *Columbia Human Rights Law Review* 36, no. 2 (2005): 365–426; Soennecken, "Shifting Up and Back."

10 "U.N. Awards Medal to Canada for Its Contributions to Cause of Refugees," *Los Angeles Times*, 7 October 1986, https://www.latimes.com/archives/la-xpm-1986-10-07-mn-5066-story.html.

11 Molly Fee and Rawan Arar, "What Happens When the United States Stops Taking in Refugees?," *Contexts* 18, no. 2 (2019): 18–23, https://doi.org/10.1177/1536504219854713.

12 John Paul Tasker, "Canada Prepared to Welcome an 'Unlimited Number' of Ukrainians Fleeing War, Minister Says," *CBC News*, 3 March 2022, https://www.cbc.ca/news/politics/canada-unlimited-number-ukrainians-1.6371288.

13 Laura Marchand, "Canada Promised to Bring in 40,000 Afghan Refugees. Only 8,500 Have Arrived," *CBC News*, 13 March 2022, https://www.cbc.ca/news/canada/montreal/ukraine-afghan-refugees-1.6381826.

14 *The History of Resettlement: Celebrating 25 Years of the ATCR* (Geneva: UN Refugee Agency, 2019), 24, https://www.unhcr.org/5d1633657.pdf; "Global Refugee Statistics," UNHCR, accessed 7 December 2021, https://www.unhcr.ca/in-canada/refugee-statistics/. Figures for 2020

are impacted by the halting of resettlement programs due to COVID-19 and the subsequent closure of the border. During this period, the United States and Canada had comparable figures, with Canada resettling 9,228 individuals and the United States 9,586.
15 For instance, the United States has started a program to support Afghan refugees through private sponsorship. See Stef W. Knight, "U.S. Will Now Allow Private Citizens to Sponsor Afghan Refugees," *Axios*, 25 October 2021, https://www.axios.com/2021/10/25/afghan-refugee-private-sponsorship-biden.
16 Rebecca Hamlin, "International Law and Administrative Insulation: A Comparison of Refugee Status Determination Regimes in the United States, Canada, and Australia," *Law & Social Inquiry* 37, no. 4 (2012): 933–68, https://doi.org/10.1111/j.1747-4469.2012.01292.x.
17 Sean Rehaag, "Judicial Review of Refugee Determinations: The Luck of the Draw?," *Queen's Law Journal* 38, no. 1 (2012): 1–58; Dagmar Soennecken, "The Managerialization of Refugee Determinations in Canada," *Droit et société* 84, no. 2 (2013): 291, https://doi.org/10.3917/drs.084.0291.
18 Thomas Gammeltoft-Hansen, *Access to Asylum: International Refugee Law and the Globalisation of Migration Control* (Cambridge: Cambridge University Press, 2011); David FitzGerald, *Refuge beyond Reach: How Rich Democracies Repel Asylum Seekers* (New York: Oxford University Press, 2019).
19 Alison Mountz, *The Death of Asylum: Hidden Geographies of the Enforcement Archipelago* (Minneapolis: University of Minnesota Press, 2020), 51; François Crépeau and Delphine Nakache, "Controlling Irregular Migration in Canada: Reconciling Security Concerns with Human Rights Protection," *IRPP Choices* 12, no. 1 (2006), https://irpp.org/wp-content/uploads/assets/research/diversity-immigration-and-integration/new-research-article-4/vol12no1.pdf; Gammeltoft-Hansen, *Access to Asylum*, 160n3.
20 Mountz, *The Death of Asylum*, 167.
21 For more on the construction of the category of "irregular arrivals" in the Canadian context, see Basia D. Ellis, "The Production of Irregular Migration in Canada," *Canadian Ethnic Studies* 47, no. 2 (2015): 93–112, https://doi.org/10.1353/ces.2015.0011.
22 Macklin, "Disappearing Refugees," 394.

23 Benn Proctor, "Fleeing to Canada on Foot: Reviewing the Canada-U.S. Safe Third Country Agreement," Wilson Center, 4 April 2017, 5, https://www.wilsoncenter.org/sites/default/files/media/documents/article/fleeing_to_canada_on_foot_stca_final_04-04-2017.pdf.
24 Canadian Council for Refugees, Amnesty International, and the Canadian Council of Churches, "Leading Human Rights Groups Challenge Safe Third Country Agreement at Supreme Court of Canada," Canadian Council for Refugees, 4 October 2022, https://ccrweb.ca/en/media/stca-scc-hearing-oct-2022.
25 Mireille Paquet and Robert Schertzer, *Irregular Border Crossings and Asylum Seekers in Canada: A Complex Intergovernmental Problem* (Montreal: Institute for Research on Public Policy, 2020).
26 This includes Bill C-11, "An Act to Amend the Immigration and Refugee Protection Act and the Federal Courts Act," 3rd sess., 40th Parliament, 2010, https://www.parl.ca/LegisInfo/en/bill/40-3/c-11?view=about; Bill C-31, "An Act to Amend the Immigration and Refugee Protection Act, the Balanced Refugee Reform Act, the Marine Transportation Security Act and the Department of Citizenship and Immigration Act," 1st sess., 41st Parliament, 2012, https://www.parl.ca/LegisInfo/en/bill/41-1/c-31.
27 Idil Atak and François Crépeau, "The Securitization of Asylum and Human Rights in Canada and the European Union," 233–34; Mountz, *The Death of Asylum*, 178–83.
28 Atak and Crépeau, "The Securitization of Asylum and Human Rights in Canada and the European Union," 233–34. Illustratively, none of the 550 refugee claimants who arrived by boat in 2010 were deemed inadmissible to Canada for their ties to terrorist organizations, and only 4 were deemed inadmissible for other causes.
29 Sean Rehaag, Janet Song, and Alexander Toope, "Never Letting a Good Crisis Go to Waste: Canadian Interdiction of Asylum Seekers," *Frontiers in Human Dynamics* 2 (2020), https://doi.org/10.3389/fhumd.2020.588961.
30 Paquet and Schertzer, *Irregular Border Crossings and Asylum Seekers in Canada*, 8–9.
31 Audrey Macklin and Joshua Blum, *Country Fiche: Canada* (Brussels: Asile: Global Asylum Governance and the European Union's Role, 2021), 10,

https://www.asileproject.eu/wp-content/uploads/2021/03/Country-Fiche_CANADA_Final_Pub.pdf.
32 Macklin and Blum, *Country Fiche: Canada*; Rehaag, Song, and Toope, "Never Letting a Good Crisis Go to Waste."
33 "Asylum Seekers Can Use Roxham Road Crossing in Quebec as Pandemic Ban Lifted," *Global News*, 23 November 2021, https://globalnews.ca/news/8396543/asylum-seekers-quebec-roxham-road-crossing-reopens/.
34 "Additional Protocol to the Agreement between the Government of Canada and the Government of the United States of America for Cooperation in the Examination of Refugee Status Claims from Nationals of Third Countries," Government of Canada, 29 March 2022, https://www.canada.ca/en/immigration-refugees-citizenship/corporate/mandate/policies-operational-instructions-agreements/agreements/safe-third-country-agreement/additional-protocol.html.
35 Lama Mourad and Kelsey P. Norman, "Transforming Refugees into Migrants: Institutional Change and the Politics of International Protection," *European Journal of International Relations* 26, no. 3 (2020): 687–713, https://doi.org/10.1177/1354066119883688.
36 "UNHCR Comments on CIC Paper Entitled 'Refugee Resettlement Eligibility and Selection Criteria: Implementation Policy,'" UNHCR, 11 August 2000, http://ccrweb.ca/sites/ccrweb.ca/files/static-files/elighcr.htm (emphasis added).
37 "'Targeted for Extermination': Harper Says Prioritizing Christian and Religious Minority Refugees Isn't Discriminatory," *National Post*, 10 October 2015, https://nationalpost.com/news/politics/targeted-for-extermination-harper-says-prioritizing-christian-and-religious-minority-refugees-isnt-discriminatory.
38 "Determining Whether the Applicant Has the Ability to Establish in Canada (REF-OVS-4-6)," Government of Canada, last modified 26 February 2021, https://www.canada.ca/en/immigration-refugees-citizenship/corporate/publications-manuals/operational-bulletins-manuals/refugee-protection/resettlement/eligibility/ability-establish.html.
39 "UNHCR Resettlement Handbook: Country Chapter – Canada," UNHCR, revised February 2018, https://www.unhcr.org/protection

/resettlement/3c5e55594/unhcr-resettlement-handbook-country-chapter-canada.html.
40 To learn more about the variations in terms of public and private components of these programs, see Rachel McNally, "Equally Public and Private Refugee Resettlement: The Historical Development of Canada's Joint Assistance Sponsorship Program," *Refuge: Canada's Journal on Refugees* 39, no. 1 (2023): 1–17, https://doi.org/10.25071/1920-7336.40941.
41 For more on the longer history that led to the adoption of private sponsorship as a model in Canada, see Shauna Labman and Geoffrey Cameron, eds., *Strangers to Neighbours: Refugee Sponsorship in Context* (Montreal: McGill-Queen's University Press, 2020).
42 Michael J. Molloy and James C. Simeon, "The Indochinese Refugee Movement and the Launch of Canada's Private Sponsorship Program," *Refuge: Canada's Journal on Refugees* 32, no. 2 (2016): 3–8, https://doi.org/10.25071/1920-7336.40412.
43 Audrey Macklin, Kathryn Barber, Luin Goldring, Jennifer Hyndman, Anna Korteweg, Shauna Labman, and Jona Zyfi, "A Preliminary Investigation into Private Refugee Sponsors," *Canadian Ethnic Studies* 50, no. 2 (2018): 38.
44 Shauna Labman, "Private Sponsorship: Complementary or Conflicting Interests?," *Refuge: Canada's Journal on Refugees* 32, no. 2 (2016): 72–4, https://doi.org/10.25071/1920-7336.40266.
45 "Bill C-11: An Open Letter," Canadian Council for Refugees, April 2010, https://ccrweb.ca/en/bill-c-11-open-letter. This bill included a "Designated Countries of Origin" list, which instituted a different process for refugees who came from countries on this list that Canada deemed "safe" (forty-two countries), including a six-month bar on work permits, no avenue for appeal to the Refugee Appeals Division, and a 36-month bar on the Pre-removal Risk Assessment. This policy was eliminated in practice in 2019, when the Canadian government removed all countries from the list. See "Canada Ends the Designated Country of Origin Practice," Immigration, Refugees and Citizenship Canada, 17 May 2019, https://www.canada.ca/en/immigration-refugees-citizenship/news/2019/05/canada-ends-the-designated-country-of-origin-practice.html. This followed two successful court challenges: see Macklin and Blum, *Country Fiche: Canada*, 7.
46 Labman, "Private Sponsorship."

47 FitzGerald, *Refuge beyond Reach*.
48 Sergio Carrera, Meltem Ineli Ciger, Lina Vosyliute, and Leiza Brumat, "The EU Grants Temporary Protection for People Fleeing War in Ukraine: Time to Rethink Unequal Solidarity in EU Asylum Policy," *CEPS Policy Insights*, no. 2022-09 (March 2022), https://www.ceps.eu/ceps-publications/eu-grants-temporary-protection-for-people-fleeing-war-in-ukraine/.
49 Rhythm Sachdeva, "'Night and Day': Lawyers Say Canada Offers More Support to Ukrainian Refugees than Afghans," *CTV News*, 23 March 2022, https://www.ctvnews.ca/canada/night-and-day-lawyers-say-canada-offers-more-support-to-ukrainian-refugees-than-afghans-1.5831685; Naomi Alboim and Karen Cohl, "Canada Needs a Unified Approach for People Fleeing Ukraine and Afghanistan," *Globe and Mail*, 4 April 2022, https://www.theglobeandmail.com/opinion/article-canada-needs-a-unified-approach-for-people-fleeing-ukraine-and/; Anthony Fong and Zamir Saar, "Canada Needs to Be as Welcoming to Afghan Refugees as It Is to Ukrainians," *The Conversation*, 25 May 2022, https://theconversation.com/canada-needs-to-be-as-welcoming-to-afghan-refugees-as-it-is-to-ukrainians-182363.
50 Lama Mourad and Stephanie Schwartz, "In Gaza, Civilian Evacuation Looks like Forced Displacement. That Cannot Be the Way Forward," *Globe and Mail*, 21 November 2023, https://www.theglobeandmail.com/opinion/article-in-gaza-civilian-evacuation-looks-like-forced-displacement-that-cannot/.
51 Christl Dabu, "Canada's Immigration Minister Says There Isn't a Hard Cap on Temporary Visa Program for Palestinians," *CTV News*, 9 January 2024, https://www.ctvnews.ca/canada/canada-s-immigration-minister-says-there-isn-t-a-hard-cap-on-temporary-visa-program-for-palestinians-1.6718089.
52 Marie Woolf, "Nearly 1,000 Palestinians Apply to Come to Canada, but Can't Exit Gaza," *Globe and Mail*, 29 January 2024, https://www.theglobeandmail.com/politics/article-nearly-1000-palestinians-apply-to-come-to-canada-but-cant-exit-gaza/; Heather Yourex-West, "Ottawa Says Only a Handful of Visas Have Been Approved for Gaza Refugees with Relatives in Canada," *Global News*, 20 March 2024, https://globalnews.ca/news/10370994/gaza-refugees-relatives-canada-visas/; Yasmine Hasan and Peter Zimonjic, "Canada Promised Temporary Visas

for 1,000 People Trapped in Gaza. Zero Have Made It Out," *CBC News*, 5 April 2024, https://ici.radio-canada.ca/rci/en/news/2062726/canada-promised-temporary-visas-for-1-000-people-trapped-in-gaza-zero-have-made-it-out; Yasmine Hasan and John Paul Tasker, "Palestinian Canadians Say Their Families Are Dying in Gaza While They Wait to Come to Canada," *CBC News*, 6 February 2024, https://www.cbc.ca/news/politics/palestinian-canadians-visa-delays-1.7105188.
53 Mountz, *The Death of Asylum*.
54 James Milner, Mustafa Alio, and Rez Gardi, "Meaningful Refugee Participation: An Emerging Norm in the Global Refugee Regime," *Refugee Survey Quarterly* 41, no. 4 (2022): 565–93, https://doi.org/10.1093/rsq/hdac007.
55 FitzGerald, *Refuge beyond Reach*, 257–8; Marie-Bénédicte Dembour, "Interception-at-Sea: Illegal as Currently Practiced – Hirsi and Others v. Italy," *Strasbourg Observers* (blog), 1 March 2012, https://strasbourgobservers.com/2012/03/01/interception-at-sea-illegal-as-currently-practiced-hirsi-and-others-v-italy/.

Conclusion

Security amid Transition: Canada in the Next Decade

AISHA AHMAD

As Canadians look ahead to the next decade, multiple perils lie on the horizon. The world is undergoing a major change in the balance of power, as a rising China and a resurgent Russia challenge US dominance across Africa, Latin America, the Middle East, and Asia. This new world is comprised not of one singular international order, but of multiple, competing, and overlapping orders and spheres of influence.[1] As this great power transition unfolds, the danger of inadvertent escalation to major war is very serious.[2] Russia's invasion of Ukraine, Israel's war in Palestine, and China's manoeuvres against Taiwan represent volatile flashpoints with the potential to trigger wider wars. Meanwhile, India is emerging as a fourth great power, and is projected to become the world's second-largest economy (after China) this century.[3] Although the United States has tried to enhance cooperation with India to balance against China, it has also levelled grave allegations that Indian operatives have been involved in assassination operations on American and Canadian soil.[4]

As US hegemony declines and this new multipolar world order emerges, Canada will need to exercise tremendous caution in its interactions with powerful rivals.[5] Many ideas and attitudes that served Canada during the era of American preponderance will need to be jettisoned. Hegemonic hubris has no place in this uncertain and volatile world order, and haughty "tough talk" in the diplomatic arena is dangerous. In this time of great change, Canada should aim to navigate this transition as peacefully as possible, and it should work intently on de-escalating the threat of direct great power conflict. Of course, as a mid-sized power, there are limits to what Canada can do to steer great powers towards peace; however, there are also subtle opportunities for global influence. This is not the first time Canada has navigated stormy great power politics. During the Cold War, the country strived to position itself as a responsible and peace-promoting middle power, and thus gained a strong reputation for diplomacy and soft power influence.[6] Although staunchly allied with the United States and NATO, Canada simultaneously endeavoured to increase global cooperation among all member states through multilateral institutions. Canada enjoyed the security of a close alliance with the United States, but it also worked hard to build its reputation for diplomacy and peacekeeping abroad. These soft power skills were especially valuable to Canada – and the world – during the Cold War.

Over the past twenty years, however, these soft skills have eroded, and arguably disappeared. After 9/11, Canada was called on to fulfill its alliance responsibilities to the United States, and thus spent two decades involved in various counter-insurgency missions that were by some accounts doomed to fail.[7] During this period, Canada prioritized alliance commitments and war fighting, and did little to maintain its diplomatic and peacekeeping reputation. Despite its loud declarations about maintaining the "rules-based international order," Canada stood by its allies, even when those allies broke the rules. Canada also parroted the American slogan "we don't negotiate with terrorists," reinforced by a culture of tough talk and groupthink in its foreign service. These cognitive biases persisted right up until the United States signed a deal with the Taliban, rendering Canada's longest-ever military mission a failure.

Indeed, the events of 2021 and 2022 were a harsh wake-up call for the Americans. In November 2021, less than three months after the Taliban victory, China tested a hypersonic missile that was so advanced that it shocked the Pentagon.[8] By its own admission at that time, the United States was years behind Chinese hypersonic missile technology, a gaping disparity that US general Mark Milley, chairman of the Joint Chiefs of Staff, referred to as close to a "Sputnik" moment.[9] In response, the United States dramatically increased its defence spending in this area to catch up with China; at the time of writing, however, America remains behind in the hypersonic arms race.

By 2022, the Americans also found themselves embroiled in a renewed military standoff with the Russians, triggered by Moscow's full-scale military invasion of the Ukraine. Although the United States and its NATO allies have thus far refused to get directly involved in the Ukraine conflict, the alliance has provided Kyiv with a massive amount of military aid to push back the Russians. This influx of weapons and ammunition has helped to prevent a Russian victory, but so far has proved insufficient to defeat Moscow outright. The United States also failed to bring about universal condemnation of Russia, which rendered its heavy economic sanctions against Moscow less effective. Not only has Russia been able to withstand these sanctions, but it has also managed to enhance its diplomatic relationships and alliances around the world, thus balancing against NATO.

The most notable alliance in this emerging multipolar order is between China and Russia themselves. Building on decades of diplomatic effort, Moscow and Beijing have forged a strategic partnership and "friendship with no limits."[10] Moreover, since 2022 both countries have also significantly extended their diplomatic and security reach across Africa and the Middle East. In February 2023, Russian foreign minister Sergei Lavrov embarked on a successful whirlwind trip across the Middle East and Africa to win new allies. During that same month, Russia and China completed a joint naval exercise with South Africa. In March 2023, China brokered a peace deal between Iran and Saudi Arabia, a feat that the United States had failed to achieve. Great power influence in the MENA region has been further affected by Israel's war in Palestine, which has left the United States increasingly isolated on the world stage for its support of Tel Aviv.

In response to its apparent waning global influence, the United States has tried to shore up support in African, Middle Eastern, and Asian states. For example, after the Solomon Islands pivoted to the Chinese sphere, in May 2023 the United States scurried to seal a new security deal with Papua New Guinea. Similarly, after Mali and Burkina Faso pivoted towards Russian, in February 2023 Secretary of State Antony Blinken and Vice-President Kamala Harris hurriedly moved to reinforce the United States' relationships in neighbouring Niger and Ghana. The effort proved too little, too late: Niger suffered a coup only six months later, and it has since entered Russia's sphere of influence.[11] America has also suffered a significant loss of influence in the Middle East, especially since the eruption of violence in Israel and Palestine. In late 2023, as Israel's bombardment of Gaza caused tens of thousands of civilian casualties, nearly every country in the world demanded a ceasefire at the UN General Assembly.[12] Yet, the Americans stood alone at the UN Security Council and single-handedly vetoed a resolution that called for a humanitarian ceasefire in Gaza.[13] The veto sparked widespread outrage, and further contributed to America's already declining influence on the world stage. In fact, Washington's hawkish choices have arguably made it easier for the Chinese and Russians to "harness a wave of sympathy for the Palestinians and to position themselves as champions of humanitarian values and peace."[14]

Indeed, the shift in the global balance of power is measured not only by hard power metrics, but also by this type of soft power influence. By these metrics, the United States has lost considerable moral credibility on the world stage in recent years, further worsened by its bellicose position on the Israeli war in Palestine. Even America's strategies for promoting democracy and human rights have different consequences in a multipolar world order. For example, in response to China's rising influence, the United States and its democratic allies – especially Canada – have considered limiting their cooperation to "like-minded" democratic nations.[15] In contrast, neither Russia nor China has any set of political preconditions for cooperation with other countries, and both are willing to do business with many different types of governments, democratic and undemocratic alike. Beijing has even opened talks with the Taliban regime in Afghanistan, in order to advance their mutual economic interest. In the competition for soft power influence, the

United States and Canada are considering limiting who they cooperate with, whereas China and Russia are opening their doors.

As the global balance of power shifts, the most urgent international security issue concerns how to manage this transition without an eruption of war between the great powers. Of course, the United States, China, and Russia are deeply afraid of sparking a direct confrontation with one another, and the knowledge that all three powers are able to trigger a world-ending nuclear war is clearly a reason to pause. Indeed, the dangers of escalation are so high that Presidents Biden, Jinping, and Putin have repeatedly stated that they do not want a direct war between their countries. For example, when Biden visited war-torn Kyiv to shore up support for Ukraine's fight against Russia, the Americans communicated this with Moscow hours beforehand to ensure that there would be no chance of an accident that could lead to Armageddon.[16] Nevertheless, as this power transition unfolds, there are countless risks of accidental escalation. In June 2023, for example, Canada and the United States conducted a naval mission in the Taiwan Strait – a move that Beijing considers threatening to its core security interests. This naval mission provoked a sudden and dangerous reaction from a Chinese warship in the area, which very nearly resulted in American, Canadian, and Chinese ships colliding in contested waters.[17] As this example shows, even though the dominant powers in the international system do not want to go to war, it is still entirely possible that they could accidentally trigger a series of events that rapidly result in global catastrophe.

Given these extreme risks, it is disconcerting that too many Canadian leaders have abandoned the difficult but necessary work of quiet diplomacy and de-escalation, seemingly to score political points with domestic audiences. Rather than seeking to establish off-ramps for all of the great powers, Canadian leaders have either shut down diplomatic channels or have publicly disparaged Russia and China.[18] This approach, which Canada cultivated during the era of American hegemony, is now outdated, self-defeating, and exceptionally dangerous. While insulting Moscow and Beijing may win politicians a few points on the nightly news, the fact is that Canada has no independent ability to intimidate either Russia or China. It is foolish to poison communication channels with powerful enemy states, and there are serious consequences to escalatory talk and poor diplomatic engagement with great powers. To successfully navigate the emerging world order, Canada must change its approach, and not only refresh the soft power skills it once had during the Cold War era, but also build stronger capabilities in mastering quiet diplomacy across "enemy lines."

Most significantly, this rise in great power conflict coincides with an urgent need for global cooperation. While the United States, Russia, and China jockey for power, climate change is projected to threaten billions of lives around the world. The latest scientific evidence shows that the planet is breaching the 1.5°C threshold, which is the target set by the 2015 Paris Accords as a hard limit on global warming.[19] The scientific consensus is that, once over this threshold, the earth will experience a cascading and irreversible series of catastrophic environmental impacts and disasters lasting several decades. These projected impacts include floods, wildfires, droughts, ecosystem collapse, agricultural failure, food insecurity, famine, and mass migration in the hundreds of millions.[20] These consequences are so severe that robust international cooperation is imperative. Yet, instead of engaging in coordinated action aimed at shoring up human security, rival great powers have already used climate negotiations as a cheap political bargaining tool.[21] To successfully mitigate the catastrophic consequences of climate change, Canada must encourage all parties to engage in respectful, collaborative, good-faith agreements by nurturing robust cooperation with rivals and even enemies. A strong diplomatic approach to climate change may also lay the foundation for urgently needed cooperation in other critical areas, such as managing and controlling rapidly advancing technologies like artificial intelligence.

Considering these system-level changes, it is clear that Canada faces a very different threat landscape today than it did in the past twenty years. There are both traditional and non-traditional security concerns on the near horizon. Alongside the risk of direct conflict between great powers are a plethora of new crises, such as climate-driven disasters and new threats in cyberspace and artificial intelligence. Canada also faces serious internal vulnerabilities, as deep-rooted problems of racial and gender discrimination persist inside Canadian foreign, defence, and security institutions. Not only do these biases undermine effective policymaking, but they also render Canadian society easily exploitable by hostile foreign states who might wish to cultivate domestic unrest.

Canada will need to welcome new experts and leaders to effectively tackle these many challenges, and adopting an inclusive security approach is essential for success. This expansion should focus on including diverse voices in policy discussions, especially those historically excluded from decision-making circles in Ottawa. Moreover, because groupthink is difficult to eradicate among those already infected, anyone whose expertise is based on the failed missions of the past two decades – especially those who demonstrate an inability to engage in critical self-reflection or who are defensive when faced with dissenting perspectives – should be invited to retire. In their place, a fresh cohort of leaders should step in, and immediately introduce rigorous instruments to protect themselves against groupthink and other cognitive biases. By normalizing "challenge sessions," encouraging dissenting perspectives, and eradicating groupthink, Canada's foreign and defence institutions will be better equipped to confront new threats on the horizon, including crises that Canada may unwittingly play a role in creating.

It is not a law of nature that great power competition must result in global war.[22] In these volatile times, what states choose to do – or not do – determines whether tensions will escalate or de-escalate. How leaders think and behave can produce dramatically different outcomes on the world stage, and the ideas Canadians adopt will shape the future world that we live in. Provocation begets provocation. Trust begets trust. At this time of great power transition, every action that Canada takes will help co-construct the security landscape of the twenty-first century. With hundreds of millions of lives hanging in the balance, it is imperative that the best and brightest are involved in these decisions.

Ask Women Experts

This volume features an all-star roster of women security experts from across Canada. Each contributor is an established and decorated scholar, highly regarded as a leader in her field. But why include only women? The reason is that for many decades, men have exercised a monopoly in security studies, and have become go-to contacts in Canada's defence and security communities. While we agree that our male colleagues have valuable things to say, this exclusion of women experts in policy circles is both absurd and dangerous. Although increasing diversity in decision-making circles does not guarantee perfect outcomes, excluding women and minorities inevitably increases the risk of groupthink, cognitive biases, and mistakes. Leaders in Canadian defence and security should invite women experts to the table, and there are plenty of highly qualified Canadian women to ask.

To help undo the outdated biases that have undermined Canada's foreign affairs and defence communities in the past, this book flips the narrative. It includes only women security experts from top Canadian academic institutions whose work is unequivocally considered the best in the business. To serve the informed non-specialist reader, it showcases their expert insights in short, accessible, jargon-free chapters. The volume is therefore best used as both a remedy against bias and an introduction to the issues covered therein. Yet, because it is a survey of the field, it should be treated as a springboard to building deeper knowledge. The next stage in this learning process is to engage with the substantive research of the authors gathered here.

Each of our contributors has a significant research portfolio, which readers are welcome to explore. Part 1 began with a hard-hitting chapter by Carla Norrlöf that uncovered the domestic political reasons for American hegemonic decline. Given that Canada's security depends enormously on American dominance, this unfolding change in the balance of power is arguably the most significant factor affecting Canadian security and defence today. Those interested in understanding American hegemony – and its decline – would do well to read Norrlöf's classic book *America's*

Global Advantage, alongside her article on hegemonic decline in *International Affairs.*[23]

Following this strong start, Stéfanie von Hlatky and Hannah Hollander then mapped out the challenges facing the NATO alliance in the years ahead, especially as the conflict between Russia and Ukraine continues to spiral. As a member of the alliance, Canada would be implicated in any direct conflict between a NATO member and Russia, thereby raising the potential for a major global war. Readers interested in this subject will want to review von Hlatky's book *American Allies in Times of War,* as well as her 2020 co-authored articles on NATO in *International Politics* and the *Journal of Global Security Studies.*[24] Continuing this theme of great power competition, Andrea Charron and Danielle Cherpako's chapter looked at the defence of the Arctic region, where Canada finds itself competing with Russia, the United States, and China. Charron's specialized publications and reports on Arctic security and cooperation are essential reading for those concerned about the future of this region.[25] Turning specifically to China, Lynette Ong presented a novel account of Beijing's global strategy, particularly its successful economic coercion of rival states. Since China emerged as a dominant global power, its relationship with the United States – and with Canada – has dramatically deteriorated. Those who wish to better understand this rising great power should read Ong's highly acclaimed books *Outsourcing Repression* and *The Street and the Ballot Box.*[26] The section concluded with Bessma Momani's analysis of the Middle East and North Africa, a region in which China is quickly gaining influence. Readers who are concerned about Canada's influence in the MENA region will benefit tremendously from Momani's most recent co-edited volume, *Middle Power in the Middle East,*[27] as well as her many other books and publications.

Section 2 moved from traditional to more non-traditional security issues. We started with a strong chapter by Katharina Coleman and Lou Pingeot on Canadian support for UN peacekeeping. Although peacekeeping has historically been a big part of Canada's foreign policy, Coleman and Pingeot explain how this mandate has evolved since its inception. Tracking Ottawa's waning influence in this area, the authors present a compelling argument for why – and how – Canada can reinvigorate its leadership on the peacekeeping file. Readers who are interested in the future of peacekeeping will be interested in Coleman's 2022 co-authored book *Token Forces*, as well as her recent articles in such high-profile venues as the *Journal of Peace Research*, *International Affairs*, and *International Peacekeeping*.[28]

Next, Leah West presented a cutting-edge chapter on cybersecurity, which called out Canada's lack of preparedness in that area and recommended how Canada can develop new laws and policies to address these serious vulnerabilities. Those interested in these thorny legal issues will want to read West's co-authored book *National Security Law*, as well as her multiple scholarly publications on Canadian cybersecurity and intelligence gathering.[29]

Building on this theme of unpreparedness, the following chapter by Nirupama Agrawal presented a critical look at Canada's disaster and emergency management systems and recommended a new "whole-of-society" approach to managing future emergencies. For those interested in Canada's disaster management systems, Agrawal has written a field-defining textbook, *Natural Disasters and Risk Management in Canada*, and has recently co-authored an article on civil-military cooperation in nature-triggered disasters for the *Canadian Journal of Emergency Management*.[30]

The next two chapters in this section addressed issues related to climate change. Kathryn Harrison delved into the science and business of the energy industry to explain how climate change politics will affect Canadian economic and environmental security. Readers may wish to read Harrison's book *Global Commons, Domestic Decisions* for a closer look at climate change politics.[31] Sarah Burch and Janetta McKenzie's chapter addressed the risks in "securitizing" climate change and offered a human security perspective on how Canada can successfully address these extreme risks. Burch's co-authored textbook *Understanding Climate Change* would be a helpful guide for those wishing to better understand both the science and the policy underlying these issues.[32] Burch, McKenzie, and Harrison have all published extensive peer-reviewed research on climate change and energy industry policies, which will serve as a solid foundation for readers wishing to deepen their knowledge of these topics.[33]

Lastly, section 3 examined how issues of identity and inclusivity affect Canadian security. It opened with my chapter on groupthink and cognitive biases in Canadian institutions, wherein I flagged a lack of diversity and dissenting perspectives in Canada's foreign policy and defence communities as key reasons for its mission failures. Those curious about the fieldwork that went into my analysis may wish to read my book *Jihad & Co.*, or my recent academic articles on complex conflicts.[34] The next chapter, by Megan MacKenzie and Nicole Wegner, offered a hard-hitting look at sexual and racial bias in the Canadian Armed Forces, and argued that these violent and discriminatory practices create serious security vulnerabilities for Canada. Readers who are interested in MacKenzie and Wegner's research will be keen to read their co-authored book *Feminist Solutions for Ending War*.[35]

The next two chapters offered equally tough critiques of the Canadian security establishment. Cheryl Lightfoot and Chelsea Parker's chapter spotlighted the systematic abuse of Indigenous communities by Canadian security institutions; their powerful research calls into question *whose* security Canada is interested in protecting. Readers interested in learning more about Indigenous security will find Lightfoot's book *Global Indigenous Politics* of interest, as well as her other recent publications on reconciliation, self-determination, and defence.[36] Following this strong chapter on Indigenous rights, Jasmin Zine presented a scathing critique of how Canadian security institutions profiled and surveilled innocent Muslim communities inside Canada. Zine's chapter in this volume builds on material from her new book *Under Siege*,[37] which is an excellent resource for readers interested in racism and Islamophobia in the Canadian security community. Building on this important discussion of Islamophobia, Lama Mourad's chapter revealed how Canada has also securitized refugees from Arab countries, suggesting that these stark discrepancies are the result of deep-seated biases. Readers who are keen to learn more about mass displacement and refugee politics will find Mourad's peer-reviewed articles on forced migration to be helpful.[38]

Wider Networks, Deeper Knowledge

The contributors to this edited volume are some of the most decorated security and defence scholars in the country. As we conclude this volume, however, I would like to spotlight a few other outstanding researchers – all women scholars at Canadian academic institutions – who, while not contributors to this particular volume, are nonetheless leaders in the field of security. Although this list is by no means exhaustive, keen learners will find these scholars, as well as those in the "Must-Read Books List" appendix, a solid springboard for building wider networks and deeper research.

Readers who are primarily concerned with power politics will be interested in several top-tier academic books. Kristen Hopewell's exceptional *Clash of Powers* investigates the economics of American hegemony and probes the reasons behind the United States' trade wars with China.[39] Diana Fu's multiple award–winning *Mobilizing without the Masses* offers a rare look inside China's politics and economy, and is based on unparalleled field research.[40] Those curious about India's future prospects in this competition will find Kanta Murali's economic analysis in *Class, Caste, and Capital* tremendously insightful.[41] Malinda Smith's edited volume *Securing Africa* is a foundational reading on post-9/11 counterterrorism policy.[42]

Turning to Russia, Juliet Johnson's highly acclaimed *Priests of Prosperity* offers a novel look at central banking in post-Soviet Europe, and it is an essential read for anyone trying to understand the Russian economy.[43] Lisa Sundstrom's co-authored book *Courting Gender Justice* offers a rare insight into the risks and challenges of human rights and civil society activism in Russia.[44] On the Russia-Ukraine war, readers will find essential historical context in Marta Dyczok's *Ukraine Calling*, Joan DeBardeleben's co-edited volume *EU-Russian Relations in Crisis*, and Maria Popova's prize-winning *Politicized Justice in Emerging Democracies*.[45] Popova's 2024 co-authored volume, titled *Russia and Ukraine*, masterfully connects these histories to the current conflict.[46]

Canadian women are also at the forefront of new areas of security research. Stephanie Carvin's *Stand on Guard* addresses a wide range of new threats to Canada's national security, from extremism to cybersecurity.[47] Wendy Wong's groundbreaking *We, the Data* examines how rights are affected in our unprecedented digital age, in which individuals are treated as commodities.[48] For more traditional human security questions, there are several leading scholars to follow. Jennifer Welsh has penned several acclaimed books, including a co-authored volume, *The Responsibility to Prevent*, probing legal, ethical, and practical considerations in efforts to prevent mass atrocities.[49] Nergis Canefe's *Crimes against Humanity* presents a novel analysis of whether or not international legal instruments are equipped to deal with atrocities perpetrated by states.[50] Shireen Hassim, the Canada 150 Research Chair in Gender and African Politics at Carleton University, has written several books on women, peace, and security that are without parallel.[51] Newer to this arena is Nadège Compaoré, an emerging academic leader in natural resource governance and extractive industries in Africa, a subject that is highly relevant to Canadian mining investments and economic interests on the continent.[52]

Those wishing to engage with the inclusive security research agenda will want to read Pam Palmater's *Indigenous Nationhood and Warrior Life*,[53] as well as Debra Thompson's award-winning book on race called *The Schematic State*.[54] On gender and war, readers may wish to review Siobhan Byrne's research on Northern Ireland and Israel-Palestine,[55] as well as Yolande Bouka's research on Rwanda and Kenya.[56] Those interested in refugee issues will benefit from Megan Bradley's books on forced migration,[57] as well as Yasmeen Abu-Laban's *Containing Diversity*, which probes Canada's biased treatment of refugees and other immigrants.[58] A valuable complement to Abu-Laban's research is Yang-Yang Zhou's scholarly articles showing how inclusive refugee practices can promote positive outcomes for host states.[59]

These are just a few of the many outstanding Canadian women scholars in the field of security. The roster of experts noted here and in the "Must-Read Books List" is by no means exhaustive.[60] I have spotlighted only a handful of women experts based in Canadian academic institutions who specialize in well-recognized topics related to national and international security. A more global survey of women experts across countries – and a more inclusive definition of security – would have resulted in a list many hundreds of pages long. Nevertheless, even this quick snapshot of Canadian talent unequivocally proves that there is no shortage of women experts in security studies, and therefore never an excuse for anyone in Canada to convene an all-male security panel or expert committee. Nor is there ever a reason for a professor to put forward a syllabus on national or international security that excludes women experts. The fact is that Canadian women are lead researchers on some of the best and most lauded scholarship in security studies. Any university instructor worth their salt will assign them and cite them.

It is hoped that this book will encourage scholars, public servants, and senior leaders across Canada to update their contact lists and include diverse women experts from across the country. We must ensure that the best and brightest are invited to advise, warn, and lead. The wider and more inclusive our networks, the more informed and prepared Canada will be to face the challenges ahead. The world is changing quickly and the culture of our foreign affairs and defence communities must also change if Canada is to survive – and thrive – in the emerging global order.

NOTES

1 Amitav Acharya, "After Liberal Hegemony: The Advent of a Multiplex World Order," *Ethics & International Affairs* 31, no. 3 (2017): 271–85, https://doi.org/10.1017/S089267941700020X; Amitav Acharya, *The End of American World Order* (New York: John Wiley & Sons, 2018).
2 A.F.K. Organski, *World Politics,* 2nd ed. (New York: Random House, 1968); John J. Mearsheimer, *The Tragedy of Great Power Politics,* updated ed. (New York: W.W. Norton, 2014); Joshua R. Itzkowitz Shifrinson, *Rising Titans, Falling Giants: How Great Powers Exploit Power Shifts* (Ithaca, NY: Cornell University Press, 2018); Evelyn Goh, "US Dominance and American Bias in International Relations Scholarship: A View from the Outside," *Journal of Global Security Studies* 4, no. 3 (2019): 402–10; Ketian Zhang, "Cautious Bully: Reputation, Resolve, and Beijing's Use of Coercion in the South China Sea," *International Security* 44, no. 1 (2019):

117–59, https://doi.org/10.1162/isec_a_00354; Fiona S. Cunningham and M. Taylor Fravel, "Dangerous Confidence? Chinese Views on Nuclear Escalation," *International Security* 44, no. 2 (2019): 61–109, https://doi.org/10.1162/isec_a_00359.

3 Bhaskar Chakravorti and Gaurav Dalmia, "Is India the World's Next Great Economic Power?," *Harvard Business Review*, 6 September 2023, https://hbr.org/2023/09/is-india-the-worlds-next-great-economic-power.

4 Justin Ling, "India Is the Latest Member of a Growing Assassination Club," *Foreign Policy*, 22 January 2024, https://foreignpolicy.com/2024/01/14/assassination-club-india-nijjar-saudi-arabia-russia-united-states/.

5 Kristen Hopewell, *Clash of Powers: US-China Rivalry in Global Trade Governance* (Cambridge: Cambridge University Press, 2020); Kristen Hopewell, "Power Transitions and Global Trade Governance: The Impact of a Rising China on the Export Credit Regime," *Regulation & Governance* 15, no. 3 (2021): 634–52, https://doi.org/10.1111/rego.12253; Kristen Hopewell, "Strategic Narratives in Global Trade Politics: American Hegemony, Free Trade, and the Hidden Hand of the State," *Chinese Journal of International Politics* 14, no. 1 (2021): 51–86, https://doi.org/10.1093/cjip/poaa020; Kristen Hopewell, "When the Hegemon Goes Rogue: Leadership amid the US Assault on the Liberal Trading Order," *International Affairs* 97, no. 4 (2021): 1025–43, https://doi.org/10.1093/ia/iiab073; Acharya, *The End of American World Order*; Acharya, "After Liberal Hegemony."

6 Geoffrey Hayes, "Canada as a Middle Power: The Case of Peacekeeping," in *Niche Diplomacy: Middle Powers after the Cold War*, ed. Andrew F. Cooper (London: Palgrave Macmillan, 1997), 73–89, https://doi.org/10.1007/978-1-349-25902-1_4; Fen Osler Hampson and Dean F. Oliver, "A Pulpit Diplomacy: A Critical Assessment of the Axworthy Doctrine Essay," *International Journal* 53, no. 3 (1998): 379–406; Kim Richard Nossal, "Pinchpenny Diplomacy: The Decline of Good International Citizenship in Canadian Foreign Policy Essay," *International Journal* 54, no. 1 (1998–9): 88–105; Carl Ungerer, "Influence without Power: Middle Powers and Arms Control Diplomacy during the Cold War," *Diplomacy & Statecraft* 18, no. 2 (2007): 393–414, https://doi.org/10.1080/09592290701322572; Paul Meyer, "George Ignatieff: A Feisty Disarmament Diplomat in the

Cold War Era," *International Journal* 78, nos. 1–2 (2023): 263–79, https://doi.org/10.1177/00207020231178924.

7   David Kilcullen, *The Accidental Guerrilla: Fighting Small Wars in the Midst of a Big One* (New York: Oxford University Press, 2009); David Kilcullen, *Counterinsurgency* (New York: Oxford University Press, 2010); Gershon Adela, "A Force for the Right Purpose? Rethinking Western COIN Interventions in Africa's Sahel," *Journal of Military and Strategic Studies* 22, no. 3 (2023), https://jmss.org/article/view/77361; Federmán Rodríguez, "American and Canadian Engagements in the Afghanistan Intervention: A Neoclassical Realist Point of View," *Canadian Foreign Policy Journal* 29, no. 1 (2023): 93–109, https://doi.org/10.1080/11926422.2023.2193419.

8   Geoff Ziezulewicz, "Pentagon: Yes, We Are Still Lagging behind China's Hypersonics," *Navy Times*, 18 April 2023, https://www.navytimes.com/news/your-navy/2023/04/18/pentagon-yes-we-are-still-lagging-behind-chinas-hypersonics/; Zuzanna Gwadera, "Intelligence Leak Reveals China's Successful Test of a New Hypersonic Missile," International Institute for Strategic Studies, 18 May 2023, https://www.iiss.org/online-analysis/online-analysis/2023/05/intelligence-leak-reveals-chinas-successful-test-of-a-new-hypersonic-missile/.

9   David E. Sanger and William J. Broad, "China's Weapon Tests Close to a 'Sputnik Moment,' U.S. General Says," *New York Times*, 27 October 2021, https://www.nytimes.com/2021/10/27/us/politics/china-hypersonic-missile.html.

10 Alexander Korolev, "How Closely Aligned Are China and Russia? Measuring Strategic Cooperation in IR," *International Politics* 57, no. 5 (2020): 760–89, https://doi.org/10.1057/s41311-019-00178-8; Artyom Lukin, "The Russia–China Entente and Its Future," *International Politics* 58, no. 3 (2021): 363–80, https://doi.org/10.1057/s41311-020-00251-7.

11 Morgane Le Cam, "Niger Chooses Russia over Europe," *Le Monde*, 6 December 2023, https://www.lemonde.fr/en/le-monde-africa/article/2023/12/06/niger-chooses-russia-over-europe_6318064_124.html.

12 "UN General Assembly Votes by Large Majority for Immediate Humanitarian Ceasefire during Emergency Session," *UN News*, 12 December 2023, https://news.un.org/en/story/2023/12/1144717.

13 Mallory Moench, "U.S. Faces Backlash for Vetoing U.N.'s Gaza Ceasefire Call," *Time*, 9 December 2023, https://time.com/6344440/us-vetoes-un-resolution-gaza-ceasefire-backlash/; Anna Gordon, "U.S. Is Called Out

after Voting against Gaza Ceasefire," *Time*, 13 December 2023, https://time.com/6452308/us-votes-against-un-gaza-ceasefire-reactions/.

14 Yaroslav Trofimov, "China and Russia Claim Moral High Ground over Palestinian Deaths," *Wall Street Journal*, 8 November 2023, https://www.wsj.com/world/china-and-russia-claim-moral-high-ground-over-palestinian-deaths-4ee351a5; Zhao Ziwen, "China, Russia Vow to Boost Brics Influence, Slam West's 'Confrontational Policy,'" *South China Morning Post*, 11 January 2024, https://www.scmp.com/news/china/diplomacy/article/3248066/china-and-russia-push-israel-gaza-ceasefire-and-two-state-solution-foreign-ministers-vow-boost-brics.

15 Kerry Buck and Michael W. Manulak, "Friend-Shoring Canada's Foreign Policy?," *Policy Magazine*, 29 October 2022, https://www.policymagazine.ca/friend-shoring-canadas-foreign-policy/; Steven Chase, "Western Countries Already Embracing 'Friend-Shoring' to Reduce Trade with Authoritarian Regimes, Freeland Says," *Globe and Mail*, 17 October 2022, https://www.theglobeandmail.com/politics/article-canada-trade-allies-freeland-friendshoring/; Bingjun Tang, "Potential Friend-Shoring in the Indo-Pacific: Why a Value-Based Approach to Trade Will Set Canada Back on Its Indo-Pacific Strategy," *Canadian Foreign Policy Journal* 29, no. 1 (2023): 110–13, https://doi.org/10.1080/11926422.2023.2199457.

16 Kathryn Watson and Bo Erickson, "U.S. Alerted Russia to Biden's Ukraine Visit for 'Deconfliction Purposes,' White House Says," *CBS News*, 20 February 2023, https://www.cbsnews.com/news/biden-ukraine-kyiv-visit-russia-deconfliction-white-house/.

17 Ben Blanchard, Laurie Chen, and Laurie Chen, "US Navy Shows Chinese Warship's 'Unsafe Interaction' Near Taiwan," Reuters, 5 June 2023, https://www.reuters.com/world/us-navy-releases-video-chinese-warships-unsafe-interaction-near-taiwan-2023-06-05/.

18 Dylan Robertson, "Joly Won't Meet Her Russian Counterpart, but Is Open to Working with China," *CBC News*, 12 November 2022, https://www.cbc.ca/news/politics/joly-lavrov-meeting-asean-g20-1.6649918; Dylan Robertson, "Internal Docs Suggest Trudeau Wants China Blocked from Pacific Rim Trade Deal," *National Post*, 7 June 2023, https://nationalpost.com/news/internal-docs-suggest-trudeau-wants-china-blocked-from-pacific-rim-trade-deal; "G20: Xi Accuses Trudeau of Leaks to Media about China-Canada Relations," *BBC News*, 16 November 2022, https://www.bbc.com/news/world-asia-china-63654337.

19 Nicola Jones, "When Will Global Warming Actually Hit the Landmark 1.5°C Limit?," *Nature* 618, no. 7963 (2023): 1, https://doi.org/10.1038/d41586-023-01702-w; Jeff Tollefson and Kenneth R. Weiss, "Nations Approve Historic Global Climate Accord," *Nature* 528, no. 7582 (2015): 315–16, https://doi.org/10.1038/528315a; World Meteorological Organization and World Meteorological Organization, *WMO Global Annual to Decadal Climate Update (Target Years: 2023–2027)* (Geneva: WMO, 2023).

20 W. Neil Adger et al., "Urbanization, Migration, and Adaptation to Climate Change," *One Earth* 3, no. 4 (2020): 396–9, https://doi.org/10.1016/j.oneear.2020.09.016; Mia A. Benevolenza and LeaAnne DeRigne, "The Impact of Climate Change and Natural Disasters on Vulnerable Populations: A Systematic Review of Literature," *Journal of Human Behavior in the Social Environment* 29, no. 2 (2019): 266–81, https://doi.org/10.1080/10911359.2018.1527739; Julien Boulange, Naota Hanasaki, Dai Yamazaki, and Yadu Pokhrel, "Role of Dams in Reducing Global Flood Exposure under Climate Change," *Nature Communications* 12, no. 1 (2021): 417, https://doi.org/10.1038/s41467-020-20704-0; Jessica E. Halofsky, David L. Peterson, and Brian J. Harvey, "Changing Wildfire, Changing Forests: The Effects of Climate Change on Fire Regimes and Vegetation in the Pacific Northwest, USA," *Fire Ecology* 16, no. 1 (2020): 4, https://doi.org/10.1186/s42408-019-0062-8; Nerilie J. Abram et al., "Connections of Climate Change and Variability to Large and Extreme Forest Fires in Southeast Australia," *Communications Earth & Environment* 2, no. 1 (2021): 1–17, https://doi.org/10.1038/s43247-020-00065-8; M.C. Kirchmeier-Young, N.P. Gillett, F.W. Zwiers, A.J. Cannon, and F.S. Anslow, "Attribution of the Influence of Human-Induced Climate Change on an Extreme Fire Season," *Earth's Future* 7, no. 1 (2019): 2–10, https://doi.org/10.1029/2018EF001050; Phudoma Lama, Mo Hamza, and Misse Wester, "Gendered Dimensions of Migration in Relation to Climate Change," *Climate and Development* 13, no. 4 (2021): 326–36, https://doi.org/10.1080/17565529.2020.1772708; Zia Mehrabi, "Food System Collapse," *Nature Climate Change* 10, no. 1 (2020): 16–17, https://doi.org/10.1038/s41558-019-0643-1; Benjamin Kipkemboi Kogo, Lalit Kumar, and Richard Koech, "Climate Change and Variability in Kenya: A Review of Impacts on Agriculture and Food Security," *Environment,*

Development and Sustainability 23, no. 1 (2021): 23–43, https://doi.org/10.1007/s10668-020-00589-1.
21 Michael Schuman, "Where U.S.-China Competition Leaves Climate Change," *The Atlantic*, 21 November 2022, https://www.theatlantic.com/international/archive/2022/11/us-china-relations-climate-change/672170/.
22 Organski, *World Politics*; Alexander Wendt, "Anarchy Is What States Make of It: The Social Construction of Power Politics," *International Organization* 46, no. 2 (1992): 391–425, https://doi.org/10.1017/S0020818300027764; Yi Feng, "Friction, Competition, or Cooperation? Menu of Choice for the United States and China – A Power Transition Perspective," in *World Order Transition and the Atlantic Area: Theoretical Perspectives and Empirical Analysis*, ed. Fulvio Attinà (Cham, Switzerland: Springer International, 2021), 39–66, https://doi.org/10.1007/978-3-030-63038-6_3.
23 Carla Norrlöf, *America's Global Advantage: US Hegemony and International Cooperation* (Cambridge: Cambridge University Press, 2010); Carla Norrlöf, "Hegemony and Inequality: Trump and the Liberal Playbook," *International Affairs* 94, no. 1 (2018): 63–88, https://doi.org/10.1093/ia/iix262.
24 Stéfanie von Hlatky, *American Allies in Times of War: The Great Asymmetry* (Oxford: Oxford University Press, 2013); Stéfanie von Hlatky and Michel Fortmann, "NATO Enlargement and the Failure of the Cooperative Security Mindset," *International Politics* 57, no. 3 (2020): 554–72, https://doi.org/10.1057/s41311-020-00240-w; Heidi Hardt and Stéfanie von Hlatky, "NATO's About-Face: Adaptation to Gender Mainstreaming in an Alliance Setting," *Journal of Global Security Studies* 5, no. 1 (2020): 136–59, https://doi.org/10.1093/jogss/ogz048.
25 Andrea Charron, "The Northwest Passage: Is Canada's Sovereignty Floating Away?," *International Journal* 60, no. 3 (2005): 831–48, https://doi.org/10.2307/40204066; Andrea Charron, "Canada and the Arctic Council," *International Journal* 67, no. 3 (2012): 765–83; Andrea Charron, "Canada, the Arctic, and NORAD: Status Quo or New Ball Game?," *International Journal* 70, no. 2 (2015): 215–31; Andrea Charron, "NORAD's Maritime Warning Mission: The Most Overlooked, yet Critically Important Mission for the Foreseeable Future," *Canadian Naval Review*, 1 June 2020, https://www.navalreview.ca/2020/06/norads

-maritime-warning-mission-the-most-overlooked-yet-critically
-important-mission-for-the-foreseeable-future/.
26 Lynette H. Ong, *Outsourcing Repression: Everyday State Power in Contemporary China* (Oxford: Oxford University Press, 2022); Lynette H. Ong, *The Street and the Ballot Box*, new ed. (Cambridge: Cambridge University Press, 2022).
27 Thomas Juneau and Bessma Momani, eds., *Middle Power in the Middle East: Canada's Foreign and Defence Policies in a Changing Region* (Toronto: University of Toronto Press, 2022).
28 Katharina P. Coleman and Xiaojun Li, *Token Forces: How Tiny Troop Deployments Became Ubiquitous in UN Peacekeeping* (Cambridge: Cambridge University Press, 2022); Katharina P. Coleman and Benjamin Nyblade, "Peacekeeping for Profit? The Scope and Limits of 'Mercenary' UN Peacekeeping," *Journal of Peace Research* 55, no. 6 (2018): 726–41, https://doi.org/10.1177/0022343318775784; Katharina P. Coleman, "Downsizing in UN Peacekeeping: The Impact on Civilian Peacekeepers and the Missions Employing Them," *International Peacekeeping* 27, no. 5 (2020): 703–31, https://doi.org/10.1080/13533312.2020.17933 28; Katharina P. Coleman and Brian L. Job, "How Africa and China May Shape UN Peacekeeping beyond the Liberal International Order," *International Affairs* 97, no. 5 (2021): 1451–68, https://doi.org/10.1093/ia/iiab113; Katharina P. Coleman, "African Peacekeeping," *International Affairs* 98, no. 5 (2022): 1828–9, https://doi.org/10.1093/ia/iiac180.
29 Craig Forcese and Leah West, *National Security Law*, 2nd ed. (Toronto: Irwin Law, 2020); Leah West and Craig Forcese, "Judicial Supervision of Anti-terrorism Laws in Comparative Democracies," in *Research Handbook on International Law and Terrorism*, ed. Ben Saul (Cheltenham, UK: Edward Elgar, 2020), 465–78, https://www.elgaronline.com/display/edcoll/9781788972215/9781788972215.00041.xml; Leah West, Thomas Juneau, and Amarnath Amarasingam, eds., *Stress Tested: The COVID-19 Pandemic and Canadian National Security* (Calgary: University of Calgary Press, 2021), http://hdl.handle.net/1880/114134; Leah West, "The Perilous Prerogative: An Argument for Legislating Defence Intelligence in Canada," *Canadian Public Administration* 65, no. 4 (2022): 585–600, https://doi.org/10.1111/capa.12498.
30 Nirupama Agrawal, *Natural Disasters and Risk Management in Canada: An Introduction* (New York: Springer Nature, 2018); Nirupama Agrawal,

Indra Adhikari, and Nathan Yiu, "Disaster Risk in Canada: A Data-Driven Discussion," *Canadian Journal of Emergency Management* 1, no. 2 (2021): 7–25.
31 Kathryn Harrison and Lisa McIntosh Sundstrom, eds., *Global Commons, Domestic Decisions: The Comparative Politics of Climate Change* (Cambridge, MA: MIT Press, 2010).
32 Sarah L. Burch and Sara E. Harris, *Understanding Climate Change: Science, Policy, and Practice*, 2nd ed. (Toronto: University of Toronto Press, 2021).
33 Fatima Denton et al., "Accelerating the Transition in the Context of Sustainable Development," in *Climate Change 2022: Mitigation of Climate Change: Working Group III Contribution to the Sixth Assessment Report of the Intergovernmental Panel on Climate Change*, ed. Priyadarshi R. Shukla et al. (Cambridge: Cambridge University Press, 2022), 2816–2915, https://doi.org/10.1017/9781009157926; Sarah Burch et al., "Building Urban Resilience through Sustainability-Oriented Small- and Medium-Sized Enterprises," *Urban Transformations* 4, no. 1 (2022): 12, https://doi.org/10.1186/s42854-022-00041-9; Linda Westman, Janetta McKenzie, and Sarah Lynn Burch, "Political Participation of Businesses: A Framework to Understand Contributions of SMEs to Urban Sustainability Politics," *Earth System Governance* 3 (March 2020): 100044, https://doi.org/10.1016/j.esg.2020.100044; Kathryn Harrison, "The Politics of Carbon Pricing," *Nature Climate Change* 8, no. 10 (2018): 852, https://doi.org/10.1038/s41558-018-0289-4; Kathryn Harrison, "Political Institutions and Supply-Side Climate Politics: Lessons from Coal Ports in Canada and the United States," *Global Environmental Politics* 20, no. 4 (2020): 51–72, https://doi.org/10.1162/glep_a_00579.
34 Aisha Ahmad, *Jihad & Co.: Black Markets and Islamist Power* (Oxford: Oxford University Press, 2017); Aisha Ahmad, "The Long Jihad: The Boom–Bust Cycle behind Jihadist Durability," *Journal of Global Security Studies* 6, no. 4 (2021): ogaa048, https://doi.org/10.1093/jogss/ogaa048; Aisha Ahmad, "'We Have Captured Your Women': Explaining Jihadist Norm Change," *International Security* 44, no. 1 (2019): 80–116, https://doi.org/10.1162/isec_a_00350; Aisha Ahmad and Ousmane Diallo, "A Winning Team of Losers: The Logic of Jihadist Coalitions in Civil Wars," *Journal of Global Security Studies* 8, no. 1 (2023): ogac029, https://doi.org/10.1093/jogss/ogac029.

35 Nicole Wegner and Megan MacKenzie, *Feminist Solutions for Ending War* (London: Pluto Press, 2021).
36 Sheryl Lightfoot, *Global Indigenous Politics: A Subtle Revolution* (London: Routledge, 2016); Sheryl Lightfoot, "Indigenous Peoples and Canadian Defence," in *Canadian Defence Policy in Theory and Practice*, ed. Thomas Juneau, Philippe Lagassé, and Srdjan Vucetic (Cham, Switzerland: Springer International, 2020), 217–31, https://doi.org/10.1007/978-3-030-26403-1_13; Sheryl R. Lightfoot, "Decolonizing Self-Determination: Haudenosaunee Passports and Negotiated Sovereignty," *European Journal of International Relations* 27, no. 4 (2021): 971–94, https://doi.org/10.1177/13540661211024713; Sheryl Lightfoot, "Indigenous Disruptions: How Indigenous Self-Determination Practices Can Deepen and Expand International Theory," in *Globalizing International Theory: The Problem with Western IR Theory and How to Overcome It*, ed. A. Layug and John M. Hobson (London: Routledge, 2022), 200–18.
37 Jasmin Zine, *Under Siege: Islamophobia and the 9/11 Generation* (Montreal: McGill-Queen's University Press, 2022).
38 Lama Mourad and Kelsey P. Norman, "Transforming Refugees into Migrants: Institutional Change and the Politics of International Protection," *European Journal of International Relations* 26, no. 3 (2020): 687–713, https://doi.org/10.1177/1354066119883688; Maja Janmyr and Lama Mourad, "Categorising Syrians in Lebanon as 'Vulnerable,'" *Forced Migration Review*, no. 57 (February 2018); Lama Mourad, "Brothers, Workers or Syrians? The Politics of Naming in Lebanese Municipalities," *Journal of Refugee Studies* 34, no. 2 (2021): 1387–99, https://doi.org/10.1093/jrs/feab012.
39 Kristen Hopewell, *Clash of Powers: US-China Rivalry in Global Trade Governance* (Cambridge: Cambridge University Press, 2020).
40 Diana Fu, *Mobilizing without the Masses: Control and Contention in China* (Cambridge: Cambridge University Press, 2017).
41 Kanta Murali, *Caste, Class, and Capital: The Social and Political Origins of Economic Policy in India*, Ill. ed. (Cambridge: Cambridge University Press, 2017).
42 Malinda S. Smith, ed., *Securing Africa: Post-9/11 Discourses on Terrorism* (Farnham, UK: Routledge, 2010).
43 Juliet Johnson, *Priests of Prosperity: How Central Bankers Transformed the Postcommunist World*, Ill. ed. (Ithaca, NY: Cornell University Press, 2016).

44 Lisa McIntosh Sundstrom, Valerie Sperling, and Melike Sayoglu, *Courting Gender Justice: Russia, Turkey, and the European Court of Human Rights* (New York: Oxford University Press, 2019).
45 Marta Dyczok, *Ukraine Calling: A Kaleidoscope from Hromadske Radio 2016–2019* (Stuttgart: Ibidem Press, 2021); Tom Casier and Joan DeBardeleben, eds., *EU-Russia Relations in Crisis: Understanding Diverging Perceptions* (London: Routledge, 2019); Maria Popova, *Politicized Justice in Emerging Democracies: A Study of Courts in Russia and Ukraine* (New York: Cambridge University Press, 2012).
46 Maria Popova and Oxana Shevel, *Russia and Ukraine: Entangled Histories, Diverging States* (Medford, UK: Polity, 2024).
47 Stephanie Carvin, *Stand on Guard: Reassessing Threats to Canada's National Security* (Toronto: University of Toronto Press, 2021).
48 Wendy H. Wong, *We, the Data: Human Rights in the Digital Age* (Cambridge, MA: MIT Press, 2023).
49 Serena K. Sharma and Jennifer M. Welsh, eds., *The Responsibility to Prevent: Overcoming the Challenges of Atrocity Prevention* (Oxford: Oxford University Press, 2015).
50 Nergis Canefe, *Crimes against Humanity: The Limits of Universal Jurisdiction in the Global South* (Cardiff: University of Wales Press, 2021).
51 Anne-Marie Goetz and Shireen Hassim, eds., *No Shortcuts to Power: African Women in Politics and Policy Making* (London: Zed Books, 2003); Shireen Hassim, *Women's Organizations and Democracy in South Africa: Contesting Authority* (Madison: University of Wisconsin Press, 2006); Shireen Hassim, Tawana Kupe, Eric Worby, eds., *Go Home or Die Here: Violence, Xenophobia and the Reinvention of Difference in South Africa* (Johannesburg: Wits University Press, 2008); Shireen Hassim, *The ANC Women's League: Sex, Gender and Politics* (Athens: Ohio University Press, 2015).
52 W.R. Nadège Compaoré, "Africa Mining Vision: Prospects and Challenges for Implementing Countries," Institute for Peace and Security Studies, 2 October 2017, https://policycommons.net/artifacts/1444130/africa-mining-vision/2075863/ on 29 Mar 2024. CID: 20.500.12592/b0bvbj; W.R. Nadège Compaoré, "Rise of the (Other) Rest? Exploring Small State Agency and Collective Power in International Relations," *International Studies Review* 20, no. 2 (2018): 264–71, https://doi.org/10.1093/isr/viy036; W.R. Nadège Compaoré and Nathan Andrews,

"Temporality, Limited Statehood, and Africa's Abandoned Mines," in *The Oxford Handbook of Comparative Environmental Politics*, ed. Jeannie Sowers, Stacy D. VanDeveer, and Erika Weinthal (Oxford: Oxford University Press), 592–608, https://doi.org/10.1093/oxfordhb/9780197515037.013.46; J. Andrew Grant, W.R. Nadège Compaoré, Matthew I. Mitchell, and Mats Ingulstad, "'New' Approaches to the Governance of Africa's Natural Resources," in *New Approaches to the Governance of Natural Resources: Insights from Africa*, ed. J. Andrew Grant, W.R. Nadège Compaoré, and Matthew I. Mitchell (London: Palgrave Macmillan, 2015), 3–24, https://doi.org/10.1057/9781137280411_1.

53 Pamela Palmater and Niigaanwewidam James Sinclair, *Indigenous Nationhood: Empowering Grassroots Citizens* (Halifax, NS: Fernwood Publishing, 2015); Pamela Palmater, *Warrior Life: Indigenous Resistance and Resurgence* (Halifax, NS: Fernwood Publishing, 2020).

54 Debra Thompson, *The Schematic State: Race, Transnationalism, and the Politics of the Census*, repr. ed. (Cambridge: Cambridge University Press, 2018).

55 Siobhan Byrne and Allison McCulloch, "Gender, Representation and Power-Sharing in Post-Conflict Institutions," *International Peacekeeping* 19, no. 5 (2012): 565–80, https://doi.org/10.1080/13533312.2012.721990; Siobhan Byrne, "Troubled Engagement in Ethnicized Conflict," *International Feminist Journal of Politics* 16, no. 1 (2014): 106–26, https://doi.org/10.1080/14616742.2012.757020; Siobhan Byrne and Allison McCulloch, "Gendering Power-Sharing," in *Power-Sharing: Empirical and Normative Challenges*, ed. Allison McCulloch and John McGarry (London: Routledge, 2017), 250–67.

56 Yolande Bouka, "Nacibazo, 'No Problem': Moving Behind the Official Discourse of Post-Genocide Justice in Rwanda," in *Emotional and Ethical Challenges for Field Research in Africa: The Story Behind the Findings*, ed. Susan Thomson, An Ansoms, and Jude Murison (London: Palgrave Macmillan, 2013), 107–22, https://doi.org/10.1057/9781137263759_9; Marie E. Berry, Yolande Bouka, and Marilyn Muthoni Kamuru, "Implementing Inclusion: Gender Quotas, Inequality, and Backlash in Kenya," *Politics & Gender* 17, no. 4 (2021): 640–64, https://doi.org/10.1017/S1743923X19000886.

57 Megan Bradley, *Refugee Repatriation: Justice, Responsibility and Redress*, repr. ed. (Cambridge: Cambridge University Press, 2014); Megan

Bradley, Ibrahim Fraihat, and Houda Mzioudet, *Libya's Displacement Crisis: Uprooted by Revolution and Civil War*, ill. ed. (Washington, DC: Georgetown University Press, 2015); Megan Bradley, *The International Organization for Migration: Challenges, Commitments, Complexities* (London: Routledge, 2020).

58 Yasmeen Abu-Laban, Ethel Tungohan, and Christina Gabriel, *Containing Diversity: Canada and the Politics of Immigration in the 21st Century* (Toronto: University of Toronto Press, 2022).

59 Yang-Yang Zhou and Andrew Shaver, "Reexamining the Effect of Refugees on Civil Conflict: A Global Subnational Analysis," *American Political Science Review* 115, no. 4 (2021): 1175–96, https://doi.org/10.1017/S0003055421000502; Yang-Yang Zhou, Guy Grossman, and Shuning Ge, "Inclusive Refugee-Hosting Can Improve Local Development and Prevent Public Backlash," *World Development* 166 (June 2023): 106203, https://doi.org/10.1016/j.worlddev.2023.106203.

60 Although I wish I could acknowledge all of Canada's outstanding women security experts by name, I can only offer a small snapshot of their work here. Any oversights are wholly unintentional.

Appendix: Must-Read Books List

This list features a small selection of the many outstanding peer-reviewed academic books published by women security experts from across Canada. Using a "big tent" definition of security, these books cover topics of relevance to both traditional and non-traditional security scholars and practitioners. You will therefore find books on American hegemony, Russian oligarchs, Chinese political repression, Canadian foreign policy, UN peacekeeping, ethnic conflict and genocide, climate change policy, race relations, and more. There are also books focusing on particular countries or regions that are of importance to Canadian foreign affairs, such as Russia, Ukraine, India, the Middle East, Africa, and Latin America. The authors come from a diverse mix of disciplinary backgrounds and perspectives.

Of course, this list is not exhaustive, and readers should consider it a mere starting point. To have included all research – books and journal articles – published by all of Canada's women security experts around the world would have made this an impossibly long list. Instead, this appendix showcases only a small handful of social science books written or edited by women security experts who happen to be based at Canadian universities at the time of writing.

Beyond those featured on this list, there are many other outstanding Canadian women security experts all around the world who have written excellent books, but who are not featured here because they are not presently at a Canadian university. There are also many other scholars who choose not to write academic books, and instead only publish their research in peer-reviewed journals. This is especially true in the STEM fields, where scientific journal articles are much more common than scholarly books. Because our women experts working on climate change and cybersecurity publish their research in top-tier science journals, they are therefore not seen on this list; but that doesn't mean they don't exist.

This preliminary list therefore represents only a fraction of the excellent scholarship produced by women security experts in Canada. And yet, it proves that there is no shortage of women experts whose research directly addresses the most pressing national and international security concerns facing the country in the years ahead. Given this abundance of expertise, there is no excuse for an all-male syllabus, advisory group, expert panel, or decision-making committee on national security in this country. Including diverse perspectives, then, is not only a necessary professional practice for any functioning organization – it is also very easy to accomplish.

Changing Systems

This section includes books that cover more traditional subjects in security studies, such as Canadian foreign affairs and defence, American power projection, NATO and Russia, Chinese politics, and other topics in alliance formation and great power politics. These books will be of interest to readers who are primarily concerned with how changes in the global balance of power can affect Canadian national security.

Carvin, Stephanie. *Stand on Guard: Reassessing Threats to Canada's National Security.* Toronto: University of Toronto Press, 2021.
– (and Thomas Juneau). *Intelligence Analysis and Policy Making: The Canadian Experience.* Stanford, CA: Stanford University Press, 2021.
– (and Thomas Juneau and Craig Forcese), eds. *Top Secret Canada: Understanding the Canadian Intelligence and National Security Community.* Toronto: University of Toronto Press, 2021.
– (and Michael John Williams). *Law, Science, Liberalism and the American Way of Warfare: The Quest for Humanity in Conflict.* New York: Cambridge University Press, 2014.

Charron, Andrea (and James Fergusson). *NORAD: In Perpetuity and Beyond.* Montreal: McGill-Queen's University Press, 2022.
Desai, Radhika. *Geopolitical Economy: After Us Hegemony, Globalization and Empire.* Halifax, NS: Fernwood Publishing, 2013.
–. *Capitalism, Coronavirus and War: A Geopolitical Economy.* Abingdon, UK: Routledge, 2022.
Fu, Diana. *Mobilizing without the Masses: Control and Contention in China.* Cambridge: Cambridge University Press, 2017.
Hopewell, Kristen. *Breaking the WTO: How Emerging Powers Disrupted the Neoliberal Project.* Stanford, CA: Stanford University Press, 2016.
–. *Clash of Powers: US-China Rivalry in Global Trade Governance.* Cambridge: Cambridge University Press, 2020.
Gilady, Lilach. *The Price of Prestige: Conspicuous Consumption in International Relations.* Chicago: University of Chicago Press, 2018.
Habib, Jasmin (and Virginia R. Dominguez). *America Observed: On an International Anthropology of the United States.* New York: Berghahn Books, 2016.
Kitchen, Veronica M. *The Globalization of NATO: Intervention, Security and Identity.* Abingdon, UK: Routledge, 2010.
Lane, Andrea (and Brian Bow), eds. *Canadian Foreign Policy: Reflections on a Field in Transition.* Vancouver: UBC Press, 2021.
Macdonald, Laura (and David Carment and Jeremy Paltiel), eds. *Canada and Great Power Competition: Canada among Nations 2021.* Cham, Switzerland: Palgrave Macmillan, 2022.
Martel, Stéphanie. *Enacting the Security Community: ASEAN's Never-Ending Story.* Standford, CA: Stanford University Press, 2022.
Momani, Bessma (and Thomas Juneau), eds. *Middle Power in the Middle East: Canada's Foreign and Defence Policies in a Changing Region.* Toronto: University of Toronto Press, 2022.
Norrlöf, Carla. *America's Global Advantage: US Hegemony and International Cooperation.* Cambridge: Cambridge University Press, 2010.
Ong, Lynette H. *Outsourcing Repression: Everyday State Power in Contemporary China.* Oxford: Oxford University Press, 2022.
–. *The Street and the Ballot Box.* Cambridge: Cambridge University Press, 2022.
Popova, Maria, and Oxana Shevel. *Russia and Ukraine: Entangled Histories, Diverging States.* Cambridge: Polity Press, 2024.
Simpson, Erika. *NATO and the Bomb: Canadian Defenders Confront Critics.* Montreal: McGill-Queens University Press, 2002.
Sloan, Elinor C. *Modern Military Strategy: An Introduction.* London: Routledge, 2016.

–. *Security and Defence in the Terrorist Era*. Montreal: McGill-Queen's University Press, 2005.
Su, Anna. *Exporting Freedom: Religious Liberty and American Power*. Cambridge, MA: Harvard University Press, 2016.
von Hlatky, Stéfanie. *American Allies in Times of War: The Great Asymmetry*. Oxford: Oxford University Press, 2013.
Wang, Juan. *The Sinews of State Power: The Rise and Demise of the Cohesive Local State in Rural China*. New York: Oxford University Press, 2017.
Welsh, Jennifer. *At Home in the World: Canada's Global Vision for the 21st Century*. Toronto: HarperPerennial, 2010.
–. *The Return of History: Conflict, Migration, and Geopolitics in the Twenty-First Century*. Toronto: House of Anansi Press, 2016.

Evolving Threats

This section includes books on a range of evolving and emerging security concerns, including civil wars, conflict economies, peacekeeping, diaspora politics, cybersecurity, disasters, and climate change. It also includes books that shed light on the political and economic landscape of important countries and regions in the world, particularly those areas where Canada has strong security interests, such as Russia, Ukraine, the Middle East, Latin America, and Africa. These books will be of interest to readers who are interested in the intersection between comparative politics and international security, as well as those who are interested in complex and multidimensional security problems.

Agathangelou, Anna (and Nevzat Soguk), eds. *Arab Revolutions and World Transformations*. New York: Routledge, 2014.
Agrawal, Nirupama. *Natural Disasters and Risk Management in Canada: An Introduction*. New York: Springer Nature, 2018.
Ahmad, Aisha. *Jihad & Co.: Black Markets and Islamist Power*. Oxford: Oxford University Press, 2017.
Bell, Colleen. *The Freedom of Security: Governing Canada in the Age of Counter-Terrorism*. Vancouver: UBC Press, 2011.
Bonner, Michelle D. *Policing Protest in Argentina and Chile*. Boulder, CO: Lynne Rienner Publishers, 2014.
–. *Tough on Crime: The Rise of Punitive Populism in Latin America*. Pittsburgh: University of Pittsburgh Press, 2019.

Brûlé, Sarah-Myriam Martin. *Evaluating Peacekeeping Missions: A Typology of Success and Failure in International Interventions.* London: Routledge, 2016.
Brunnée, Jutta (and Daniel Bodansky and Ellen Hey), eds., *The Oxford Handbook of International Environmental Law.* Oxford: Oxford University Press, 2007.
– (and Daniel Bodansky and Lavanya Rajamani). *International Climate Change Law.* Oxford: Oxford University Press, 2017.
– (and Meinhard Doelle and Lavanya Rajamani), eds. *Promoting Compliance in an Evolving Climate Change Regime.* Cambridge: Cambridge University Press, 2012.
– (and Silke Goldberg, Richard Lord, and Lavanya Rajamani), eds. *Climate Change Liability: Transnational Law and Practice.* Cambridge: Cambridge University Press, 2012.
– (and S.J. Toope). *Legitimacy and Legality in International Law: An Interactional Account.* Cambridge: Cambridge University Press, 2010.
Buchanan, Ruth (and Peer Zumbansen), eds. *Law in Transition: Human Rights, Development and Transitional Justice.* London: Bloomsbury, 2016.
Burch, Sarah L., and Sara E. Harris. *Understanding Climate Change: Science, Policy, and Practice.* 2nd ed. Toronto: University of Toronto Press, 2021.
Canefe, Nergis. *Crimes against Humanity: The Limits of Universal Jurisdiction in the Global South.* Cardiff: University of Wales Press, 2021.
Coleman, Katharina P. *International Organisations and Peace Enforcement: The Politics of International Legitimacy.* Cambridge: Cambridge University Press, 2007.
– (and Markus Kornprobst and Annette Seegers), eds. *Diplomacy and Borderlands: African Agency at the Intersections of Orders.* Abingdon, UK: Routledge, 2019.
– (and Xiaojun Li). *Token Forces: How Tiny Troop Deployments Became Ubiquitous in UN Peacekeeping.* Cambridge: Cambridge University Press, 2022.
– (and Thomas K. Tieku). *African Actors in International Security: Shaping Contemporary Norms.* Boulder, CO: Lynne Rienner Publishers, 2018.
Deonandan, Kalowatie (and Michael L. Dougherty), eds. *Mining in Latin America: Critical Approaches to the New Extraction.* Abingdon, UK: Routledge, 2016.
Dyczok, Marta. *Ukraine Calling: A Kaleidoscope from Hromadske Radio 2016–2019.* Stuttgart: Ibidem Press, 2021.
–. *The Grand Alliance and Ukrainian Refugees.* New York: St. Martin's Press, 2000.
Fisher, Kirsten J. *Moral Accountability and International Criminal Law: Holding Agents of Atrocity Accountable to the World.* London: Routledge, 2013.

–. *Transitional Justice for Child Soldiers: Accountability and Social Reconstruction in Post-conflict Contexts*. New York: Palgrave Macmillan, 2013.

– (and Robert Stewart), eds. *Transitional Justice and the Arab Spring*. Abingdon, UK: Routledge, 2015.

Fujii, Lee Ann.[1] *Killing Neighbors: Webs of Violence in Rwanda*. Ithaca, NY: Cornell University Press, 2011.

–. *Show Time: The Logic and Power of Violent Display*. Ithaca, NY: Cornell University Press, 2021.

Habib, Jasmin. *Israel, Diaspora, and the Routes of National Belonging*. 2nd ed. Toronto: University of Toronto Press, 2019.

Harrison, Kathryn, and Lisa McIntosh Sundstrom, eds. *Global Commons, Domestic Decisions: The Comparative Politics of Climate Change*. Cambridge, MA: MIT Press, 2010.

Hassim, Shireen. *The ANC Women's League: Sex, Gender and Politics*. Athens: Ohio University Press, 2015.

– (and Anne-Marie Goetz), eds. *No Shortcuts to Power: African Women in Politics and Policy Making*. London: Zed Books, 2003.

Hiebert, Maureen S. *Constructing Genocide and Mass Violence: Society, Crisis, Identity*. Abingdon, UK: Routledge, 2019.

Hilgers, Tina, and Laura Macdonald, eds. *Violence in Latin America and the Caribbean: Subnational Structures, Institutions, and Clientelistic Networks*. Cambridge: Cambridge University Press, 2017.

Johnson, Juliet. *Priests of Prosperity: How Central Bankers Transformed the Postcommunist World*. Ithaca, NY: Cornell University Press, 2016.

Momani, Bessma. *Arab Dawn: Arab Youth and the Demographic Dividend They Will Bring*. Toronto: University of Toronto Press, 2015.

– (and Matteo Legrenzi), eds. *Shifting Geo-economic Power of the Gulf: Oil, Finance and Institutions*. London: Routledge, 2016.

Murali, Kanta. *Caste, Class, and Capital: The Social and Political Origins of Economic Policy in India*. Cambridge: Cambridge University Press, 2017.

Peterson, Jenny. *Building a Peace Economy? Liberal Peacebuilding and the Development-Security Industry*. Manchester: Manchester University Press, 2014.

Popova, Maria. *Politicized Justice in Emerging Democracies: A Study of Courts in Russia and Ukraine*. New York: Cambridge University Press, 2012.

Sharma, Serena, and Jennifer Welsh, eds. *The Responsibility to Prevent: Overcoming the Challenges of Atrocity Prevention*. Oxford: Oxford University Press, 2015.

Simons, Penelope, and Audrey Macklin. *The Governance Gap: Extractive Industries, Human Rights, and the Home State Advantage*. London: Routledge, 2015.

Smith, Malinda S., ed. *Securing Africa: Post-9/11 Discourses on Terrorism*. London: Routledge, 2010.

West, Leah (and Craig Forcese). *National Security Law*. 2nd ed. Toronto: Irwin Law, 2020.

– (and Thomas Juneau and Amarnath Amarasingam), eds. *Stress Tested: The COVID-19 Pandemic and Canadian National Security*. Calgary: University of Calgary Press, 2021.

Wong, Wendy H. *Internal Affairs: How the Structure of NGOs Transforms Human Rights*. Ithaca, NY: Cornell University Press, 2012.

–. *We, the Data: Human Rights in the Digital Age*. Cambridge, MA: MIT Press, 2023.

Inclusive Security

This section includes books on topics related to race, gender, human rights, migration, and nationality, all of which are directly related to Canadian security concerns. They also cover topics related to both equity and justice and how these pertain to Canadian national interests, and which expand upon conventional definitions of security. These books will be of interest to readers who are interested in refugee issues, human security, feminist foreign policy, gender and security, and race and Indigeneity.

Abu-Laban, Yasmeen, Ethel Tungohan, and Christina Gabriel. *Containing Diversity: Canada and the Politics of Immigration in the 21st Century*. Toronto: University of Toronto Press, 2022.

Anderson, Miriam J. *Windows of Opportunity: How Women Seize Peace Negotiations for Political Change*. Oxford: Oxford University Press, 2016.

Bohn, Simone, and Charmain Levy, eds. *Twenty-First-Century Feminismos: Women's Movements in Latin America and the Caribbean*. Montreal: McGill-Queen's University Press, 2021.

Bradley, Megan, ed. *Forced Migration, Reconciliation and Justice*. Montreal: McGill-Queen's University Press, 2015.

–. *The International Organization for Migration: Challenges, Commitments, Complexities*. Abingdon, UK: Routledge, 2020.

–. *Refugee Repatriation: Justice, Responsibility and Redress*. Cambridge: Cambridge University Press, 2014.

– (and Cathryn Costello and Angela Sherwood), eds. *IOM Unbound? Obligations and Accountability of the International Organization for Migration in an Era of Expansion*. Cambridge: Cambridge University Press, 2023.

– (and Ibrahim Fraihat and **Houda Mzioudet**). *Libya's Displacement Crisis: Uprooted by Revolution and Civil War.* Washington, DC: Georgetown University Press, 2015.
– (and James Milner and Blair Peruniak), eds. *Refugees' Roles in Resolving Displacement and Building Peace: Beyond Beneficiaries.* Washington, DC: Georgetown University Press, 2019.
Byrne, Siobhan, and Allison McCulloch, eds. *Power-Sharing Pacts and the Women, Peace and Security Agenda.* London: Routledge, 2021.
Côté, Isabelle (and Matthew I. Mitchell and Monica Duffy Toft), eds. *People Changing Places: New Perspectives on Demography, Migration, Conflict, and the State.* New York: Routledge, 2018.
Doran, Marie-Christine (and Gabriel Blouin-Genest and **Sylvie Paquerot**), eds. *Human Rights as Battlefields: Changing Practices and Contestations.* Cham, Switzerland: Springer, 2018.
Eichler, Maya. *Gender and Private Security in Global Politics.* Oxford: Oxford University Press, 2015.
–. *Militarizing Men: Gender, Conscription, and War in Post-Soviet Russia.* Stanford, CA: Stanford University Press, 2011.
Givens, Terri E. *The Roots of Racism: The Politics of White Supremacy in the US and Europe.* Bristol, UK: Bristol University Press, 2022.
Kitchen, Veronica (and Jennifer G. Mathers), eds. *Heroism and Global Politics.* Abingdon, UK: Routledge, 2018.
Lightfoot, Sheryl. *Global Indigenous Politics: A Subtle Revolution.* London: Routledge, 2016.
Lu, Catherine. *Just and Unjust Interventions in World Politics: Public and Private.* Basingstoke, UK: Palgrave Macmillan, 2006.
–. *Justice and Reconciliation in World Politics.* Cambridge: Cambridge University Press, 2017.
MacKenzie, Megan. *Beyond the Band of Brothers: The US Military and the Myth That Women Can't Fight.* Cambridge: Cambridge University Press, 2015.
–. *Female Soldiers in Sierra Leone: Sex, Security, and Post-conflict Development.* New York: NYU Press, 2012.
– (and Nicole Wenger). *Feminist Solutions for Ending War.* London: Pluto Press, 2021.
Momani, Bessma (and Alistair Edgar and Rupinder Mangat). *Strengthening the Canadian Armed Forces through Diversity and Inclusion.* Toronto: University of Toronto Press, 2019.
Palmater, Pamela. *Warrior Life: Indigenous Resistance and Resurgence.* Halifax, NS: Fernwood Publishing, 2020.

– (and Niigaanwewidam James Sinclair). *Indigenous Nationhood: Empowering Grassroots Citizens.* Halifax, NS: Fernwood Publishing, 2015.

Robinson, Fiona. *The Ethics of Care: A Feminist Approach to Human Security.* Philadelphia, PA: Temple University Press, 2011.

Shachar, Ayelet. *Lawless Zones, Rightless Subjects: Migration, Asylum and Shifting Border.* Cambridge: Cambridge University Press, 2024.

–. *The Shifting Border: Legal Cartographies of Migration and Mobility.* Manchester: Manchester University Press, 2020.

– (and Rainer Bauboeck, **Irene Bloemraad**, and Maarten Vink), eds. *The Oxford Handbook of Citizenship.* Oxford: Oxford University Press, 2017, 2020.

Sundstrom, Lisa McIntosh (and Valerie Sperling and Melike Sayoglu). *Courting Gender Justice: Russia, Turkey, and the European Court of Human Rights.* New York: Oxford University Press, 2019.

Thompson, Debra. *The Schematic State: Race, Transnationalism, and the Politics of the Census.* Cambridge: Cambridge University Press, 2018.

von Hlatky, Stéfanie. *Deploying Feminism: The Role of Gender in NATO Military Operations.* New York: Oxford University Press, 2022.

Zine, Jasmin, ed. *Islam in the Hinterlands: Muslim Cultural Politics in Canada.* Vancouver: UBC Press, 2012.

–. *Under Siege: Islamophobia and the 9/11 Generation.* Montreal: McGill-Queen's University Press, 2022.

NOTE

1 Dr. Lee-Ann Fujii's influential work is rightly included on this list of Canadian women security scholars, and she is recognized here posthumously as a scholar from the University of Toronto.

Contributors

Dr. Aisha Ahmad is an associate professor of political science at the University of Toronto and a multiple award–winning expert on jihadist insurgencies operating in complex civil wars. She is a senior fellow at Massey College, a fellow at Trinity College, a senior researcher at the Munk School of Global Affairs, and a member of the Royal Society of Canada's College of New Scholars, Artists, and Scientists. Dr. Ahmad is the author of *Jihad & Co.: Black Markets and Islamist Power* (Oxford University Press, 2017), which was awarded both the distinguished 2017 Mershon Center Furniss Award for the best new book in international and national security and the 2018 Best Book in Comparative Politics Prize by the Canadian Political Science Association, in addition to being listed as one of the Best Books of 2018 in *Foreign Affairs*. Her article "The Security Bazaar," published in the flagship journal *International Security*, won the 2017 Best Security Article Award from the International Studies Association. Her article "The Long Jihad: The Boom-Bust Cycle behind Jihadist Durability" was awarded Best Article in the *Journal of Global Security Studies* for 2021. She is the winner of the 2024 International Studies Association's International Security Studies Section Emerging Scholar Award, which recognizes scholars who have made (through their body of publications) the most significant contribution to the field of security studies. Dr. Ahmad is also the winner of the 2018 Northrop Frye Award of Excellence for outstanding contributions to co-curricular learning and pedagogical innovation, and the 2018 recipient of the University of Toronto Scarborough's Assistant Professor Award for outstanding contributions to undergraduate teaching at U of T's Scarborough campus. She has conducted fieldwork in Afghanistan, Pakistan, Somalia, Mali, Iraq, and Lebanon, and has spent over a decade advising senior leaders in military, government, and international organizations on global security policy. Dr. Ahmad was formerly an international security fellow at the Belfer Center for Science and International Affairs at the Harvard Kennedy School and was previously the chair of the Board of Directors of Women in International Security (WIIS)-Canada.

Dr. Carla Norrlöf is a professor of political science at the University of Toronto and an internationally renowned expert on great power politics, international finance and monetary policy, global economics, and international security. She is a global authority on dollar hegemony, and the author of *America's Global Advantage: US Hegemony and International Cooperation* (Cambridge University Press, 2010). She has published with MIT Press and Oxford University Press, as well as in the *Canadian Journal of Political Science*, *Conflict Management and Peace Science*, the *Cambridge Review of International Affairs*, *Cooperation and Conflict*, *International Affairs*, the *International Political Science Review*, *International Security*, and the *Review of International Political Economy and Security Studies*. Dr. Norrlöf is a non-resident senior fellow with the Atlantic Council, and serves on the editorial board of the *International Studies Review*, the *International Studies Quarterly*, and *International Theory*. Dr. Norrlöf has testified twice before the United States Congress as part of the House Financial Services Committee hearings on *Dollar Dominance: Preserving the U.S. Dollar's Status as the Global Reserve Currency* (June 2023) and *Under the Radar: Alternative Payment Systems and the National Security Impacts of Their Growth* (September 2022). Her public commentary has appeared in *Foreign Affairs*, the *Globe and Mail*, *The Guardian*, *Le Monde*, *Newsweek*, *Project Syndicate*, and the *Washington Post*.

Hannah Hollander is an officer in the Canadian Armed Forces (CAF) who has research expertise in multilateral diplomacy, irregular warfare, and intersectional security dynamics. Hollander has a bachelor's degree in political science from the Royal Military College of Canada (RMC) and earned a master's degree in political studies from Queen's University under the supervision of Dr. Stéfanie von Hlatky. Her recent publications include the 2021 policy brief "What Is Grey Zone Deterrence?" for the Network for Strategic Analysis. She also contributed to the *Report on CJOC Defence Planning* and *The Geopolitical Impacts of*

COVID-19 (2020) with the National Security Agency. Building on her positive mentorship experience with Women in International Security (WIIS)-Canada, Hollander helped to resurrect the RMC Athena Network, which connects officer cadets to female leaders in the CAF.

Dr. Stéfanie von Hlatky is a full professor in the Department of Political Studies and the associate dean of research at Queen's University. She is the Canada Research Chair on Gender, Security, and the Armed Forces, and a nationally decorated scholar in military cooperation, NATO alliances, deterrence, gender in the armed forces, and the Women, Peace, and Security agenda. Her book *Deploying Feminism: The Role of Gender in NATO Military Operations* (Oxford University Press, 2022) provides the most comprehensive account of NATO's implementation of the Women, Peace, and Security agenda, with over one hundred interviews from strategic-level headquarters to the missions in Iraq, Kosovo, and the Baltics. Dr. von Hlatky has published six books, the most recent of which include *Going to War? Trends in Military Operations* (McGill-Queen's University Press, 2016), *Countering Violent Extremism and Terrorism* (McGill-Queen's University Press, 2020), *Transhumanizing War* (McGill-Queen's University Press, 2020), and *Total Defence Forces in the Twenty-First Century* (McGill-Queen's University Press, 2023). Dr. von Hlatky is the honorary colonel at the Princess of Wales' Own Regiment, the co-director of the Canadian Defence and Security Network, and was the founder of Women in International Security (WIIS)-Canada. She has previously held positions at Georgetown University's Center for Peace and Security Studies, the Woodrow Wilson International Center for Scholars in Washington, DC, Dartmouth College, and the Center for Security Studies at ETH Zurich.

Danielle Cherpako is an associate political affairs officer with the United Nations Department of Peace Operations, and has research expertise in Canadian foreign policy, Arctic and northern policy, the use of sanctions, and the use of truth commissions. She holds a master of arts in political studies from the University of Manitoba, Canada, for which she received the Governor General's Gold Academic Medal, a Social Sciences and Humanities Research Council of Canada Graduate Scholarship, and a J.W. Dafoe Political Studies Fellowship. Cherpako has conducted community-based research with the Misipawistik Cree Nation as part of a fellowship with the Samuel Centre, has worked as a research assistant with the National Centre for Truth and Reconciliation, and has also worked and volunteered with the Canadian International Council Winnipeg Branch. She has previously worked with the North American and Arctic Defence Security Network, the Centre for Defence and Security Studies, the Canadian International Council, and Transport Canada, among other organizations. She has also volunteered with the United Nations Global Information Management Assessment and Analysis Cell on COVID-19.

Dr. Andrea Charron is a professor of international relations and director of the Centre for Defence and Security Studies at the University of Manitoba, as well as a nationally recognized expert on Arctic security, NATO, NORAD, and Canadian defence policy. Dr. Charron has published several books on global security and sanctions regimes, including *NORAD: In Perpetuity and Beyond* (McGill-Queen's University Press, 2022), *The Legacy of 9/11: Views from North America* (McGill-Queen's University Press, 2023), and *UN Sanctions and Conflict: Responding to Peace and Security Threats* (Routledge, 2011). She is the network co-lead for the North American and Arctic Security Network, an operations node co-lead for the Canadian Defence and Security Network, and a global fellow for the Wilson Center in Washington, DC. She serves on the editorial boards of the *Canadian Foreign Policy Journal*, the *Canadian Naval Review*, and the *Canadian Army Journal*. Dr. Charron has been awarded the Students' Teacher Recognition Award for the Faculty of Arts (2021), the Faculty of Arts Teaching Award (2019), and the Faculty of Arts Internationalization Award (2019) at the University of Manitoba. She is regularly asked to provide guest lectures at Canadian Forces College and to provide testimony to Senate and House of Commons' committees.

Dr. Lynette H. Ong is a professor of political science at the Munk School of Global Affairs and Public Policy at the University of Toronto and an internationally recognized authority on Chinese politics. She is a senior fellow at the Asia Society Policy Institute, a faculty fellow at the Schwartz Reisman Institute for Technology and Society, and an appointed senior fellow at the Asia Society's Center for China Analysis in New York City. Dr. Ong is the author of *Outsourcing Repression: Everyday State Power in Contemporary China* (Oxford University Press, 2022), which has won multiple international best book awards from the American Political Science Association, the American Sociological

Association, and the International Studies Association, including the Distinguished Contribution to Scholarship in Political Sociology from the American Sociological Association. Her other monographs include *The Street and the Ballot Box: Interactions between Social Movements and Electoral Politics in Authoritarian Contexts* (Cambridge University Press, 2022) and *Prosper or Perish: Credit and Fiscal Systems in Rural China* (Cornell University Press, 2012). Her peer-reviewed publications have appeared in *Perspectives on Politics, Comparative Politics, China Quarterly,* and *China Journal,* among others. Dr. Ong was the 2023 recipient of the Faculty of Arts and Science Dean's Research Excellence Award at the University of Toronto. She has delivered expert testimonies before the United States Congress's US-China Economic and Security Review Commission and Canada's House of Commons Special Committee on Canada-China Relations on numerous occasions. Her public commentary has been published by *The Economist, Foreign Affairs,* the *Washington Post,* and the *Globe and Mail*.

Dr. Bessma Momani is a full professor of political science and the associate vice-president, international at the University of Waterloo, and a renowned global authority on Middle Eastern politics and economics. Dr. Momani is a senior fellow at the Centre for International Governance Innovation, a non-resident fellow at the Arab Gulf States Institute in Washington, DC, a governor of the International Development Research Council, and a Fulbright Scholar. She has authored and co-edited ten books and over eighty scholarly, peer-reviewed journal articles and book chapters on the topics of international affairs, the economics and politics of the Middle East, and diversity and inclusion. Dr. Momani was a non-resident senior fellow at both the Brookings Institution and Stimson Center, a consultant to the International Monetary Fund, a visiting scholar at Global Affairs Canada and Georgetown University's Mortara Center, and a 2015 fellow of the Pierre Elliott Trudeau Foundation. From 2018 to 2022 she sat on the National Security Transparency Advisory Group to advise Public Safety Canada. She also spearheaded the Pluralism Project, which explored the link between Canadian diversity and economic prosperity and led to funding grants from Immigration, Refugees and Citizenship Canada to bring racialized women into the Canadian economy and from Heritage Canada to study the impact of disinformation on ethnocultural communities. She sits on the editorial board of the *Canadian Foreign Policy Journal.* Dr. Momani was awarded the

2016 University of Waterloo Excellence in Arts Teaching Award and the University of Waterloo Outstanding Performance Award. She is a frequent contributor to international media on international affairs and writes op-eds for the *Globe and Mail*.

Dr. Katharina P. Coleman is an associate professor of political science at the University of British Columbia and a world-leading expert on international organizations and peace operations, with a regional specialization in sub-Saharan Africa. Dr. Coleman has published several books, including *Token Forces: How Tiny Troop Deployments Became Ubiquitous in UN Peacekeeping* (Cambridge University Press, 2022), as well as *Diplomacy and Borderlands: African Agency at the Intersections of Orders* (Routledge, 2019) and *African Actors in International Security: Shaping Contemporary Norms* (Lynne Rienner, 2018). Her published academic work on peace operations includes analyses of financing models, force generation, gendered workplaces, national staff, rapid deployment, and the evolving roles of regional organizations. In addition to her academic publications, she has authored several policy reports on UN peacekeeping, including a primer on peacekeeping financing for the 2015 High-Level Independent Panel on Peace Operations. She currently serves on the Technical Committee of the United Nations' Elsie Initiative Fund for Uniformed Women in Peace Operations.

Dr. Lou Pingeot is a postdoctoral fellow at the Centre for International Policy Studies, University of Ottawa, and an expert on international interventions and the role of police forces. She is the author of *Police Peacekeeping: The UN, Haiti, and the Production of Global Social Order* (Oxford University Press, 2023), and has published in leading academic journals, including *International Studies Quarterly*, *Third World Quarterly*, and *International Peacekeeping*. Dr. Pingeot is an associate editor of the *Journal of Intervention and Statebuilding* and has conducted extensive fieldwork on policing in United Nations peacekeeping operations. Her research lies at the intersection of global historical sociology, postcolonialism, and international practice theory, and investigates the links between external and internal security.

Dr. Leah West is an associate professor of international affairs at the Norman Paterson School of International Affairs, Carleton University, specializing in national security law, international humanitarian law, and cyber operations. Dr. West is a nationally recognized authority on national security law, counterterrorism, and public international law. She completed her SJD at the University of Toronto in 2020, where she studied the application of the Charter of Rights and Freedoms to state conduct in cyberspace. Beyond her SJD, Leah obtained an LLM in international humanitarian and national security from the University of Ottawa, a JD from the University of Toronto, an MA in intelligence from the American Military University, and a degree from the Royal Military College of Canada. In addition to her many published academic articles, Dr. West has co-authored two books on law and national security in Canada: *National Security Law* (Irwin Law, 2021) and *Stress Tested: The COVID-19 Pandemic and Canadian National Security* (University of Calgary Press, 2021). Prior to her appointment at Carleton, Dr. West served as counsel with the Department of Justice in the National Security Litigation and Advisory Group. She has appeared before the Supreme Court of Canada, the Federal Court in designated proceedings, and the Security Intelligence Review Committee. Before her law career, Dr. West served for a decade as an armoured officer in the Canadian Army, and was deployed to Afghanistan in 2010.

Dr. Nirupama Agrawal is a professor and founding faculty member in York University's Disaster and Emergency Management program since 2005. She has a PhD in water resources from Kyoto University and a master's in hydrology from the Indian Institute of Technology Roorkee, and over thirty-five years of professional experience. Her wide-ranging research includes threat assessment of potential natural, intentional, and technological hazards, public safety, disaster resilience in a changing climate, and the use of geospatial technologies for decision making. She has mentored over seventy students, published over ninety refereed articles and book chapters, two books, one edited volume, and co-guest-edited three special issues for the journals *Natural Hazards* and *Sustainability*. Her *Tsunami Travel Time Atlas*, an early warning resource for the Atlantic Ocean, is the first of its kind. Her textbook *Natural Disasters and Risk Management in Canada: An Introduction*, published by Springer, is one of the most used textbooks in emergency management. Dr. Agrawal is an adjunct professor at the United Nations University Institute for Water, Environment and Health and a co-director of the Canadian Defence and Security Network's MINDS project on domestic operations.

Dr. Kathryn Harrison is a professor of political science at the University of British Columbia (UBC) and a world-renowned expert on environmental, climate, and energy policy. Dr. Harrison is currently chair of the Expert Advisory Panel on Climate Mitigation of the Canadian Climate Institute and a member of the British Columbia Climate Solutions Council. She is the author of the book *Passing the Buck: Federalism and Canadian Environmental Policy* (UBC Press, 1996), co-author of *Risk, Science, and Politics* (McGill-Queen's University Press, 1994), and co-editor of *Global Commons, Domestic Decisions: The Comparative Politics of Climate Change* (MIT Press, 2010). She has published extensively in edited volumes and journals, including the *Canadian Journal of Political Science*, the *Canadian Journal of Economics*, the *Journal of Policy Analysis and Management*, and *Global Environmental Politics*. Dr. Harrison's many awards include Fulbright Fellowships, the Gilbert White Fellowship at Resources for the Future, the UBC Killam Research Fellowship, the K.D. Srivastava Prize from UBC Press, and the John Vandercamp Prize for the best article of the year in *Canadian Public Policy*. She has previously served as senior associate dean and acting dean in UBC's Faculty of Arts and has advised governments from the local to the international levels. She has worked in the oil industry and has also served as a policy analyst for both Environment Canada and the United States Congress.

Dr. Sarah Burch is a professor in the Department of Geography and Environmental Management and Canada Research Chair in Sustainability Governance and Innovation at the University of Waterloo. She is a national authority on climate change and sustainability challenges, the executive director of the Waterloo Climate Institute, and a fellow at the Balsillie School of International Affairs. Dr. Burch was a lead author of the United Nations' *Sixth Assessment Report* of the Intergovernmental Panel on Climate Change (winner of the Nobel Peace Prize in 2007) and has helped to lead expert input into the development of Canada's first National Adaptation Strategy. Her book *Understanding Climate Change: Science, Policy, and Practice* (University of Toronto Press, 2021) expertly addresses the climate crisis from both scientific and public policy angles. Dr. Burch taught the first massive open online course on climate change, which reached thousands of students in over 130 countries. She was named to the Royal Society of Canada's College of New Scholars in 2017, one of Canada's Top 40 Under 40 in 2018, and one of Canada's Clean 50 in 2021. Dr. Burch leads the international partnership–based research project TRANS-FORM: Accelerating Sustainability Entrepreneurship Experiments in Local Spaces and is the director of the Sustainability Policy Research on Urban Transformations (SPROUT) Lab.

Dr. Janetta McKenzie is an expert on energy policy development, natural gas certification, and industrial decarbonization in Canada. She has a PhD in geography from the University of Waterloo, as well as an MSc in conflict studies from the London School of Economics and a master's degree from the Department of Government and International Relations at the University of Sydney. Dr. McKenzie's doctoral research analyzes the efficacy of pipeline regulation in Canada and the United States. She is currently the manager of the oil and gas program at the Pembina Institute. Prior to joining the institute, she worked on regulatory compliance for TC Energy and contributed to a variety of research projects on international climate governance.

Dr. Megan MacKenzie is a professor and the Simons Chair in International Law and Human Security at the School for International Studies at Simon Fraser University. She is a world-leading expert on military culture, and has directed research projects on gender integration, masculinities in war, military suicide, and military sexual violence. Dr. MacKenzie has published several books, including *Good Soldiers Don't Rape: The Stories We Tell about Military Sexual Violence* (Cambridge University Press, 2023) and *Beyond the Band of Brothers: The US Military and the Myth that Women Can't Fight* (Cambridge University Press, 2015). She is a co-research lead in the Research Network on Women Peace and Security based at McGill University and is also involved in a research hub on images and international relations, based at the University of Copenhagen. Dr. MacKenzie is a leading authority on postconflict transitions and feminist solutions to ending war. Her work in this area includes projects on disarmament programs, amnesty provisions in peace agreements, and truth and reconciliation commissions. She was previously a fellow at the Belfer Center for Science and International Affairs at the Harvard Kennedy School.

Dr. Nicole Wegner is a lecturer in politics and international relations at Waipapa Taumata Rau (University of Auckland) in Aotearoa (New Zealand). She is an internationally recognized expert in critical military studies and feminist international relations, using feminist approaches to studying war, militarization, critical security studies, and gendered violence in global politics. Dr. Wegner is the author of the book *Martialling Peace: How the Peacekeeper Myth Legitimises Warfare* (Edinburgh University Press, 2023) and a co-editor, with Dr. Megan MacKenzie, of the book *Feminist Solutions for Ending War* (Pluto Press, 2022). She has published feminist security research in multiple academic journals, including the *International Journal: Canada's Journal of Global Policy Analysis*, the *International Feminist Journal of Politics*, *Critical Military Studies*, *International Political Sociology*, and *Global Studies Quarterly*.

Chelsea Parker specializes in non-state governance, state weakness, and civil conflict. She holds a master's degree in political science from the University of British Columbia and has conducted research on a wide range of projects and reports at the Institute of Critical Indigenous Studies and in the Department of Political Science. Parker is enthusiastic about work that advances decolonization and focuses on bottom-up, community-informed institution building. She has a background in front-line work in Ecuador as a family and street outreach worker, working in various capacities with women and children. She currently works in the non-profit sector, focused predominantly on anti-violence initiatives.

Dr. Sheryl Lightfoot (Anishinaabe) is a professor in the Department of Political Science and the School of Public Policy and Global Affairs at the University of British Columbia (UBC). She is a world-leading expert on global Indigenous politics, Indigenous diplomacy, social movements, and critical international relations. Dr. Lightfoot specializes in complex questions involving Indigenous peoples' rights, specifically how those rights are claimed and negotiated. Her work explores both practical and theoretical aspects of the implementation of Indigenous rights globally, as well as in domestic contexts. She has published several high-impact books, including *The Handbook of Indigenous Public Policy* (Edward Elgar Publishing, 2024), *Global Indigenous Politics: A Subtle Revolution* (Routledge, 2016), and *Indigenous Peoples and Borders* (Duke University Press, 2023). Dr. Lightfoot has also published numerous academic articles and book chapters, and her research has appeared in such journals as the *International Journal of Human Rights*, *Native American and Indigenous Studies*, and the *European Journal of International Relations*. She was the Canada Research

Chair in Global Indigenous Rights and Politics from 2013 to 2023, and between 2018 and 2023 she served as UBC's senior adviser on Indigenous affairs, leading the development and implementation of the Indigenous Strategic Plan across UBC. In 2023–4, she served as chair of the United Nations Expert Mechanism on the Rights of Indigenous Peoples.

Dr. Jasmin Zine is a professor of sociology and religion and culture at Wilfrid Laurier University and an internationally recognized authority on Islamophobia, anti-Muslim racism, and education and social justice. Her recent book, *Under Siege: Islamophobia and the 9/11 Generation* (McGill-Queen's University Press, 2022), was named on the *Hill Times* list of Best Books of 2022 and explores the experiences of the millennial generation of Canadian Muslim youth who came of age during the global war on terror and times of heightened anti-Muslim racism. Dr. Zine won the Wilfrid Laurier University Merit Award in 2009, 2015, and 2022, and is the author of a major report entitled *Canadian Islamophobia Industry: Mapping Islamophobia's Eco-System in the Great White North* (2022), conducted in partnership with the Islamophobia Studies Center and the Islamophobia Research and Development Project at the University of California, Berkeley. She is an affiliated faculty member with the Islamophobia Research and Documentation Project at UC Berkeley, and co-founder and vice-president of the International Islamophobia Studies Research Association. As an education consultant, she has developed award-winning curriculum materials that address Islamophobia and anti-Muslim racism, and has served as a consultant on combating Islamophobia for the Council of Europe, the Office for the Democratic Institutions and Human Rights at the Organization for Security and Cooperation in Europe, and the United Nations Educational, Scientific and Cultural Organization, developing international guidelines for educators and policymakers on combating Islamophobia and discrimination against Muslims.

Dr. Lama Mourad is an assistant professor at the Norman Paterson School of International Affairs at Carleton University, and an international expert on the intersection of forced migration, local governance, and the politics of borders, with a regional focus on the Middle East. Her work has been published in both academic and public outlets, including the *Journal of Refugee Studies, Middle East Law and Governance, Forced Migration Studies,* and the *European Journal of International*

Relations, as well as the *Globe and Mail*, *The Atlantic*, *Lawfare*, the *Washington Post's Monkey Cage*, and the *Toronto Star*. Dr. Mourad's research has garnered major recognition. In 2020, she was awarded the APSA-Migration & Citizenship Section's Best Dissertation award for her thesis *Open Borders, Local Closures: Decentralization and the Politics of Local Responses to the Syrian Refugee Influx in Lebanon*. She has been supported by a number of institutions and agencies, including the Harvard Kennedy School's Middle East Initiative, the Social Sciences and Humanities Research Council, the International Development Research Centre, as well as by project- and issue-specific grants from the Project on Middle Eastern Political Science and the American Political Science Association's First Generation Scholar's Initiative. She has previously held fellowships at Perry World House, University of Pennsylvania, and with the Middle East Initiative at the Harvard Kennedy School of Government.

Index

Act: (2001) Anti-terrorism, 204; (2001) Canadian Immigration and Refugee Protection, 207; (1984) CSIS, 117–18; 201; (2019) Communications Security Establishment, 116, 123; (1982) Constitution, 191, 199; (1988) Emergencies, 129; (2022) Emergencies, 129; (1999) Emergency Preparedness, 129; (1876) Indian, 191; (1976) Immigration, 224
Afghanistan, 4, 13–14, 50–3, 89, 152, 155, 163–4, 166–9, 175, 180, 204, 238, 240, 281; Canada's Afghanistan mission, 169
Africa, 8–9, 55, 86, 96, 104–5, 169, 237, 239, 245, 249, 260
Alberta, 79, 129, 141
Arctic: communities, 149; Council, 65, 70, 72, 255; Inuit homelands, 66–9, 72–3; search and rescue (SAR), 65–9
Argentina, 153
artificial intelligence (AI), 111, 127, 242–3
Australia, 76, 81, 126, 150, 155

Biden, Joe, 42, 48, 53, 64, 96, 103, 105, 218, 241
Brazil, 103, 153
British Columbia, 9, 11, 15, 126, 131, 138, 149, 195
Burkina Faso, 240

Canada: and the United States, 12–13, 36, 129, 133, 167, 207, 241; visible minorities in, 36, 43
Canada Border Services Agency, 223
Canada Energy Regulator (CER), 143
Canada Revenue Agency (CRA), 205
Canadian: foreign policy, 245, 247; women, 244, 248–50, 263; values, 35
Canadian Armed Forces (CAF), 7, 10, 14–15, 18, 57, 63, 68–70, 88, 90, 117–18, 120, 125, 127–8, 131–2, 134, 164, 170, 178–84, 247, 281
Canadian Coast Guard (CCG), 63, 67–9
Canadian intervention in Somalia, 16
Canadian mission to Haiti, 170
Canadian Security and Intelligence Services (CSIS), 113, 114, 117–18, 120, 127, 170, 212
canola, 79, 80–2

carbon tax, 155
Centre for Cyber Security, 114
Charter of Rights, 191, 205, 221
China, 4, 7–8, 10, 19, 31–5, 50, 54, 59, 62, 64–6, 75–83, 86, 90, 94, 101, 104–5, 107, 121, 203, 237–42, 245, 248, 266, 282; and Iran, 54, 79, 92, 94, 239; and Russia, 65, 104, 239; and Saudi Arabia, 239
Chrétien, Jean, 89
civil war, 89, 169
Civilian Air Search and Rescue Association (CASARA), 63, 69
climate change, 66, 138, 148, 152, 156, 157; refugees, 151
Cold War, 4, 49–50, 55, 58, 63, 100, 106, 151, 155, 165, 238, 242
collective security, 50, 57–8
counter-insurgency, 51, 103, 238
counterterrorism, 3, 10, 51, 105, 248
COVID-19, 50, 76, 91, 99, 102, 104, 114, 125–30, 153, 157, 222; anti-vaccine protests, 127–8
cyber: activities, 116; Convention on Cybercrime, 119; espionage, 111, 114; infrastructure, 112; operations, 111, 114; security threats, 50, 183; space, 10, 112, 118, 119, 120, 243; tools, 113

decarbonization, 11, 13, 149–50, 156–7
de-escalation, 65, 241
democracy, 4, 38, 40, 54, 56–7, 87, 89–90, 92–3, 101, 116–17, 240; liberal, 106, 153
digital security, 133

economic: coercion, 8, 75–8, 82–3, 245; decoupling, 75; security, 11, 15, 189, 194

economy, 6, 12, 33, 40, 79–80, 126, 133, 139, 144, 151, 237, 248
Egypt, 89–90, 94, 96, 99
emergency management, 125–30, 132–3, 183, 246
escalation, 3, 17, 59–60, 76, 157, 198, 237, 241
espionage, 111, 113–14, 117, 127. *See also* spy
Europe, 16, 19, 36, 51, 65, 81, 86, 143, 185, 204, 213, 217, 228, 248
European Court of Human Rights, 228
European Union (EU), 32, 55, 81, 143, 226

feminism, 6, 14, 26–7, 56, 87, 178, 181, 247, 269
First Nations, 15, 193–4, 197; Assembly of, 193
Five Eyes, 120, 208, 222
Foucault, Michel, 210
Freeland, Chrystia, 82

gas, 11, 13, 65, 138, 139, 140, 141, 142, 143, 144, 145, 148, 149, 150, 154
Gaza, 42, 86–7, 91–2, 102, 104, 155, 218, 226–7, 240
gender-based violence, 126
gender inequity, 18, 243
Global North, 217, 218, 223, 225–6, 228
Global South, 105, 218, 219, 226
globalization, 131
great power conflict, 4, 20, 238, 242
G7, 117, 148

Haiti, 100, 103, 126, 170. *See also* Canadian mission to Haiti
Harper, Stephen, 89, 167, 224

Harris, Kamala, 42, 105, 240
human rights, 7, 38, 87, 100–3, 106, 188–93, 195–8, 209, 240, 248; violations of, 189, 195
human security, 5, 7, 13, 50, 56, 62–3, 69, 125, 149, 150–2, 157, 185, 242, 246, 249, 269
humanitarian: aid agencies and community-based organizations, 128; assistance, 57; catastrophe, 51; ceasefire, 47,100, 242; emergencies, 126; pathways, 226, 227, 228; values, 240
hybrid war, 54
hypersonic weapons, 65, 238–9

Ibn Khaldûn, 41; *asabiyyah*, 41–2
Ikenberry, G. John, 38
Immigration and Refugee Board of Canada, 220
India, 8, 101, 203, 237, 248, 268
Indigenous: human rights, 15, 188–9, 190–1, 193–4, 196–7, 247; Inuit communities, 66–9, 72–3; lands and territories, 190. *See also* First Nations
insecurity: food, 92; gendered, 179; job, 105; water, 155
International Energy Agency (IEA), 140–5
international law, 10, 112, 114, 118–21
Iran, 54, 79, 92, 94, 239
Iraq, 14, 50, 52–3, 58, 89–90, 165
Islamophobia, 16, 37, 170, 203–6, 208, 211–12, 247
Israel, 8, 42, 48, 55, 86–92, 102, 152, 155, 172, 204, 218, 237–9, 240, 249; Israel-Hamas war, 55, 86, 218. *See also* Gaza
Italy, 35, 153, 228

Kyoto Protocol, 139

Layton, Jack, 168
Lebanon, 14, 17, 93, 219
LGBTQ+, 132
liberal international order, 32, 38, 43, 88, 91, 107
Liberal Party of Canada, 11, 31, 38, 40, 166, 167
Libya, 50, 52, 89–90, 92, 94, 261

Mali, 14, 100, 105, 169, 240
Manitoba, 7, 79
Middle East and North Africa (MENA) region, 8–9, 16, 36, 55, 86–96, 237, 239, 240, 245
military: exceptionalism, 179, 182; families, 180; sexual violence, 14, 15, 179, 181–4; suicide, 14, 178–81
multiculturalism, 35, 40, 188
Myanmar, 203

NATO, 6–7, 36, 47, 49, 50–9, 64–5, 71, 73, 86, 88–90, 99, 104–5, 112–13, 120, 127, 133, 163, 165–6, 171–2, 183, 238–9, 245, 271; and Canadian security, 5, 7–8, 10, 13, 16–17, 20, 32, 77, 88, 118, 125, 127, 164, 184, 198, 204, 222, 244, 247; intervention, 105; Policy on Women, Peace, and Security, 50; 2 per cent defence spending, 57–8
New Democratic Party (NDP), 168
NORAD, 7, 64, 70–1
North Korea, 54, 77
Northwest Territories, 125, 129, 131
nuclear: war, 19, 77, 241; weapons, 4, 130

Obama, Barack, 168
Ontario, 7, 16, 37, 129–31, 136, 149, 194, 197, 203
Ontario Emergency Management Strategy Action Plan, 130
Ottawa, 10, 36, 70–2, 81, 89, 126, 136, 195, 243, 245

Pakistan, 14, 101, 164, 167
Palestine, 8, 48, 86–7, 91–5, 152, 203–4, 227, 237, 240, 249
Paris: Accords, 242; Agreement, 138–9, 140, 142, 144, 154, 156
peace agreement: ceasefire, 47, 100, 240, 242; negotiated, 53, 99, 145, 167
pipeline: Coastal GasLink, 194; Colonial, 126, 133; Nord Stream, 149; regulation, 13; Trans Mountain, 144
Poilievre, Pierre, 42, 48
pork, 79–82
poverty, 91–2, 155, 181

Quebec, 37, 72, 149, 194, 203, 222

racism, 16, 37–41, 43, 45–7, 178, 193, 203, 212, 226, 247
refugees, 16–17, 54, 95, 148, 155, 204, 213, 217, 219–29, 247–9
residential schools, 189, 195
right-wing populism, 152–3
Royal Canadian Mounted Police (RCMP), 63, 209, 223
Russia, 4, 7, 10, 19, 32, 33, 41, 47, 50, 51–9, 62–6, 71–2, 81, 90, 99, 101–7, 112–15, 121, 149, 152, 172, 177, 183, 219, 237, 239, 240–5, 248, 253, 259; invasion of Ukraine, 31, 49, 53–5, 65, 99, 101, 105, 107, 125, 143, 149, 152, 172, 219, 237

Safe Third Country Agreement (STCA), 218–19, 221–3, 228
Sahel, 169
Saudi Arabia, 86–7, 94, 239
September 11 attacks (9/11), 16, 88, 165, 204, 206, 209–12, 219, 238, 248, 258, 269, 271
sexual: abuse, 195; harassment, 181; integrity of the individual, 117; misconduct, 170, 178, 183, 184; violence. *See also* military: sexual violence
soft power, 4, 238, 240, 242
Somalia, 14, 100, 169
South Africa, 239
South Korea, 76, 77, 78
spy, 64, 75, 77, 113. *See also* espionage
Sudan, 218
Syria, 22, 89–90, 92, 94, 224, 226

Taliban, 52–3, 152, 166–9, 171, 220, 238, 240
Terminal High Altitude Area Defense (THAAD), 77–8
terrorism, 10, 113–14, 117, 125–8, 204–5, 207–8
trade, 6, 32–6, 75–80, 82–3, 89, 149–50, 166, 193, 214, 248
trucker convoy, 36, 43, 129, 153, 157
Trudeau, Justin, 48, 78, 89, 129
Trump, Donald, 31, 34–7, 42, 53, 56–7, 64, 103, 153, 168, 203, 219, 221–2

Ukraine, 32–3, 50–8, 62–5, 81, 102, 104, 112–15, 133, 143, 155, 235, 239, 241–8, 263–8

Index   289

unemployment, 91–2
United Arab Emirates, 82
United Kingdom, 35, 53, 78, 101, 114, 150, 155, 208
United Nations (UN), 7, 16, 51, 90, 99, 148, 151, 153, 156, 189, 192–3, 195–6, 219; Committee on the Elimination of Racial Discrimination, 192; Declaration on the Rights of Indigenous Peoples (UNDRIP), 189, 196–8; General Assembly, 42, 47, 95, 104–5, 240; High Commission for Refugees (UNHCR), 217, 219, 223, 225, 228; Intergovernmental Panel on Climate Change, 148; intervention, 163; peace operations, 100, 102–3, 105, 107; peacekeeping, 88, 99–107, 245; Security Council (UNSC), 10, 90, 101–2, 104–5, 240; stabilization, 106; Framework Convention on Climate Change (UNFCCC), 139, 151, 156

United States, 4, 6, 31–8, 40–3, 53, 56–9, 63–5, 70, 75, 77–8, 86–9, 91, 95, 101, 104, 113–15, 126–9, 132–3, 143, 150–5, 165–6, 169, 180, 203, 208, 217–22, 228, 237–42, 245, 248; Federal Emergency Management Authority (FEMA), 129; hegemony of, 4, 6, 32, 38, 78, 237, 244; State Department, 13

Wanzhou, Meng, 76, 79
Wet'suwet'en, 194, 197
white nationalist, 34, 37, 203
wildfires, 125–6, 131, 138, 148–9, 242
women, 13, 17–20, 87, 132, 166–8, 178, 181–2, 193, 244, 248–50, 263, 264; experts, 17–20, 244, 249–50, 264
World Health Organization, 5, 126

xenophobia, 34–8, 43, 203–4

Yemen, 89, 92, 94

UTP insights

Books in the Series

- Aisha Ahmad (ed.), *Securing Canada's Future: Vital Insights from Women Experts*
- Ingrid Leman Stefanovic (ed.), *Conversations on Ethical Leadership: Lessons Learned from University Governance*
- Sue Winton, *Unequal Benefits: Privatization and Public Education in Canada*
- David A. Detomasi, *Profits and Power: Navigating the Politics and Geopolitics of Oil*
- Andrew Green, *Picking Up the Slack: Law, Institutions, and Canadian Climate Policy*
- Peter MacKinnon, *Canada in Question: Exploring Our Citizenship in the Twenty-First Century*
- Harvey P. Weingarten, *Nothing Less than Great: Reforming Canada's Universities*
- Allan C. Hutchinson, *Democracy and Constitutions: Putting Citizens First*
- Paul Nelson, *Global Development and Human Rights: The Sustainable Development Goals and Beyond*
- Peter H. Russell, *Sovereignty: The Biography of a Claim*
- Alistair Edgar, Rupinder Mangat, and Bessma Momani (eds.), *Strengthening the Canadian Armed Forces through Diversity and Inclusion*
- David B. MacDonald, *The Sleeping Giant Awakens: Genocide, Indian Residential Schools, and the Challenge of Conciliation*
- Paul W. Gooch, *Course Correction: A Map for the Distracted University*
- Paul T. Phillips, *Truth, Morality, and Meaning in History*
- Stanley R. Barrett, *The Lamb and the Tiger: From Peacekeepers to Peacewarriors in Canada*
- Peter MacKinnon, *University Commons Divided: Exploring Debate and Dissent on Campus*
- Raisa B. Deber, *Treating Health Care: How the System Works and How It Could Work Better*
- Jim Freedman, *A Conviction in Question: The First Trial at the International Criminal Court*

- Christina D. Rosan and Hamil Pearsall, *Growing a Sustainable City? The Question of Urban Agriculture*
- John Joe Schlichtman, Jason Patch, and Marc Lamont Hill, *Gentrifier*
- Robert Chernomas and Ian Hudson, *Economics in the Twenty-First Century: A Critical Perspective*
- Stephen M. Saideman, *Adapting in the Dust: Lessons Learned from Canada's War in Afghanistan*
- Michael R. Marrus, *Lessons of the Holocaust*
- Roland Paris and Taylor Owen (eds.), *The World Won't Wait: Why Canada Needs to Rethink Its International Policies*
- Bessma Momani, *Arab Dawn: Arab Youth and the Demographic Dividend They Will Bring*
- William Watson, *The Inequality Trap: Fighting Capitalism Instead of Poverty*
- Phil Ryan, *After the New Atheist Debate*
- Paul Evans, *Engaging China: Myth, Aspiration, and Strategy in Canadian Policy from Trudeau to Harper*

www.ingramcontent.com/pod-product-compliance
Lightning Source LLC
Chambersburg PA
CBHW030307080526
44584CB00012B/467